AF505841

Exile Armies

# Exile Armies

Edited by

## Matthew Bennett
*Senior Lecturer in Communication and Management Studies, Royal Military Academy Sandhurst*

and

## Paul Latawski
*Senior Lecturer in Defence and International Affairs, Royal Military Academy Sandhurst*

palgrave macmillan

Editorial Matter, Selection, Introduction and Conclusion
© Matthew Bennett and Paul Latawski 2005
Chapters 1–12 © Palgrave Macmillan 2005

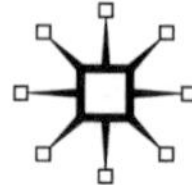

All rights reserved. No reproduction, copy or transmission of this
publication may be made without written permission.

No paragraph of this publication may be reproduced, copied or transmitted
save with written permission or in accordance with the provisions of the
Copyright, Designs and Patents Act 1988, or under the terms of any licence
permitting limited copying issued by the Copyright Licensing Agency,
90 Tottenham Court Road, London W1T 4LP.

Any person who does any unauthorized act in relation to this publication
may be liable to criminal prosecution and civil claims for damages.

The authors have asserted their rights to be identified
as the authors of this work in accordance with the Copyright,
Designs and Patents Act 1988.

First published 2005 by
PALGRAVE MACMILLAN
Houndmills, Basingstoke, Hampshire RG21 6XS and
175 Fifth Avenue, New York, N.Y. 10010
Companies and representatives throughout the world

PALGRAVE MACMILLAN is the global academic imprint of the Palgrave
Macmillan division of St. Martin's Press, LLC and of Palgrave Macmillan Ltd.
Macmillan® is a registered trademark in the United States, United Kingdom
and other countries. Palgrave is a registered trademark in the European
Union and other countries.

ISBN 0–333–94564–6 hardback

This book is printed on paper suitable for recycling and made from fully
managed and sustained forest sources.

A catalogue record for this book is available from the British Library.

Library of Congress Cataloging-in-Publication Data
Exile armies / edited by Matthew Bennett and Paul Latawski.
      p.   cm.
   Includes bibliographical references and index.
   ISBN 0–333–94564–6
   1. Exile Armies—History—20th century.   2. Military history,
   Modern—20th century.   I. Bennett, Matthew, 1954–   II. Latawski,
   Paul C. (Paul Chester), 1954–

   D431.E94 2004
   355—dc22

                                                           2004048755

10   9   8   7   6   5   4   3   2   1
14   13   12   11   10   09   08   07   06   05

Printed and bound in Great Britain by
Antony Rowe Ltd, Chippenham and Eastbourne

# Contents

# List of Table

# Preface

This project owes its origins to a study day held at the Royal Military Academy Sandhurst in February 1999 devoted to the subject of exile armies. As the day progressed it became evident that the diverse case studies examined yielded a number of common themes and experiences that merited further exploration. Exile armies are not a particularly new phenomenon, but they are not well studied in political and military terms. This book aims to offer a contribution to filling that gap.

Although the majority of case studies in this book are historical in nature, the issues that are raised undoubtedly have relevance for the contemporary problems of post-Cold War international security. With state failure a major concern in the international security environment, the political and military dynamics of exile armies echo to some extent the predominant intrastate conflict that is characterized by warring factions. As in the experience of many exile armies, political fragmentation is a dilemma not easily overcome. Similarly, the would-be interveners of the international community are confronted with difficult choices regarding which groups to back in seeking a lasting resolution to intrastate conflicts. In this context, the problems associated with exile armies have a certain resonance.

This book and the earlier study day are the product of the efforts of many people who deserve thanks for their input into the project. We would like to thank the contributors who provided stimulating discussion and ideas on the study day that eventually transmogrified into the chapters that make up this volume. We would also like to thank our families who patiently endured the gestation of this project.

For those of us contributing to the book who are civil servants there is one more duty to perform by issuing a necessary disclaimer: the analysis, opinions and conclusions expressed or implied in this book are those of the authors alone. They do not necessarily represent the views of the Royal Military Academy Sandhurst, the UK Ministry of Defence or any other government agency.

Matthew Bennett
Paul Latawski

# List of Contributors

**Matthew Bennett** is a Senior Lecturer at the Royal Military Academy Sandhurst in Communication and Management Studies, and a medieval historian interested in both the ethos and practice of warfare. His publications include an atlas of medieval warfare for Cambridge University Press and a score of articles. He also works on Christian/Jewish/Muslim interaction.

**Keith Blackmore** is a Senior Lecturer in Defence and International Affairs at the Royal Military Academy Sandhurst. His main research interests the politics of the Middle East and British power projection east of Suez in the 1950s and 1960s.

**Anthony Clayton** was a senior Lecturer at the Royal Military Academy between 1965 and 1999. He is the author of *France, Soldiers and Africa, Three Marshals of France*, and *The Wars of French Decolonisation*. Currently he is working on a history of the French Army in the First World War.

**Alan Brown** lectures in history and politics at Selby College, North Yorkshire. His doctoral research examined the political and military relationship between the British government and the Czechoslovak government-in-exile during the Second World War, concentrating on the Czechoslovak Air Force. His new book, *Airmen in Exile*, extends that theme to examine the experiences of other European émigrés.

**Stuart Gordon** is a Senior Lecturer in Defence and International Affairs at the Royal Military Academy Sandhurst. His research interests include Peace Support Operations, British Foreign and Defence Policy. His latest publications include: *British Internationalism and the Ethical Foreign Policy: the Road to Sierra Leone?* (London: Kings' College, Centre for Defence Studies, September 2000).

**Robin Havers** is a Senior Lecturer in War Studies at the Royal Military Academy Sandhurst. His main research interests are the war in the Far East during the Second World War. His book on the experiences of British and Australian prisoners of war entitled *Reassessing the Japanese POW experience: The Changi POW Camp, 1942–45* (Curzon Press, 2001).

**James Higgs** is a Senior Lecturer in Defence and International Affairs at the Royal Military Academy Sandhurst. His main research interests include civil–military relations and security in Africa with a particular interest in defence policy in the Republic of South Africa. He is a Research Associate of the South African Institute of International Affairs (SAIIA).

**Paul Latawski** is a Senior Lecturer in Defence and International Affairs at the Royal Military Academy Sandhurst. He is an Associate Fellow at the Royal United Services Institute for Defence Studies, London and an Honorary Visiting Fellow at the School of Slavonic and East European Studies, University of London. His principal research interests include contemporary Poland and security in Central Europe. He has published extensively on these topics.

**Christopher Mann** is a Senior Lecturer in War Studies at the Royal Military Academy Sandhurst. He is a holder of a doctorate from the Department of War Studies, King's College London. He specializes in Scandinavian military history in the twentieth century.

**Sean McKnight** is Deputy Head of the Department of War Studies at the Royal Military Academy Sandhurst. He has published work on media relationship, race and recruitment in the British Army, the Iran–Iraq war and modern Iraq. He is currently working on Venetian fortifications in the Eastern Mediterranean.

**Martin A. Smith** is a Senior Lecturer in Defence and International Affairs at the Royal Military Academy Sandhurst. His main research interests are in the fields of international and European security and his most recent book is *NATO in the First Decade after the Cold War* (The Hague: Kluwer 2000).

**Edmund Yorke** is a Senior Lecturer in Defence and International Affairs at the Royal Military Academy Sandhurst. He has specialized in British Empire and Commonwealth political and military affairs with his books and articles ranging from colonial war studies to contemporary African peacekeeping. He has recently published two colonial siege studies of Mafeking (1900) and Rorkes Drift (1879).

# List of Abbreviations

| | |
|---|---|
| ADP | *Alliance Democratie de Peuples* |
| AFDL | Alliance of Democratic Forces for the Liberation of Congo |
| ANC | African National Congress |
| APLA | Azanian Peoples Liberation Army |
| BSF | Border Security Force |
| CDR | Coalition for the Defence of the Republic |
| CEF | *Corps Expéditionnaire Français* |
| CIA | Central Intelligence Agency |
| CNDR | *Conseil National de Resistance pour la Democratie* |
| DBLE | Demi-Brigade |
| EBR | East Bengal Regiment |
| EPR | East Pakistan Rifles |
| FAR | *Forces Armées Rwandaises* |
| FAZ | Forces of Zaire |
| FIC | Free Iraqi Council |
| FRELIMO | Front for the Liberation of Mozambique |
| FROLIZI | Front for the Liberation of Zimbabwe |
| ICS | Indian Civil Service |
| IFP | Inkatha Freedom Party |
| IIL | Indian Independence League |
| IJA | Imperial Japanese Army |
| INA | Indian National Army |
| INC | Iraqi National Congress |
| KDP | Kurdish Democratic Party |
| KFOR | Kosovo Force |
| KLA | Kosovo Liberation Army |
| KRN | *Krajowa Rada Narodowa* – National Home Council |
| LDK | Democratic League of Kosovo |
| MDC | Movement for Democratic Change |
| MK | *Umkhonto weSizwe* – Spear of the Nation |
| MRND | Movement for Reconciliation and National Development |
| MRP | *Movimiento Revolucionario del Pueblo* |

| | |
|---|---|
| MTB | Motor Torpedo Boat |
| MUP | Serbian Police |
| NATO | North Atlantic Treaty Organization |
| NCO | Non-Commissioned Officer |
| NHM | Norges Hjemmefront museum (Norwegian Resistance Museum) |
| NKVD | Narodnaya Kommissya Vevnutrikh Dyel – People's Commission of Internal Affairs (Soviet security service) |
| NRA | National Resistance Army |
| NS | *Nasjonal Samling* – National Union |
| OAS | Organization of American States |
| OSCE | Organization for Security and Cooperation in Europe |
| PAC | Pan Africanist Congress |
| PKK | Turkish Kurdish Workers Party |
| POW | Prisoner of War |
| PRO | Public Record Office |
| PRP | *Parti de la Revolution Populaire* |
| PSZ | *Polski Sły Zbrojne* – Polish armed forces |
| PUK | Patriotic Union of Kurdistan |
| RMT | *Régiment de Marche de Tchad* |
| RPF | Rwandan Patriotic Front |
| SACP | South African Communist Party |
| SADF | South African Defence Force |
| SAIRI | Supreme Assembly for the Islamic Revolution in Iraq |
| SANDF | South African National Defence Force |
| SOE | Special Operations Executive |
| TA | Territorial Army |
| TRC | Truth and Reconciliation Commission |
| UCK | *Ushtria Çlirimitare e Kosovës* |
| UDF | United Democratic Front |
| UDI | Unilateral Declaration of Independence |
| UN | United Nations |
| US | United States |
| USA | United States of America |
| UNITA | *Uniao Nacional para a Independencia Total de Angola* |
| VJ | *Vojska Jugoslavije* – Yugoslav Army |
| ZANLA | Zimbabwe African National Liberation Army |

| | |
|---|---|
| ZANU | Zimbabwe African National Union |
| ZAPU | Zimbabwe African People's Union |
| ZIPA | Zimbabwe Peoples Army |
| ZIPRA | Zimbabwe Peoples Revolutionary Army |
| ZLP | Zimbabwe Liberation Platform |
| ZNA | Zimbabwean National Army |
| ZNLWVA | Zimbabwean National Liberation War Veteran Association |
| ZPP | *Związek Patriotów Polskich* – Union of Polish Patriots |

# Introduction

*Matthew Bennett and Paul Latawski*

The aim of *Exile Armies* is to explore the common problems associated with military forces operating outside their homelands. Indeed, the purpose of the book is to identify those features of exile armies that will inform our current understanding of their nature and limitations in both military and political terms. The utility of this is shown by the fact that exile armies are not simply a historical phenomenon but a feature that has a continuing resonance today in many post-Cold War regional conflicts. As a subject of academic study, exile armies have not been subject to scrutiny as subjects in their own right or given comparative treatment. Although exile governments of various political persuasions have been examined by historians and social scientists, and governments in exile from the perspective of specialists in international law, their associated armies have not been given comparable examination.[1] The literature on governments in exile, however, does provide a useful starting point to develop a definition and typology for exile armies.

Yossi Shain has defined an exile government as 'opposition groups that struggle from outside their home territory to overthrow and replace the regime in their independent, occupied or claimed home country'. He goes on to say that 'as such, they vie for the support of their national constituencies at home and in diaspora, and appeal for international assistance'.[2] Reflecting this view, the sociologist Alicja Iwańska argues that governments in exile are entities 'without either territory or power' and are 'social movements whose central, and sometimes single goal is that of implementing radical change in their home countries'.[3] Dependency is also a key attribute according to Iwańska; 'exiled government is rooted in its host country'.[4] In terms of international law, this dependency is underscored by the precarious status of governments in exile. Stefan Talman notes 'the predominant view in legal literature' demonstrates that 'the term "government in exile" does not denote special legal status or an independent subject of international law but indicates the domicile of a "government".'[5]

From the range of definitions presented above, it is clear that governments in exile share a number of common features. The idea of return to homeland is central to the raison d'être of any exile government. In addition, its dependence on its host state is an inescapable reality giving them a significant vulnerability if not an ephemeral quality. Their objectives can range from the pursuit of a radical or even revolutionary reshaping of their destination country to simply realizing the return of a constitutional and democratically elected government driven abroad by war and defeat or domestic rebellion or coups. Given the fact that governments in exile are 'accompanied by (the remains of its defeated) armed forces or raises such forces in the host country'[6] it can be assumed that such military forces share the distinctive characteristics and problems of the exile government. From these general features of the government in exile it is possible to construct a definition of exile armies:

> An exile army is an armed force that for both political and military reasons bases its operations outside its homeland. Its central political and military objective is to return to its place of origin. An exile army derives its legitimacy from a government that claims a line of succession to previously existing state institutions or through a *sui generis* national liberation movement or political organization seeking to alter by revolutionary means the existing political order in its homeland. Therefore the military attributes of an exile army can reflect a continuum ranging from the army of a 'normal' state to that of an insurgent force pursuing its aims through irregular warfare.

The book is arranged in two parts. The first deals with the Second World War, with the majority of the studies covering the Allied experience: the Norwegians, Czechoslovaks, Poles and French (listed here in rising order of the size of their forces). Of these nations, only the Norwegians and French were able to establish regimes that represented the ideals and ideology of the majority of the participants in the exile forces; the former a constitutional monarchy the second a seemingly fragile but remarkably resilient republic. The Czechoslovaks and Poles became part of the Soviet Empire, from which they were unable to disentangle themselves, despite their efforts in 1967 and 1956 onwards respectively, until the collapse of Communism in 1989–91. So even being on the 'winning side' did not ensure that the aspirations of the exiles and their armed forces were realized in a post-conflict environment. In contrast, the supporters of the Japanese-led Indian National Army (INA) may have been deemed to back the wrong side. Yet, ironically perhaps, the independence initiatives, which had lain at the heart of the INA's formation, did make a substantial contribution to the withdrawal of the British less than two years after the end of the Second World War.

The Cold War, which ensued between the United States of America and the Soviet Union, did change the global political landscape for two generations. It has just been noted how two European countries were drawn into the latter's Eastern Bloc. The limits of so-called superpowers were well exposed in the Cuban debacle of 1961, when anti-Communist exiles found that America was not the fount of liberation that they had hoped. The stakes were raised significantly in the ensuing missile crisis, which brought the world to the brink of nuclear war, but both sides pulled back and instead engaged in a series of proxy wars. These are not the focus of this volume, however, and the most significant conflict, in Vietnam, did not involve exile forces. So, in the second part of the collection, the emphasis shifts to Africa, with excursions into the subcontinent and the Middle East. Just how important a role a regional power such as India could play in supporting a successful independence movement, is shown in the successful establishment of Bangladesh, after a short war. The situation in Africa was much more long and drawn out with the majority populations of South Africa and Southern Rhodesia/Zimbabwe taking decades to create a political environment sensitive to their needs. The differing resolutions and outcomes of those conflicts represent the very different approaches and leadership of Nelson Mandela and Robert Mugabe. The chaotic, and yet to be resolved, situation of the Great Lakes region of Central Africa shows that not all such issues are susceptible to resolution in the context of failed states.

The studies of exile forces in Iraq and in Kosovo, point up the uncertainty of outcome even after a major regional conflict. The constraints of geography, legitimacy and will on behalf of the international community, or at least some of its major players, profoundly affected the outcome for the Iraqi dissidents and the Albanian Kosovars. Balkan state-building was dealt a bloody nose by NATO, seeking to prevent further genocide. In contrast, Saddam Hussein's regime was allowed the time and the political space to crush uprisings against it, and so defer its demise for over a decade. This, too, after a previous decade of exhausting war with Iran. The humiliation of the first Gulf War was insufficient to undermine the Ba'athist state without considerable Western support for potential exile governments and internal rebellions. On the other hand, the Kosovars were able to gain self-rule, and Serbia a return to democracy through the efforts of the KLA and its powerful protectors.

What this volume shows, not least, is that there is no perfect model for exile forces to achieve their aims. In stark contrast to the propositions of 1960s theorists, whether protagonists of Marxist historical forces or the reactive fears expressed in the 'domino theory', what is striking about the case studies examined in this collection is the diversity and uncertainty of outcomes. Circumstances clearly alter cases. The variety of local and immediate political and strategic decisions can have a dramatic impact on the success or failure of exile forces. In some cases this was the result of dramatic and swift military action, yet in more a 'slow burn' can be observed to achieve the desires of the exiled community. So the studies that follow should not be seen as prescriptive, providing evidence for what will or will not work for exile forces, but as expressions of a complex environment in which they operated.

## Notes

1. See Alcja Iwańska, *Exiled Governments: Spanish and Polish: An Essay in Political Sociology* (Cambridge, MA: Schenckman Publishing Company, Inc., 1981), Yossi Shain (ed.), *Governments-in-Exile in Contemporary World Politics* (London: Routledge, 1991) and Stefan Talman, *Recognition of Governments in International Law: With Particular Reference to Governments in Exile* (Oxford: Clarendon Press, 1998).
2. Yossi Shain, 'Introduction: Governments-in-Exile and the Age of Democratic Transitions', in Shain (ed.), *Governments-in-Exile in Contemporary World Politics*, p. 2.
3. Iwańska, *Exiled Governments: Spanish and Polish: An Essay in Political Sociology*, p. 21.
4. *Ibid.*
5. Talman, *Recognition of Governments in International Law: With Particular Reference to Governments in Exile*, pp. 15–16.
6. *Ibid.*, p. 267.

# Part I
# The Second World War

# 1
## 'The Army of Lords': The Independent Czechoslovak Brigade 1940–45

*Alan Brown*

The Czechoslovak land forces that reorganized in Britain during the desperate summer of 1940 were in part the remnants of the Czechoslovak Army eliminated by the diplomatic vandalism at Munich. The few who rejected defeat managed to escape first to Poland, where they were gently but firmly urged to continue their travels; and then to Romania, Yugoslavia, Hungary or the Soviet Union. Others headed west to France, but yet again they were to be disappointed. France, like Poland, had no desire to provoke the Germans by openly accepting military refugees from the Protectorate, for Berlin had declared all former citizens of the Czech lands to be subjects of the Reich. The French, therefore, felt inclined to keep everything Czechoslovak at arm's length even as the battle of France began in 1940. The air force contingent, numbering about a thousand men, were held back until the last desperate hours when only a very small percentage saw action. Similarly, the army group – nearly 11,000 strong – was hastily set into action. As France moved towards defeat, so the exiled groups, including Czechoslovak soldiers, converged on western ports in the hope of escaping to Britain.

### The ambivalent welcome in Britain

Only 4,000 of the known 11,000 Czechoslovak army personnel had made their escape to Britain. Many Czechoslovaks in France had opted for voluntary demobilization as they had families or reserved occupations there while others were repatriated back to the Protectorate or Slovakia. Of those who eventually found their way to Britain, by far the largest percentage had come originally from Czechoslovakia and felt no strong ties to France. On their arrival, the Czechoslovaks were located at a holding camp in Cholmondeley Park in Cheshire. In the eyes of the

British leaders, fully two-thirds of the men had thrown in their lot with the Germans, and this sent every wrong signal imaginable.

That these events dismayed influential men in Whitehall can be seen clearly in the minutes of the War Cabinet of late June 1940. Both military and civilian sections of the government spoke of caution when dealing with the Czechoslovak group, and Lord Halifax put a fine point on it when he urged that the contingent needed 'a quick comb-out' before giving them guns. Two things added substance to these views. In the first place, the Home Office, the Air Ministry, the intelligence services and even the Prime Minister Winston Churchill himself had cast doubts upon the fighting spirit or political reliability of Czechoslovak nationals long before they arrived in any great numbers. Second, within days of their arrival at Cholmondeley Park, some five hundred men had been removed and interned for stirring up political and racial trouble in the camp. At a later date, most of them were transferred into the Pioneer Corps, the British Army's dustbin for problematic individuals. The men were predominantly communists, who had fought with the republicans in the Spanish Civil War. This proved to be an isolated incident, but it went a long way to reinforce the prejudices held by men of power. As a result, whether it was justified or not, the Czechoslovak Brigade was earmarked for a quiet life.

There was also a much deeper political dimension to this. Edvard Beneš, the former Czechoslovak President, was busily restoring his political fortunes. Taking advantage of the chaos caused by the French collapse, he had been petitioning the Foreign Office on an almost daily basis with a demand for the establishment of a Provisional Czechoslovak Government and for the immediate reconstitution of the army and air force as independent fighting units. This last point was to prove anathema to the Air Ministry, but on the question of political recognition, Lord Halifax swept aside the many earlier objections to involving Beneš in the political process by pointing out that the Czechoslovaks then in the country would have to be looked after 'whether or not' Beneš was granted his wishes. But Beneš was not to be satisfied with this. His long-term goal was not only the liberation of the Czechoslovak State, but also the complete erasure of the stain of Munich. To achieve this, he needed to maximize every resource at his disposal, but his position in England was politically precarious. His only option was to increase his prestige and hope that as the war drew to a close he might be able to force Czechoslovak matters on to the agenda.

As part of his strategy Beneš sought to obtain fully independent status for the exile Czechoslovak forces, so that they might stand as legitimate representatives of their homeland and with him as Commander-in-Chief. The Air Ministry flatly refused to do this, arguing that a small air force of some 1,600 men could barely function without the assistance of British ground crew making independence both impractical and unrealistic. As for the War Office, it had no such objections to the formation of a separate Czechoslovak Army unit. Beneš had thus chosen very sensitive matters over which to do battle, and on the two occasions he tried to secure independent status for his air force, he was firmly put in his place by the Air Ministry, the second attempt being far more bitterly contested than the first. To make matters worse, he persisted in trying to ride two horses at once; that is, to have a fully functioning air force and an army group up to strength and capable of taking its place in the line when the time came. His problem was that he only had enough men to achieve one of these aims, not both. Recruitment for the Czechoslovak forces in exile was sparse indeed. After the initial wave of escapees had been assimilated, attempts to drum up enthusiasm in America came to little, and by 1942 the trickle of new escapees from occupied Europe dwindled to almost nothing. To cover losses in the air, he was forced to draw men from the army group – much against the wishes of his Chief of Staff, General Sergej Ingr – and he was told by both the Secretary of State for Air, Archibald Sinclair and, the Foreign Secretary, Anthony Eden that he should choose which force he wanted to remain active, sacrificing the other for the sake of manpower provision. He refused to make that choice; therefore, for the whole of the war both the army and air force groups were permanently under strength.

## The development of the Czechoslovak Brigade

From the first day of the exodus from France, the Prime Minister, Winston Churchill had insisted that all the European groups be given every assistance in their reorganization. From his standpoint, this was primarily an exercise in propaganda directed toward the United States and the Dominions, so he directed the Chiefs of Staff to furnish him with weekly reports on the allied contingents. A trawl through these summaries reveals that the Czechoslovak Brigade was by the winter of 1940 fully equipped as an infantry battalion with anti-tank sections and field gun batteries with a total strength of about 3,000 men. Morale was described in October as 'good and improving', but very soon a secret report was issued to the War Office recommending that both the Polish and Czechoslovak contingents should be kept in the Britain 'until the such time as the re-occupation of their own countries is feasible and likely to be unopposed'.[1] In the long run, this policy had no impact on the Poles, but shaped Czechoslovak fortunes.

In January 1941, the Brigade received an influential visitor. Robert Bruce Lockhart had been appointed by the Foreign Office as political representative to the Provisional Czechoslovak Government. He received this brief because of his close association with Beneš and Czechoslovakia's first President Tomáš Masaryk in the inter-war years. On Czechoslovak matters, he was completely trusted by the Foreign Office. He visited the Brigade's new home at Leamington Spa (where a memorial to them stands to this day) in company with Beneš and the Polish leader General Władysław Sikorski. Lockhart's report of the visit contained the following observations:

> The Brigade contains a considerable percentage of bespectacled individuals upon whose frames the modern British battle-dress... hung clumsily. It was difficult to distinguish an officer from a private, and I formed the impression that here was democracy on the march, with certain manifest weaknesses and inherent virtues which have already stood the test of a harrowing experience in France. Two themes prevailed: gratitude to, and admiration for, this country, and bitterness against France. Several men used the same phrase: 'In France we were treated like dogs – here we are handled as men.' Like all people who have been enslaved for long periods, the Czechoslovaks are well versed in the arts of concealment... but I believe sincerely today that the spirit of the Czechoslovak forces in Britain is good.[2]

This report went directly to the Eden, largely upon the latter's insistence that anything connected with the exiled forces which contributed to a reliable impression should be brought to his attention first. Bruce Lockhart was moved to the Political Warfare Executive in 1941 when Philip Nichols became British ambassador to the fully recognized Czechoslovak government, but he was still consulted regularly, though unofficially, by Beneš and Jan Masaryk on diplomatic affairs.

By April 1941, the Brigade had been further visited by various British and Czechoslovak personalities, all of whom had pronounced the unit to be a fine body of men. Training proceeded throughout the summer, and by the early autumn the British Inspector General of Allied Contingents, General Sir George Cory, declared the Brigade ready for action when the moment arrived. But what action, and when? That much was still to be decided. A confidential memorandum circulated within the

War Office that October determined that allied groups from the west might conceivably be utilized in a general assault on occupied Europe, leading inevitably to the liberation of their own countries. But groups from the east should either be fully integrated into the invasion of France or, given the new circumstances of the Soviet entry into the war, be prepared for a transfer to the eastern front.

But these were not the practical considerations in 1942. The reports reaching Churchill had become quarterly by this time, and all parties acknowledged that the Czechoslovak Brigade was significantly under strength and likely to remain so in the foreseeable future. In London, Beneš was still under heavy pressure from the British to transfer more men to the air force, but still he remained adamant. For some time there had been a group of Czechoslovaks in the Middle East, men who had been trained and organized as an anti-aircraft battery. This unit had served with distinction in the defence of Tobruk, and it was suggested to Beneš that they be brought to Britain to address the acute manpower shortages. Reluctantly, he concurred. Further reinforcements came from the less fanatical communist sympathizers who were interned in 1940. Realizing now that the Soviet Union was in need of help, many volunteered for service with the Brigade again. About 150 men were released from the Pioneers and re-enlisted. This clearly demonstrates how flawed Beneš's manpower policy was at its core. A couple of years before, those same men who re-joined the Brigade were political outcasts; now the President they had so roundly condemned needed every man he could get.[3]

As the war entered its middle years, and still no prospect of a European offensive was in sight, both the British and Czechoslovak authorities recognized that the Brigade could not be deployed as an infantry unit and function effectively in the field. The solution was to reorganize the group into an Armoured Brigade that needed fewer men. By the middle of 1942, the total strength of the group was 700 officers and 2,670 other ranks, but nearly 400 of the officers – mainly older men nearing demobilization age – undertook general duties with the ranks. This gave, on paper at least, a healthier ratio of officers to men, roughly 1 to 9. As the reorganization plan matured into 1943, the War Office admitted that even then the group would still be under strength. The full complement of a British armoured brigade at this time was 352 officers and 4,542 other ranks, whereas the Czechoslovaks could only muster 490 officers and 2,395 men indicating that there were 39 per cent too many officers and 47 per cent too few of the other ranks. It was agreed that some further manipulation might reduce the officer strength, but there was simply no hope of doubling the numbers in the ranks. This meant that they would always be short of a full field battalion. A further injection of men from the Middle East and the Pioneers would help matters, but in no way could they meet the full war establishment. The Czechoslovaks felt the lack of recruits harder than many other exile armies.

The conversion to an armoured brigade began in June 1943. Equipment was slow to arrive at first, but the Chiefs of Staff report declared that all ranks were 'very pleased' at the prospect of the new role for the Czechoslovak Army. At roughly the same time, a deployment policy had been finally agreed, more relevant now that the initial planning for Operation Overlord was under way. A directive stated that the Brigade would not be used on the initial assaults by sea, 'but they will be retained in general reserve and employed as an armoured formation in a later phase of the operations'.[4] This satisfied Beneš who wanted to return home with an experienced army group as the core of his future rearmament policies; and it suited the British who for political reasons did not want the Brigade rendered unfit for operations through rapid attrition. This was the eventual distillation of a series of meetings conducted at the end of 1942 between representatives of the British and Czechoslovak governments. In December 1942, Philip Nichols informed the Foreign Office that the Brigade should be 'blooded' in battle 'since they could never hold up their heads in Prague unless they have been in actual combat with the Germans'. He accepted that some of the men had been involved in the retreat from France, but that they would receive no welcome in their own country until and unless they fought the Germans in later stages of the war:

> The dilemma is plain. The Brigade must go into action but it must not be decimated. If...it was to be put in the forefront of the battle, it might well lose half its effectives, with the result that Beneš and his Government would be reduced to the use of something under 2,000 men. It seems to follow that the future employment...must be regarded largely from the political as opposed to the military angle; that the method of its employment is in fact a political rather than a military question. [The Brigade] should play its part, but should not be called upon to make heavy sacrifices.

Nichols further had claimed that he had mentioned all of this to the Czechoslovak Foreign Minister, Jan Masaryk, who 'entirely agreed'.[5]

## Into action: Siege of Dunkirk

As 1944 began and D-Day approached, the re-named Independent Czechoslovak Armoured Brigade was fully equipped with Cromwell tanks and stood ready to play its part when called upon to do so. Some surplus officers had been posted to the Soviet Union to replace casualties within the 3,000-strong Czechoslovak infantry brigade fighting on the eastern front, and the release of the men from the Middle East had brought the group near to its official war establishment. As the prospect of real action drew near after four long years of training, Beneš visited the Brigade on the eve of their departure for France. Beneš reminded them that the British had been their hosts and their friends, but also that the Red Army would receive them with honour. It was stirring stuff, but Beneš was unaware as to exactly what his Army would be doing in France and his desire for a glorious entry into Prague was to be bitterly disappointed.

The reconnaissance parties for the Brigade arrived in France on 27 August 1944 to liase with other allied commanders and prepare the assembly points for the full contingent. Attached to the 21st Army Group, the Brigade's total strength was now 238 officers and 3,936 other ranks – still under strength, but capable of functioning as an effective unit in certain circumstances. After arriving in France, the armoured brigade moved to the Falaise area for further training. On 24 September, a meeting between General Ingr and the British Chief Liaison Officer, determined that no first line reinforcements were available. British war establishments for reinforcements were generally fixed at 10 per cent, but with the Brigade already under strength and the likelihood of any liberated men stepping forward for service being remote, it was clear that they could withstand scarcely any casualties at all. Nine days later they received their battle orders. They were to proceed to Dunkirk and contain a substantial German garrison. The enemy numbers were estimated at 15,000 men of all ranks, and though strictly a job for an infantry brigade, the Czechs were told that this would be 'an excellent way of giving them their initial battle experience'.[6]

At the same time, there was a ray of hope concerning potential recruitment with the liberation of several thousand Czechs and Slovaks from occupied France. The numbers were placed at 4,000–5,000 civilians plus another 1,000 prisoners of war (POWs). In theory at least, this could easily have made up the Brigade's shortfall and probably provided the replacements as well, but there were no screening or training facilities in France, so the decision was taken to send recruits back to England pending further action. Nevertheless, the British acted quickly, and by mid-November over 900 Czechoslovaks were listed as being in basic training.

The Czechoslovak brigade moved to the perimeter of Dunkirk in Autumn 1944. The Brigade sat outside the town until the end of the war with little to do but wait upon events. The Germans had strong fortifications. Much of the landscape was flooded and their defences lay behind the flooded areas across a perimeter line of some 21 miles. Around 17,000 civilians had been voluntarily evacuated and on the first night of the investment the Germans attempted a break-out, forcing the Czechs back. Within 48 hours the positions had been re-taken, but the episode became the general pattern for many weeks and then months. According to a report compiled by the British liaison officer to the force, an air of permanence took hold and at the Brigade headquarters they gave lunches, dinners and received guests. The British liaison officer even complained that 'gin and whisky levels ran low in the first few days of the month'.[7] This same officer also reported that the Germans remained in control of the anti-aircraft positions and as a consequence several British and American aircraft were brought down because they were unaware that Dunkirk was still in enemy hands. He noted also that the French government tabled several complaints at the destruction and the potential danger presented to the 665 French nationals who had refused to leave the town back in October. When Czechoslovakia was on the point of liberation the Brigade stepped up the bombardment in an effort to force the Germans to surrender. Heavy air attacks were also scheduled, but the garrison still refused to capitulate.

## The Independent Brigade at the close of the war

With General Omar Bradley's 12th American Army Group preparing a final thrust into western Czechoslovakia, most in the Brigade hoped for a sudden change of orders to head east at all speed, but the orders never came. The British liaison officer noted that morale dipped alarmingly. Beneš was also becoming impatient and instructed General Ingr to petition the British authorities for a more active role for the Brigade only to be told that it would be too difficult to find a replacement unit. Nichols, the ambassador, reported to Eden in early April that it was politically desirable that the Brigade should have some part in the liberation. After all, it was magnificently equipped and now fully up to strength for the first time thanks to the new recruits from France. 'When asked what part they played in the victories in the west', wrote Nichols, 'it would be hard to reply that, with their equipment, all they had done was sit outside Dunkirk'. A few days later, he urged Eden to send at least a token force to the east.[8]

Then came news of a major re-shuffle in the Czechoslovak High Command. Beneš, perhaps demonstrating to the Soviets that he could install into positions of power men with knowledge of Red Army methods, replaced many of his western commanders with officers who had seen service in the east, Ingr being among the casualties. The alarm bells sounded in Whitehall. There were already intense discussions in progress regarding the repatriation of the Czechoslovak Air Force into the Soviet zone, and now it became apparent that unless swift action was taken, the entire Czechoslovak land forces may fall under Soviet influence before the men even got out of France. The 'token force' idea was soon presented to General Dwight D. Eisenhower, who immediately agreed, and early in May a group of around 150 was sent with all haste to join up with Bradley's army as they crossed into northern Bohemia. A few days later, on 9 May, the German Dunkirk garrison surrendered to the commander of the Czechoslovak Independent Armoured Brigade.[9]

Within days, the entire Brigade was sent to the Czech lands. Its first task was to relieve the American forces around Plzen, clearing the area of renegade Germans who were looting, but what the Brigade wanted to do most of all was march into Prague. That pleasure was denied them for a while because the British and the Americans were keen to obtain Soviet permission first, but on 30 May the whole force paraded triumphantly through the city before withdrawing again to the north. By June the Brigade was renamed the First Armoured Corps and given a Soviet organizational structure. Demobilization of men over 40 years of age began in July and formal application to release the Brigade from the command of American forces was made by Beneš, now returned to Prague. He was already under extreme pressure to permit the re-equipping of the force by the Red Army and one by one his western commanders were replaced or dislodged by pro-Soviet officers.

In August 1945 the *Manchester Guardian* ran an article by a Czech officer that warned of the deteriorating political situation in his country. On a happier note, he praised the people of Britain for their courage and kindness and his own countrymen for the hero's welcome they gave him and his comrades: 'They called us "the Intellectual Brigade" or "the Army of Lords", partly because we were so well fed and turned out, and partly because we never stopped talking about England'.[10] It was this willingness to talk freely and positively about their British experience that hastened the extinction of the Brigade as an independent unit. In October 1945, Philip Nichols reported to the new British Foreign

Secretary, Ernest Bevin, that since the return of the force to home territory it had been 'a valuable instrument of pro-British propaganda', adding that their discipline and appearance stood starkly in contrast to that of their countrymen who had seen service in the East. The Brigade, said Nichols, demonstrated 'the superior civilisation of the West', but a couple of sentences later he was lamenting the fact that it would now soon merge into the larger background of the Czechoslovak Army. Nichols even suspected that the Beneš government welcomed such a development, quite possibly because they were embarrassed by what the ambassador called 'this inconvenient advertisement' for the western alliance.[11] Thus by the end of 1945, the Czechoslovak Independent Armoured Brigade had effectively ceased to exist as a discrete entity, many of the men who had been with the unit since the dark days of 1940 facing an insecure future and, for more than a few, eventual imprisonment simply because of their link to the West.

## Conclusion

It would be impossible to write that the Brigade had a glorious history during its time in exile. The Czechoslovak soldiers in the west sustained casualties in France, some in the Middle East, and a few in the siege of Dunkirk, but the allied policy of keeping them far from the front line had limited their operational experience. There is evidence to suggest that Beneš and his commanders wanted it that way. He was well aware that he faced a dangerous and possibly revolutionary situation when he returned to Prague. Moreover, he made it clear time and again that he wanted an experienced, well trained core of army and air personnel ready to call upon in crisis or as the base for the reconstruction of the national defences. The Communists were equally aware of this, which is why they worked to undermine the Brigade.

In the final analysis, the Brigade and the Air Force were beacons of hope for the oppressed at home, and symbols of the reconciliation between the British and the Czechoslovaks, a way of demonstrating that Munich was a shabby crime and should be written off as a political mistake. The Brigade was also so small in number that in a major battle they risked effective destruction as a viable military formation. Neither Beneš nor the British authorities could contemplate such a disaster for political reasons if nothing else. Thus they were not given the chance to show what they were really capable of achieving in military terms, but they certainly would have risen to the occasion had the opportunity been presented to them.

## Notes

1. Inspector General's Summary, 29 November 1940, WO 193/32, Public Record Office, Kew (Hereafter PRO).
2. Bruce Lockhart to Eden, 7 February 1941, FO 371/26376, PRO.
3. An exception to this rule were Sudeten Germans, a few hundred of whom volunteered at various stages to serve with the Czechoslovak forces. All of them were refused unless they possessed some particular technical skills. It is also worth noting that the British assessment of the men interned after the Cholmondeley Park disturbances was most positive. The Inspector General described them as 'very good material' except for 15 or 20 'bad sorts'. He would have happily enlisted them into the British Army had that been politically acceptable. See: Minutes of Army Council, 14 September 1940, WO 163/48, PRO.
4. War Office Directive, 21 July 1943, WO 193/32, PRO.
5. Nichols to Roberts, 8 December 1942, FO 371/30855, PRO.
6. Allied Liaison, 24 September 1944, WO 171/175, PRO.
7. Report of the Siege of Dunkirk, undated, but probably June 1945, WO 205/1233, PRO.
8. Nichols to Eden, 3 April 1944 and 18 April 1945, FO 371/47139, PRO.
9. The report by Captain G. H. Stephenson, FO 1063/38, PRO.
10. Article in the *Manchester Guardian* 7 August 1945 as recorded in FO 371/47091, PRO.
11. Nicols to Bevin, 12 October 1945, FO 371/47093, PRO.

# 2
# French Exile Armies 1940–44

*Anthony Clayton*

The armed forces in exile of France, after the French collapse in June 1940 in which the army was traumatized by the speed and totality of its defeat, pose very special problems of understanding. To follow the confused motives, occasionally even leading to confrontation between Frenchmen in exile of one faction and Frenchmen in exile of another, it is necessary to analyse what precisely had happened in June 1940, what exactly General Charles de Gaulle came, more quickly than has sometimes been appreciated, to stand for, and on what the supporters of Vichy France, admittedly composed of many different strands, could, at least initially, agree. These different views, or at least strands within them, were to lead to two quite different groupings of armed forces in exile. Their differences were so great that even in 1944 when the armies of both perceptions had actually and with massive outside help landed in France to liberate their country, formations could not agree on unification, and continued to fight their separate battles even when in close proximity.

With hindsight, we can now see that the French collapse of 1940 and the acquiescence of the Vichy regime to a German European hegemony, an attitude that among some politicians, notably Pierre Laval, amounted to an actual approval, represented, to use the term of some modern French historians, *une fracture*, a fault line.[1] This *fracture* split down the centre the traditional post-1870 European strategic policy of France, that of the support of freedom, parliamentary democracy and resistance to authoritarianism and domination by others, in particular Germany. The Vichy regime from the start and increasingly as time passes, represented a break from that past, an acquiescent 'if you can't beat them join them' view towards Germany, a view not devoid of, albeit misguided, concern for the welfare of French people and one sincerely held, for example, by

Admiral François Darlan, who can justly be accused of self-destroying ambition but not of lack of patriotism. To summarize this view, German was the leading European power, Britain at Dunkirk had shown she was not going to help and would probably lose the war, Communism was the real danger, France's future lay in combating Communism, and within German hegemony, securing the best deal, whatever could be safeguarded. The violence and horrors of the Spanish Civil War, viewed across the Pyrenees by senior French officers and others before the war, seemed amply to justify anyone, even Adolf Hitler, who stood out against Communism.

De Gaulle and the whole Free French movement challenged this view, seeing it as gross betrayal. For the Free French of 1940–41, drawn from the widest variety of views right and left within French politics and society, the capitulation must be wrong, for many at first a simple gut reaction. The *fracture* was indefensible, if France was ever again to stand for anything with honour it could not be surrender – for many even if they doubted any ultimate victory over the Germans the fight must continue. They were fortunate in their views in having the towering personality of Charles de Gaulle to be their leader. Jean Lacouture's biography very revealingly sets out the development in de Gaulle's mind from June to July 1940, at first as a dissident soldier totally opposed to any armistice, then in a protest revolt against the capitulation, and finally a man who finds a leadership role thrust upon him, allied with a nation that from his childhood he had been brought up to dislike intensely, but with a legitimacy based on traditional moral French national policies and totally rejecting the *fracture*.[2] Lacouture suggests that one event in particular crystallized de Gaulle in his views and was in time to lead to the adhesion of many Frenchmen to his cause – the 19 July 1940 French parliament meeting offering Marshal Philippe Pétain vast personal enabling legislative powers.[3] In contradistinction, de Gaulle could justifiably begin to claim that Free France was the true, legitimate Republic.

It is only within these two frames that an understanding of France's forces in exile, after the collapse of 1940, can begin. Understanding of what de Gaulle truly represented, the significance of his stand against the *fracture* was not evident in London in the summer and autumn, faced with the clear evidence of massive support for Pétain in France itself. The Poles, Norwegians, Netherlands and Belgium had a London-based government in exile, recognized as legitimate, headed by known national figures. No one saw de Gaulle as more than a difficult French junior general with his heart in the right place even if his tongue was not, at the head of a committee that included some relatively unknown and in some cases odd characters, certainly not a body that could not conceivably meet any claim to be the legitimate government of the French nation. All that London was prepared to do politically was to recognize de Gaulle as the head of Free France, while at the same time paying for and equipping his volunteers. As time passed de Gaulle increasingly exasperated the British Prime Minister Winston Churchill, but the friction never affected British support for Free French soldiers and sailors. The most overt British support for de Gaulle came from King George VI, despite the fact that one of the King's governments, Canada, actually recognized Vichy.

The armies that were developed by both sides of the *fracture* differed sharply as a consequence of the divide. De Gaulle's forces were prepared from the outset to fight the Axis. Those on the other side, principally the North African army quietly developed by Generals Maxime Weygand and Alphonse Juin, were a 'force in being'. It was not an army whose primary aim was a return to the *metropole*, rather it sought to preserve French North Africa and be a powerful military and diplomatic card in the hand of an otherwise very weak France. It was only to become a fully combatant army in exile specifically seeking to liberate the *metropole* after the Allied landings in North Africa in November 1942.[4] Curiously there was one feature common to both these armies, each contained a very large number of men who were not born native Frenchmen.

## De Gaulle's Free French forces

Only a few soldiers rallied to de Gaulle at the outset due to Anglophobia occasioned by the evacuation of Dunkirk and resentment of British comments on the French collapse. Those who rallied included a handful of *Fusiliers Marins* (marines) from warships in British ports, a small number of *Chasseurs Alpins* and half of the survivors from an obscure demi-brigade of the *Légion Etrangère* (Foreign Legion) these latter having been withdrawn from the unsuccessful operations in Norway. The Legion demi-brigade contained a high percentage of Jews and Spanish Republicans for whom return to Vichy France could not be an option. These were all grouped in one unit, under the Legion's title of the 13th Demi-Brigade (DBLE). In Cyprus, a detached battalion of *Coloniale* infantry largely composed of Breton soldiers, and a squadron of *Spahis Marocains* also opted for de Gaulle despite the impact upon French opinion created by the Royal Navy's attack on the French fleet at Mers el-Kebir on 3 July; these were joined during the summer of 1940 by some 7,000 more men arriving by one route or another, a number from the parent *Coloniale* infantry regiment of the Cyprus battalion who escaped from Lebanon into Palestine. Colonies that declared for de Gaulle, the New Hebrides in July and those in French Equatorial Africa following the lead of Governor Felix Eboué of Chad, the successful entry of Colonel Philippe Leclerc into Cameroun and the small scale of operations in Gabon and Moyen-Congo raised the total to some 35,000; it was to reach 70,000 by early 1941.[5] While this total included many who escaped from France and other Frenchmen living in the colonies, the majority were indigenous colonial men, in particular Africans. However, due to the particular structure of the French Army, officers of *La Coloniale*, the special distinct Corps with an autonomous status akin to that of the United States Marines, and with the dual roles of sponsoring indigenous *Tirailleurs* regiments and the defence of all French colonies were more inclined to respond to de Gaulle's call. These officers were often southern Frenchmen, of lower middle class origin, both by adventurous temperament and by their absence from France less awed by spectres of the Spanish Civil War. They included generals Edgard de Larminat and Paul Legentilhomme, and more significantly for the future, Capitaine Jacques Massu.

It was agreed with the British Government in August 1940 that Free French troops would not be asked to fight against France, and in March 1941 that the British would fund the Gaullist contingent on the basis of a loan repayable after the end of the war. The loan appears to have been repaid, and in any case, from January 1943 the French were able to provide essential funding for themselves – though of course with massive American military equipment aid. The Free French interpreted the August 1940 agreement as, nevertheless, permitting them to combat individual Frenchmen who opposed them, the basis for later actions in Africa and in Syria. The Vichy regime first deprived all who supported de Gaulle of their nationality and then on 31 July announced that all who had failed to return to France by 15 August would be sentenced to death. Later Vichy legislation provided for sentences of death for all military personnel who opted to join de Gaulle, with loss of citizenship and two years hard labour for civilians. In December 1941 an Oran military tribunal sentenced *in absentia* 24 named senior Free French officers.[6] There appears, however, to have been only relatively few cases of victimizing the families of Free French personnel still in France, and it seems that in most cases dependants of Free French personnel continued to receive payment of allowances from one source or another. At a later stage in the war when the Germans stated they would execute all Free French prisoners that they took, the Free French riposte, that they would kill all German prisoners that they had captured caused the Germans to abandon their policy.

Nevertheless, Free French personnel who had escaped from France, *les métros* needed special protection. Escape was in any case exceedingly difficult, especially for those living in Occupied France hoping to escape over the Pyrenees who had first to cross a German guarded border to enter Unoccupied France. Spain, with memories of the Blum Popular Front government's support for the Republicans in the Civil War, controlled the frontier as best it could, and returned escapees caught across the border. The other preferred escape route, by boat across the Channel, soon became equally hazardous, with German air and naval surveillance. Some escapees tried to pretend they were French Canadians. Those caught trying to escape were deprived of citizenship and given sentences of hard labour often leading before long to a concentration camp. On arrival in Britain many, in particular Jews, had to be given new names and new identities to disguise their métro origin. One or two, notably Philippe de Hauteclocque, assumed a new name, in his case Jacques Leclerc, for idealistic reasons believing in the need for a spiritual rebirth, akin to entering a monastic order.[7] The métros, having left all behind, proved generally to be exceptionally well motivated.

## Free French in action 1940–43

De Gaulle's soldiers, although few in number, were soon at work. In September 1940 the two battalions of the 13th DBLE sailed on the abortive Dakar expedition without seeing action. After Colonel Leclerc's audacious landing in Cameroun, securing the colony and a little later also Moyen-Congo for de Gaulle in August 1940, the 13th DBLE and two other improvised columns formed from three *Tirailleurs Sénégalais* and local colonist units then entered and took Gabon after clashes with Vichy forces costing 30 dead. These colonies were all now in de Gaulle's hands and drafting for new Senegalese units began on a district quota system. After the rallying to de Gaulle by Eboué, the Governor of Chad, and the arrival of Leclerc at Fort Lamy, operations in southern Libya commenced. In January 1941 a handful of *Coloniale* officers (including Massu), NCOs and Chad irregulars worked with the British Long Range Desert Group. A little later Leclerc led a column of 350, mostly Senegalese and *Groupe Nomade* irregulars with one field gun and four mortars, to encircle and eventually take the Italian garrison at the Kufra Oasis. This event, at a cost of four dead and a few more wounded, had much symbolic importance for the Free French cause, the first Free French victory over the Axis. Leclerc made a prophetic address, the *Serment de Kufra*, signalling the event as part of a process only to be completed with the liberation of Strasbourg. Meanwhile, in the Eritrean campaign, the 13th DBLE together with a Senegalese battalion and the *Spahis* squadron was serving with the British and Indian forces, being the first to enter Massawa. These units were then moved to the Middle East, where they, joined by the Cyprus *Coloniale* infantry battalion, began their involvement in the theatre. Two newly recruited Senegalese battalions also arrived in Egypt from Equatorial Africa for installation guard duties.

In the June 1941 Syrian operations a small 1st Light Division composed of the DBLE, the *Coloniale* infantry, and four Senegalese battalions together with the Moroccan *Spahis* squadron participated, on occasions fighting against Vichy Legion and Senegalese units. After defeat, the majority of the Vichy forces opted for a return to France or North Africa, but de Gaulle gained almost all the Vichy Senegalese, some 1,500, together with 690 of the Vichy Legion regiment and 980 North African soldiers, mainly Moroccans. These additions led to restructuring, the best units being sent to the Western Desert and the remainder, mainly Senegalese, being retained in Syria and Lebanon to try to reassert a French presence.

The following year, 1942, saw the Free French forces both beginning to restore self-confidence in French military capabilities and gaining the respect of the British and, later, the Americans. In the disastrous summer of 1942 the 1st Free French Brigade composed of the 13th DBLE, and three *Coloniale* battalions including one recruited in the Free French Pacific territories, together with two light artillery companies fought a brilliant 15 day defensive battle at Bir Hakeim. This brigade was a little later to be joined by the Moroccan *Spahis*, now expanded to a full regiment and a third battalion for the 13th DBLE. At Alamein the Brigade again fought tenaciously, one of the Legion commanders, the Georgian Prince Dimitri Amilakvari, being killed in action. Also present at Alamein and in the pursuit across Libya was a 2nd Brigade, formed from three Equatorial African Senegalese battalions later in Tunisia joined by two more units recruited in Djibouti. All these in February 1943 were grouped together as the 1st Free French Division.

Of less real but far greater symbolic importance was the epic march of a column led by Leclerc from Chad across the Sahara to join up with Montgomery's 8th Army outside Tripoli. The infantry and light artillery of this force were again indigenous *Tirailleurs* or *Coloniale* artillerymen. Leclerc's small force went on to fight notably well and to Montgomery's great admiration, in the Mareth Line fighting and later served with the 1st Free French Division in the Tunisian campaign.

## The North African exile army

The 1940 armistice terms had allowed France to retain for internal security purposes a metropolitan army of 100,000 (the figure permitted Germany in 1919) but with restrictions on certain equipment; this force never achieved any real significance. However, for the French colonies, and in particular North Africa the Germans, as anxious for stability as the French though for different reasons, permitted a garrison of a further 100,000, later increased to 120,000 together with 33,000 later, 56,000 for West Africa, and also a small air force. The two Vichy-appointed army commanders in North Africa, Weygand and Juin, carefully built up the strength of this army, and engaged in numerous subterfuges to increase the permitted strengths by one means or another – misleading statistics, weapon caches concealed in caves, etc. Both commanders overtly saw their role as the defence of the three French North African territories, against anyone – Spain, Italy or America, or as a bargaining asset if necessary, in any final peace settlement with Germany. But they both had a hidden agenda, the preparation of a force which if circumstances so permitted could be used in an Allied liberation of France.

However strong the preferences of Juin and other carefully selected French generals in North Africa were in November 1942, they did not prevent the common phenomenon among exiles removed from home domestic realities, quarrelling. The arrival of the Anglo-American force met largely token land but very real, even if quickly overwhelmed, naval resistance. In the negotiations leading to the adhesion of the *Armée d'Afrique* to the Allied cause Juin played the most influential role, but the *Armée d'Afrique* looked for leadership to another general, Henri Giraud, brought out of France in the hope held by the Americans that he could marginalize de Gaulle, seen by them as profoundly anti-American.

The German occupation of unoccupied France served to convert the residents, civil and military, en masse to the Allied cause, and Juin saw his priority as being to contribute to the Allied forces attempting to enter Tunisia. Beginning with four battalions of Senegalese in action as early as 9 November, General Louis Koeltz's 19th Army Corps by the end of the Tunisian campaign totalled some 60,000 men in three small divisions, an armoured unit and a reserve. The Algiers Division comprised a regiment each of *Tirailleurs*, *Spahis* and *Zouaves*, with artillery and a Moroccan irregular unit of *Goums*. The Moroccan Division included a Moroccan *Tirailleurs* regiment, a Legion infantry and a Legion armoured regiment, a Senegalese battalion and a Morrocan artillery unit. The Oran Division included two Algerian and one Senegalese *Tirailleurs* regiments, a Legion infantry unit and artillery. In the armoured and general reserve units were squadrons of *Chasseurs d'Afrique*, a *Zouave* regiment, three Algerian and one Tunisian *Spahis* regiments, a further Senegalese regiment and a few artillery batteries.[8] Although much of their equipment was at the outset out-dated, the units fought well, earning American praise – and new equipment.

The sharp divisions remained however, and were summed up at the end of the campaign by Harold Macmillan, then British government minister resident in North Africa. 'The two kinds of French troops, Gaullists and Giraudists, now that there are no Germans to fight will soon start a civil war amongst themselves'.[9] Leclerc's forces were forbidden to cross into Algeria and Juin even tried to debar them from participation in the victory parade, a move countered by the appearance of Leclerc's forces at the head of the parade with the 8th Army in a place of honour, the 19th Corps units only appearing at the end. President Roosevelt's detestation of de Gaulle led him to urge Churchill to try and remove him. Churchill also believed de Gaulle to be anglophobe, authoritarian and consumed by ambition, but the British War Cabinet warned in strong terms against any attempt to remove him, so leaving Churchill as his reluctant patron.[10]

Eventually under Anglo-American brokering, an uneasy agreement was reached between Giraud and de Gaulle, which the latter soon came to dominate. Arrangements were agreed for the expansion and re-equipping of the French forces, now able to tap considerable reserves of local manpower, 175,000 French citizens (not all of French birth) and 230,000 indigenous North Africans being mobilized in accordance with early secret plans together with an increasing stream, of 25,000 by mid-1944, of *évadés* successfully crossing the Pyrenees.

De Gaulle, with an eye to the future and symbolic re-entry into Paris, ensured that an elite force, under Leclerc, would be available. Leclerc, to the annoyance of the *Armée d'Afrique* officers, was able by personal charisma and the better rates of pay on offer in British-sponsored units, to attract the manpower for what was to become the 2nd Armoured Division.

This division was composed in an attempt to reflect all interests. Most of the Africans were returned to Africa, but their achievement com-memorated in a new regiment, the proudly named *Régiment de Marche de Tchad*, (RMT). The RMT, a tank regiment, and the Moroccan *Spahis* regiment which had now been reformed to be a regiment of Europeans despite its name, maintained the Gaullist tradition; all these were composed of Leclerc's original followers, and large numbers of *évadés* and European and North African volunteers. A *Chasseurs d'Afrique* regiment and an artillery unit had *Armée d'Afrique* origins, another artillery unit was *Coloniale* from Dakar. Another armoured unit carried the name of an old pre-Revolution metropolitan French regiment, the 12th *Cuirassiers*. Engineers came from the Christian Lebanon community and logistic personnel came from as far afield as Pondicherry. A map of France was painted on all the divisions vehicles and tanks; at first only the units of Gaullist origin were permitted the addition of a Cross of Lorraine, but later the privilege was extended to the entire division after its departure from North Africa.[11]

In North Africa the expansion and re-equipment of the *Armée d'Afrique* continued throughout the summer of 1943. The Anglo-American force in the July–August 1943 Sicilian campaign included only a very small French component, a *tabor* (small battalion) of Moroccan *goums*. These were used by Patten to cover the mountain flanks of his forces during their advances on Palermo and then Messina. In late September 1943 an entirely French force transported in French warships liberated Corsica in a five day operation; the force comprised a *Bataillon de Choc*, a North African *Tirailleurs* battalion, two Moroccan *Spahis* squadrons, a group of *goums* and an artillery unit largely French.

In November 1943, however, began the *Armée d'Afrique*'s finest achievement, with the arrival – after American assent only grudgingly given – of the first units of the *Corps Expéditionnaire Français* (CEF) in Italy, unfortunately not well clothed for a severe Italian winter: – two divisions, the 2nd Moroccan Infantry Division, of a Moroccan *Spahis* and three *Tirailleurs* regiments with an artillery unit, and the 3rd Algerian Division of an Algerian *Spahis* and two *Tirailleurs* regiments together with a Tunisian *Tirailleurs* regiment and an artillery unit. A *Chasseurs d'Afrique* armoured regiment, formed from the Algeria detachments of the Vichy *Chantiers de Jeunesse* youth movement, and two *goum* units arrived a little later. By May 1944 two further divisions had arrived. Of these the Gaullist 1st Motorized Division, the new name proposed for the 1st Free French Division, included the 13th DBLE, a battalion recruited in North Africa, three Senegalese battalions, three *Coloniale* infantry battalions, two of which had been recruited in Djibouti and the third formed from survivors of the Pacific unit and *évadés*, a *Coloniale* artillery unit from Djibouti, some marines, technical staff from Syria, anti-aircraft gunners from the Antilles and *Signalles* from Pondicherry.

The 4th Moroccan Mountain Division was composed similarly to the 2nd, a regiment of *Spahis*, three regiments of *Tirailleurs* and artillery units. Other Corps units to arrive included artillery units, one recruited in the Levant, another *Chasseurs d'Afrique* regiment and a *goum* unit. The three

*Armée d'Afrique* divisions each of some 7,000 North Africans with 7,000 French officers and NCOs soon earned a high reputation, the oddly assorted Gaullist division was less well viewed. Finally a fifth division, the 9th Colonial Infantry Division, of three Senegalese regiments, one *Coloniale* armoured, one artillery and two infantry units with other smaller detachments, in total some 7,000 Europeans and 10,000 Africans, arrived in time for operations in June. The division, supported by *goums* and two special force units, also later stormed the heavily fortified island of Elba.[12]

The French Corps' past experience of cold weather conditions and mountain warfare, with special know-how in infantry mobility, surprise, night infiltration, hand-to-hand fighting and the use of mules for supply, made the North African divisions perhaps the finest in the Allied armies. In addition, in Juin, the Corps had a battlefield commander of exceptional tactical ability.[13] The Corps' greatest achievements were at Cassino and in the final stages of the advance on Rome when Moroccan *Tirailleurs* and *goums* swarmed over the Arunci mountains, surprising and putting to flight some of the best regiments in the German army. The *goums*, however, earned an evil reputation for the rapine and pillage of their Atlas warfare style, and it proved difficult to persuade the Americans to allow them to be used in later operations. After the capture of Rome and Sienna the French Corps was withdrawn to prepare for its participation in the landings in the South of France, its place assured by the Corps achievements in Italy.

The honour of being the first French troops to return from exile to the French mainland, was, nevertheless, to fall to Leclerc's 2nd Armoured Division. Retrained in Britain (much of the training, including an officer cadet school, being in Scotland) generously equipped by the Americans and commanded by Leclerc, one of the Second World War's finest divisional commanders, the division was transported to Utah Beach, Normandy on the 1st August. It was very soon in action with the US 3rd Army and to the division fell the honour of entry to Paris, an honour that was followed by stiff fighting and severe casualties in Alsace and Germany.

The much larger French contribution to the Liberation was, however, the French 1st Army of General Jean de Lattre de Tassigny, which began landing on the Riviera coast on 15 August. This force had been put together amid objections from Leclerc who refused to join it, from Juin who had wanted to continue operations in Italy, and from the Americans and British who were initially opposed to the concept of an entirely French Army; indeed it was only allowed its title of the 1st Army after the Riviera landings.

The 1st Army ultimately totalled two armoured and five infantry divisions. First ashore, alongside the American 7th Army, were four divisions. These were the 3rd Algerian Infantry Division, the 1st Free French Division proudly displaying the Cross of Lorraine on its vehicles and reverting to its old title, the 9th Colonial Infantry Division, and a fresh formation, the 1st Armoured Division composed of two *Chasseurs d'Afrique* armoured regiments, the 2nd *Cuirassiers*, metropolitan at least in name, a demi-brigade of *Zouaves* as infantry, and an artillery unit. These were supported by a general reserve of two special force units, three *tabors* of *goums*, a regiment of Senegalese, three *Coloniale* and three further *Chasseurs d'Afrique* armoured regiments, an Algerian *Spahis* reconnaissance regiment and one *Coloniale* and one *Armée d'Afrique* artillery unit. Most of these reserve units were soon posted to the front line divisions. The 2nd Moroccan Infantry Division and the 4th Moroccan Mountain Division followed soon after the initial landings, composed as in Italy with the exception that an Algerian *Tirailleurs* regiment had replaced one of the Moroccan *Tirailleurs*. Finally in September arrived the 5th Armoured Division formed at the outset of a *Chasseurs d'Afrique* and a Legion armoured regiment, a Legion infantry regiment and an artillery unit, to be joined later by an infantry unit raised in France. These divisions were grouped into two army corps, under the 1st French Army command, in September.[14]

The French 1st Army fought with flair and valour under de Lattre, another general of brilliance even if of uncertain temper.[15] Shortages of equipment often produced the *Armée d'Afrique*'s flair for improvisation. The Army campaigned on the east flank of the Americans. The North Africans swiftly raced over the mountains capturing Toulon and Marseille, and the divisions then advanced up the Rhône, fought a bitter and tenacious winter campaign in the Vosges and then, crossing the Rhine, moved on into Germany finishing the war on the shores of Lake Constance.

Several features of interest in the Liberation and Germany operations need mention as these arise from the exile formation of the French forces. First was the process of *blanchiment* that occurred in the autumn and winter of 1944–45, all Black African and a number of North African soldiers being returned home and their places filled in the regiments by young Frenchmen, mostly from the Resistance French Forces of the Interior. This exchange was done for reasons climatic, military, many of the Africans being exhausted, and political, de Gaulle seeing a need to convince Frenchmen that, at least in part, Frenchmen were liberating themselves. For this display reason Leclerc's division was often moved across large areas of France. Leclerc himself flatly refused all de Lattre's attempts to persuade him to join the 1st French Army. For Leclerc his formation had a special symbolic role as the vanguard of a national regeneration, not to be diluted or taken over. Below the surface in the French North African, particularly Algerian, units there were a few indications that the *Tirailleurs* had their own agenda on the war. On one occasion French officers were horrified to find a large flag, the banner of Abd el-Kader who has led the resistance to the French in the 1840s, in a barracks. De Lattre himself recorded his anxieties that the Algerians were beginning to see themselves as exploited by the *metropole*, '*sentiment terriblement dangereux*'.[16] The forces brought over from Algeria included two regiments of horsed *Spahis*, used against militant radicals, many Spanish, in the Toulouse area before service in the Black Forest. The Gaullist 1st Light Division, reinforced by an Algerian and further Senegalese units, was moved to the Alps in the last weeks of the war, a secondary role seen by some as a gesture of spite by Juin. Some of its units were detached for service against German-held Atlantic ports, as were others from Leclerc's division.

Finally, although the French Army had come home its heavy dependence on Africans, particularly North African troops was to leave in the minds of many Frenchmen, particularly among the military, a view that France's future independence against the new great powers, in particular '*les anglo-saxons*', could only be assured by the retention of North Africa and its manpower resources.[17] This view was to have disastrous consequences later.

Another legacy of the France's exiled armies was the institutionalization of the many personal animosities arising from the 1940 *fracture* in the ground forces. Liberated from German captivity by the Americans, General Weygand was transported to de Lattre's headquarters. At his arrival, on instructions from de Gaulle, de Lattre had to inform Weygand that he was to be taken under escort to Paris. For his departure le Lattre provided a guard of honour of picked troops, but on his arrival in Paris Weygand was incarcerated under humiliating conditions. The creator of one of France's exile armies had ordered the arrest of the creator of the other, the passions aroused by the *fracture* remaining despite victory and liberation.[18]


## Notes

1. For example, papers given at the Colloque 'Du Capitaine de Hauteclocque au Général Leclerc, Maréchal de France', by J. P. Azema and J. L. Cremieux-Brilhac, Paris, November 1997 in Christine Levisse Iouzé (ed.), *Du Capitaine de Hauteclerque au général Leclerc.* (Paris, Editions Complexe, 2000).

2. Jean Lacouture, (trans. P. O'Brian), *De Gaulle: The Rebel 1890–1944* (London, Collins Harvill, 1990), pp. xviii, xix.
3. Lacouture, *De Gaulle: The Rebel 1890–1944*, p. 255.
4. For the composition of these forces see: Anthony Clayton, *France, Soldiers and Africa* (London, Brassey's, 1988).
5. Guy Ganachaud, *Les FFL et l'Armée d'Afrique* (Paris, Tallandier, 1990), p. 13.
6. *Ibid.*, p. 14.
7. See Anthony Clayton, *Three Marshals of France* (London, Brassey's, 1991).
8. The composition of the 19th Army Corps is set out in greater detail in: Clayton, *France, Soldiers and Africa*, p. 140.
9. Harold Macmillan, *The Blast of war 1939–1945* (London: Macmillan – new Palgrave Macmillan 1967), p. 324.
10. A summary of the May 1943 crisis appears in *The Times*, 5 January 2000, p. 3 based on records released the previous day at the Public Record Office.
11. Clayton, *France, Soldiers and Africa*, pp. 141–2.
12. *Ibid.*, pp. 143–5.
13. Clayton, *Three Marshals of France*, pp. ii, iv and vii provide a biography of Juin.
14. Clayton, *France, Soldiers and Africa*, pp. 145–8.
15. For a biography of de Lattre see Clayton, *Three Marshals of France*, pp. ii, v and vii.
16. Maréchal Jean de Lattre, *Reconquerir, Ecrits 1944–1945* (Paris: Plon, 1985), letter to A. Diethelm, 9 November 1944, p. 75.
17. For an example of this view see General Goilard de Monsabert's preface to General R. Huré (ed.), *L'Armée d'Afrique, 1830–1962* (Paris: Laranzelle, 1977), p. 1. De Monsabert wrote: 'It is thanks to the *Armée d'Afrique* that France rediscovered not only the road to victory and faith in the army, but also and above all Honour and Freedom'.
18. Bernard Destremau, *Weygand* (Paris, Perrin, 1989), pp. 746–9. After trial by the High Court of Justice and further subsequent enquiries, Weygand was eventually acquitted of all charges of collaboration with the Germans.

# 3
# Polish Exile Armies, 1939–45: Manpower and Military Effectiveness

*Paul Latawski*

From the end of the eighteenth century, Polish armies in exile have been a re-occurring feature in the military history of Poland. The final partition of the Polish–Lithuanian Commonwealth in 1795 created conditions that were particularly conducive to the birth of such formations. The combination of statelessness, movements for national liberation and willing foreign patrons meant that Polish armed struggles to recover an independent state often took place on foreign soil. The earliest of these exile armies were Napoleon's Polish legions. Between 1797 and 1807 some 20,000 troops fought for the French emperor.[1] One of their marching songs, the Dąbrowski mazurka, had lyrics that spoke of returning from 'the Italian lands to Poland' (*ziemi Włoski do Polski*). It would become in due course Poland's national anthem. If the Dąbrowski mazurka demonstrates the centrality of the exile army to Polish historical consciousness, then the story of the destruction of Polish exile units in 1802–03 in Napoleon's efforts to pacify Santo Domingo in the Caribbean provides a salutary lesson on the consequences of linking national struggles to cynical foreign patrons.[2] Indeed, Tadeusz Kościuszko, the military and political leader of the Polish insurrection against the final partition in 1794 and an elder statesman among Polish exiles in France inspired a pamphlet called 'Can the Poles Fight their Way to Independence?' (*Czy Polacy mogą się wybić na niepodległość*) that appeared in 1800. The pamphlet questioned the wisdom of relying on foreign patrons in the light of the experience of Napoleon's Polish legions and argued that the Poles should look to their own resources.[3] It was advice, however, that went unheeded in the next century and a half.

During the nineteenth century, Polish exile armies took on a decidedly revolutionary hue with the slogan 'For Your Freedom and Ours' (*za wolność, naszę i waszę*) linking the Polish cause to that of other European peoples. In the 1840s, attempts to form a legion in Italy by the poet Adam Mickiewicz and the Poles fighting in the Hungarian Revolution under the command of General Józef Bem exemplified this linkage. After a hiatus in the last quarter of the nineteenth century Polish exile armies emerged during the First World War fighting on the side of all the major continental combatants. It was a Polish scale of effort not seen since Napoleon's day nor would they be the last Polish exile armies of the twentieth century.

The outbreak of the Second World War in September 1939 and the partition of independent Poland once again saw the emergence of two Polish exile armies; the first coalescing after 1939 in Western Europe, the Middle East and North Africa and closely associated with the major democratic states such as Britain and the United States. The second of these armies emerged in 1943 and was a creature of the Soviet Union. This radically different political context of the two Polish exile armies reflected a significant ideological gulf and played a major role in shaping their legitimacy and relationships with their foreign patrons. The differences between the two exile armies were not limited to their political arrangements. Each faced critical manpower shortages of a very different nature that were resolved in ways unique to their operational circumstances. This chapter will focus on the manpower issues faced by the Polish armies in exile and its impact on their military effectiveness.

## The Polish army in the West, 1939–45

The emergence of the Polish army in the West (*Polski Siły Zbrojne* – PSZ) was very much tied to the creation of a Polish government-in-exile based first in France when it was formed on 30 September 1939. Under the Premiership of Gen. Władysław Sikorski, the exile government established its seat in Angers until the French collapse in 1940 whence it moved to London. Sikorski headed the exile government until his death in a plane crash in April 1943. His successor Stanisław Mikołajczyk, a prominent leader of the Peasant Party, served until nearly the end of the war. The PSZ was the army of this exile government and both could claim continuity with the pre-war government and army. Moreover, this continuity conferred a legitimacy based not only on a legal constitutional transfer of authority from the Polish government but also on the support and allegiance of the Polish underground resistance and its political representatives in occupied Poland.[4] On this latter point, no exile government can enjoy the same legitimacy of an elected government sitting in the national capital in peacetime. Under wartime conditions, this represented in the Polish case a strong measure of legitimacy enjoyed by few governments-in-exile.

The creation of an army in exile was the product of the catastrophic defeat of Poland in September 1939. Defeat and occupation at home meant that any further armed resistance by the armed forces would have to be transferred abroad. In the wake of the September campaign, some 90,000 members of the armed forces escaped to neighbouring or nearby countries and to internment but hoping to make their way further abroad to resistance alongside Poland's British and French allies.[5] Following a French government offer to take in these evacuated soldiers, an organized evacuation scheme led to some 43,000 being transported to France by the middle of June 1940.[6] Other Polish soldiers made their way westward by whatever means that they could find until German pressure and eventual captivity for the remaining internees ended any possibility of joining Polish forces being reconstituted in France. In the nine months up to the beginning of the Battle of France in June 1940, Polish forces were reconstituted under French command. Manpower from France's sizeable Polish community augmented the soldiers who had managed to get out of Poland.[7]

The collapse of France in the summer of 1940 led to another phase in the development of the Polish army in the West. The story shifts from France to Britain and British controlled territory in the Middle East. Once it became clear that French resistance was coming to an end, Polish forces in France made their way to Britain either in organized evacuations, by way of third countries or a trickle organized by escape operations to places like Gibraltar. The only exceptions were a Polish division that crossed into Switzerland to be interned, soldiers who became prisoners of war or Polish soldiers recruited in France that opted for demobilization. The total number of service personnel that made it to Britain in July 1940 amounted to just under 20,000. In the Middle East, the Carpathian Rifle Brigade in Palestine had a strength of just under 9,000.[8]

Although the Polish armed forces in the West represented a sizeable body of soldiers, the manpower structure was not conducive to building major formations particularly against the Polish government-in-exile's ambitious plans.[9] The reality was that the army had too many officers and not enough rank and file soldiers. Moreover, the age profile of this group of officers meant that many were unsuitable for front-line service. Col. Leon Mitkiewicz, a Polish staff officer in London commented in his memoirs that there were 'too many old officers' and that there were not enough enlisted personnel. On the ratio of officers to enlisted men he rather despairingly noted that 15 to 1 was the norm but instead it was around 4 to1 in the Polish land forces in Britain.[10] Rather than creating a corps strength formation in Britain, a single division represented the most realistic proposition. Given the shortage of enlisted personnel to replace battle casualties it would, in any event, become a significant problem to address.

The evacuation of 70,000 Poles to the Middle East from the Soviet Union in August 1942 improved the manpower situation of the Polish army in the West with respect to both overall numbers and the numbers of rank and file soldiers. The bulk of this manpower would form the basis of the 2nd Polish Corps commanded by Gen. *Władysław* Anders and composed of 3rd Carpathian Rifle Division (3 Dywizja Strzelcow Karpackich), 5 Borderlands Infantry Division (5 Kresowa Dywizja Piechoty), 2nd Tank Brigade and assorted corps supporting formations. The Polish forces based in Britain also benefited from transfers from the Middle East to make up critical manpower deficiencies. Around 12,000 were sent to Britain in 1942–43.[11] The reality of the Polish army in the West was that finding more recruits from abroad was going to be very difficult. Between 1940 and 1943, 15,470 men were recruited from Poles abroad and locally resident Polish communities from a wide range of locales including Asia, Europe, Latin America, North Africa and the Middle East. Among these recruits could be counted 600 Poles who were taken as enemy prisoners of war and volunteered for service in the Polish army in the West.[12]

In 1944, the Polish army in the West participated in coalition operations in Italy and Northwest Europe. In December 1943, the 2nd Polish Corps arrived in the Italian theatre and from July 1944 the 1st Polish Armoured Division (Pierwsza Dywizja Pancerna) landed in Normandy. Although engaged in lengthy campaigns until the end of the war, 1944 witnessed three major battles involving Polish forces. The first of these was Monte Cassino in Italy where the 2nd Polish Corps played a key role in the Allied victory in that battle that cost the Poles a great many casualties. In Normandy in late August, the 1st Polish Armoured Division fought in the Falaise encirclement battle and similarly suffered significant casualties in a gritty action on the 'Mace' and Chambois to seal the pocket. Finally, the 1st Polish Independent Parachute Brigade (1 Samodzielna Brygada Spadochronowa) fought along side the British 1st Airborne Division in Operation *Market Garden* in September 1944 at Arnhem in that costly action. These three major Polish actions undoubtedly brought the issue of replacements of battle casualties to the fore. In his memoirs, Gen. Stanisław Maczek, the commander of the 1st Polish Armoured Division, notes how the loss of cadre led to a reduction in the size of elements of his division.[13] Although it would seem that heavy fighting risked the withering away of the combat power of the Polish Army in the West, in fact they managed to meet their manpower needs and maintain their combat power. This was because replacements arrived from prisoner of war camps. It was a source of manpower that would grow in importance after the Polish army in the West became engaged in combat operations.

As a result of the incorporation of large segments of Poland into Germany and German military manpower requirements, large numbers of Polish men were conscripted into the German armed forces. In the course of the war, an estimated 300,000 Poles were swept up for service in the German armed forces.[14] As a source of manpower, for the Polish Army in the West, it was seen as an important manpower pool to draw on. The II Polish Corps commander, Gen. Anders was confident that it would be a reliable source:

> General Maitland Wilson expressed concern about how the II Polish Army Corps could be reinforced in the event of heavy casualties. I answered him, as I did all my colleagues, that reinforcements will join us from the front line. We had no country behind us to get our reserves from, but we knew that at the first news of Poles fighting on the continent, all Poles, and, above all, those who had been conscripted by force into the German army, would try to join us.[15]

Gen. Anders' optimism was justified by events. His II Polish Corps ended wartime operations a larger formation than when it entered the Italian campaign with the new recruits supplied via the German army.[16] Overall, the Polish Army in Italy and Northwest Europe recruited just under 90,000 Poles who came over from the German side. By the end of the war, Poles from the German army proved to be the largest single source of recruits providing 40 per cent of the total number of recruited soldiers.[17] Without this vital source of manpower, the problem of maintaining combat effectiveness would have been far more severe and doubtless would have led to significant operational limitations.

## Stalin's Polish army, 1943–45

The formation of the Kościuszko infantry division in May 1943 marked the beginning of Stalin's Polish Army. Nominally under the direction of the Union of Polish Patriots (*Związek Patriotów Polskich* – ZPP), a front organization for Polish Communists and pro-Moscow Poles, it was in fact a Soviet creation. Sent into action in October 1943 before completing its training, the Kościuszko division suffered losses of about one-third of its strength at the battle of Lenino. From a military point of view the battle was costly and pointless; from the point of view of Stalin and Polish Communists, it served an important political role by signalling an alternative to the London Polish government-in-exile and its armed forces.[18] The Polish forces under Soviet tutelage quickly expanded from the initial base of the Kościuszko infantry division established in 1943. Drawing on Polish prisoners of war and civilians on the territory of the Soviet Union, by August 1943 the division grew into the 1st Polish Corps and by March 1944 the Soviet authorities agreed to the formation of the Polish Army in the USSR. During 1944 and 1945, the 1st Polish Corps evolved into the 1st Polish Army and in due course a 2nd Polish Army. Among its major actions in 1944 included the Magnuszew bridgehead on the Vistula and bloody fighting to relieve the embattled insurgents of the Warsaw Uprising August–October 1944. This force would fight its way across Poland and into Germany with elements of it taking part in the assault on Berlin.

The expansion of the Polish forces in the Soviet Union was, theoretically, a straightforward task. There was undoubtedly a large pool of Polish manpower to draw on within the Soviet Union. Polish prisoners of war captured during the Soviet occupation of eastern Poland in 1939 alone numbered around 230,000 to which could be added sizeable numbers of civilian Polish males of military age on Soviet territory.[19] Indeed, this recruitment pool could be broken down into six significant categories:

1.  Polish civilians from eastern Poland as well as refugees from other parts of the country deported to the interior of the Soviet Union in 1939–41;
2.  Poles mobilized into the Soviet army serving in construction battalions and military units;
3.  Poles freed by an amnesty from Soviet camps and prisons in 1941;
4.  Soviet citizens of Polish ancestry, principally officers and NCOs;
5.  Soviet officers (not of Polish ancestry) seconded to the Polish forces;
6.  Poles found among *Wehrmacht* prisoners of war.[20]

This impressive diversity of manpower sources, however, did not tell the entire story. Missing was the vital category of trained Polish officers.

Indeed, their conspicuous absence was the direct result of Soviet policy. In 1939, approximately 11,000 Polish army officers fell into Soviet hands as prisoners of war. Over 8,000 of these men were held at camps in Kozelsk, Ostashkov and Starobelsk and were executed on the order of the Soviet leadership in May 1940.[21] The surviving 3,000 officers joined the Polish army led by Anders as a consequence of the rapprochement between the Soviet Union and the Polish government-in-exile in London July 1941. The overwhelming majority of surviving officers that could be found on Soviet territory left in 1942 when Anders' Polish army was evacuated to the Middle East. Only a handful of pro-Soviet officers from the pre-war Polish army remained in the Soviet Union.[22] The most prominent of these was Zygmunt Berling. The reasons for his pro-Soviet leaning were not readily apparent. Berling served in Piłsudski's legions from November 1914, fought in the Polish-Soviet war in 1920 during which he earned a Silver Cross of the Order Virtuti Militari. In September 1939, he was arrested by the NKVD (Soviet security service) in Wilno (Vilnius) at which time he is alleged to have begun his cooperation with the Soviet authorities.[23] Although he held a series of important military posts including deputy commander-in-chief of the Polish Army in 1944, his importance was more political than military. Berling provided a thin Polish veneer to a Soviet military construction for propaganda reasons. Moreover, the Soviet authorities distrusted Berling and the clutch of Polish officers who placed themselves at their disposal. This mistrust was not entirely warranted from the Soviet perspective. Berling's outspoken views on drawing the post-war Polish–Soviet frontier further east than the Curzon line drew unfavourable comment from his Soviet masters as it did not accord to move the Polish–Soviet frontier eastwards at Poland's expense.[24] Ultimately, Stalin tolerated his 'reactionary' Polish officers for reasons that were largely political and because he had eliminated the alternatives previously available to him.

This artificially created shortage of Polish officers meant that it was necessary to use Red Army officers in the Polish forces organized in the Soviet Union. Soviet officers in the Polish army in the east according to the best estimates in the period of May 1943 to May 1945 numbered between 16,800 and 19,700. In July 1943 they represented 66 per cent of officers in the Polish army in the Soviet Union; a year later they amounted to 64.4 per cent of total officers and at the conclusion of the war 45 per cent of all officers.[25] Large numbers of Soviet officers across the spectrum of ranks held positions in the Polish army. In some branches the proportion of Soviet officers in the technical arms such as armoured forces, artillery, and signals was consistently very high (approximately 80 per cent) to the very end of the war. Polish officers only began to make inroads in the closing months of the war in these branches.[26] The Soviet domination of the senior command and staff positions was equally dominant throughout the army. This was the most important source of Soviet influence. Of the command positions in the army, 70 per cent were in the hands of Soviet officers in the Spring of 1944. In critically sensitive areas such as military intelligence, the percentage of Soviet officers reached 100 per cent.[27]

Incorporating so many Soviet officers in what was supposed to be a Polish army was not a straightforward exercise. Although Communist historiography made much of the Polish ancestry of Soviet officers, the vast majority of them could not speak Polish. This created obvious command and control problems in front-line units. It led in September 1944 to a Soviet military directive that ordered only Soviet officers who could speak Polish to wear Polish uniforms. The non-Polish speakers remained in Soviet uniforms and efforts were made to give them Polish language instruction.[28] Apart from the practical difficulties of commanding troops in the field where two languages are in use, the Soviet officers were not very popular with Polish junior officers or with other ranks whose political sympathies could scarcely be described as pro-Soviet.[29]

As the Red Army moved westwards, the overall number of Soviet officers began to fall. The crossing of the river Bug and the liberation of Lublin Poland (*Polska Lubelska*) greatly increased the Polish manpower pool available for mobilization. In 1944, under the authority of the National Home Council (*Krajowa Rada Narodowa*, KRN) the Polish Communists ambitiously decreed the creation of the 2nd Polish Army and had plans to create a Third. Despite the liberation of indisputably Polish populated territories, the Polish Communists only succeeded in raising a second army by the end of the war. So great were the shortages of Polish officers that many of those who were mobilized or pressed into service in 1944 came from underground organizations including the Home Army whose sympathies and politics linked them to the London government-in-exile.[30] The entry of Soviet forces into German territory late in the war, however, added another sizeable group of Polish officers. These were officers of the pre-war Polish army who had been in German prisoner-of-war camps since 1939. Although some would see wartime service, Communist vetting processes meant that the majority who were accepted entered the post-war army.

## Manpower and military effectiveness

Polish exile armies in the Second World War were among the largest and most diverse to be found among the Allied armies in exile. The Polish role was not merely symbolic given the size and sophistication of the force structures and capabilities found in the Polish exile armies. In the later stages of the war the Polish army made major and credible contributions to operations on two fronts, both in the west and the east. This contribution is all the more credible given the manpower challenges faced by both Polish exile armies. The nature of the manpower problems and the solutions adopted, however, were very different. Unlike the Polish forces fighting in the West, those under the aegis of the Soviet Union experienced diametrically opposite manpower issues as they suffered from a shortage of trained officers. This problem was less structural than political insofar as it was an artificially created shortfall as a result of Stalin's decision to eliminate thousands of captured Polish officers. Seconded Soviet officers who not only served a vital military function but also ensured close political control over the Polish army in the east met this critical shortfall. Less of a problem was the finding of recruits for the rank and file of the army. The manpower pool of Poles in the Soviet Union was sufficient to create sizeable formations and the further West the Red Army advanced the more Poles would become available. In the Polish army in the west, the major manpower problem concerned the need to find adequate numbers of rank and file personnel. The numbers of officers were more plentiful but their age profile was not ideally matched to the requirements for younger men to lead combat units. Thus, the most critical need for battlefield replacements was met from Poles recruited from enemy prisoners of war. It was a solution born out of the particular conditions of war that saw Poles conscripted into opposing armies – not for the first time in Poland's history. The solutions to manpower dilemmas adopted by the two Polish exile armies insured their operational effectiveness in the closing stages of the war in Europe in 1944–45. In one aspect both Polish exile armies shared a common experience; the sacrifice and heroism displayed by Polish soldiers on many battlefields added to an already formidable military tradition.

### Notes

1. Jerzy Kozlowski, 'Emigracja okresu schyłkowego Rzeczypospolitej szlacheckiej i porozbriorowa (do 1864 r.)', in Andrzej Pilch (ed.), *Emigracja z ziem polskich w czasach nowożytnych I najnowszych (XVIII–XXw.)* (Warsaw: PWN, 1984), p. 53.

2. See: Jan Pachoński and Reuel K. Wilson, *Poland's Caribbean Tragedy: A Study of Polish Legions in the Haitian War of Independence 1802–1803* (Boulder: East European Monographs, 1986), pp. 318–23.

3. Emanuel Halicz, *Partisan Warfare in 19th Century Poland: The Development of a Concept* (Odense: Odense University Press, 1975), pp. 30–54.

4. George V. Kacewicz, *Great Britain, The Soviet Union and the Polish Government in exile (1939–1945)* (The Hague: Martinus Nijhoff Publishers, 1979), p. 36.

5. Keith Sword with Norman Davies and Jan Ciechanowski, *The Formation of the Polish Community in Britain 1939–1950* (London: School of Slavonic and East European Studies, 1989), p. 37.

6. *Polskie Siły Zbrojne w drugiej wojnie światowej: kampanie na obczyźnie, tom II, część 1* (London: Instytut Historyczny im. Gen. Sikorskiego, 1959), p. 30.

7. Witold Biegański, *Wojsko Polskie we Francji 1939–1940* (Warsaw: MON, 1967), pp. 78–87.

8. *Polskie Siły Zbrojne w drugiej wojnie światowej: kampanie na obczyźnie, tom II, część 1*, pp. 233.

9. For a detailed overview see: Zbigniew Wawer, *Organizacja Polskich Wojsk Lądowych w Wielkiej Brytanii 1940–1945* (Warsaw: Bellona, 1992).

10. Leon Mitkiewicz, *Z gen. Sikorskim na Obczyźnie* (Paris: Instytut Literacki, 1968), pp. 59, 72.

11. Witold Biegański, *Regularne Jednostki Wojska Polskiego na Zachodzie* (Warsaw: MON, 1973), p. 62.

12. *Polskie Siły Zbrojne w drugiej wojnie światowej: kampanie na obczyźnie, tom II, część 2* (London: Instytut Historyczny im. Gen. Sikorskiego, 1975), pp. 126, 131.

13. Stanisław Maczek, *Od podwody do Czołga: wspomnienia wojenne 1918–1945* (Edinburgh: Tomar Publishers, 1961), p. 186.

14. Andrzej Pilch (ed.), *Emigracja z ziem polskich w czasach nowożytnych i najnowszych (XVIII–XXw.)* (Warsaw: PWN, 1984), p. 475.

15. Lt. Gen. W. Anders, *An Army in Exile: The Story of the Second Polish Corps* (London: Macmillan – new Palgrave Macmillan, 1949), pp. 152–3.

16. Biegański, *Regularne Jednostki Wojska Polskiego na Zachodzie*, p. 63.

17. Andrzej Liebich, *Na Obcej Ziemi: Polskie Siły Zbrojne 1939–1945* (London: 1947), pp. 69, 74.

18. Czeslaw Grzelak, Henryk Stańczyk and Stefan Zwoliński, *Bez możliwości wyboru: Wojsko Poliskim na froncie wschodnim 1943–1945* (Warsaw: Bellona, 1993), p. 162.

19. Wojciech Materski (ed.), *Z archiwów Sowieckich tom I: Polscy jeńcy wojenni w ZSSR*, (Warsaw: PAN-ISP, 1992), p. 9. According to various estimates the number of civilians deported from eastern Poland in 1939 numbered between 1,250,000 and 1,600,000. Included in this population were males of military age. See: Keith Sword, *Deportation and Exile: Poles in the Soviet Union, 1939–48* (London: Macmillan – new Palgrave Macmillan, 1994), p. 27.

20. The list presented here is a consolidation of the list appearing in Grzelak, 'Kształcenie kadr w Polskich Siłach Zbrojnych w ZSRR Maj 1943–lipiec 1944 r.', *Wojskowy Przegląd Historyczny*, 1–2 (January–June 1985), p. 317.

21. See note Chief of NKVD, L. Beria to J. Stalin, March 1940 in: Ewa Wosik (ed.), *Katyń: Dokumenty Ludobójstwa* (Warsaw: ISP-PAN, 1992), pp. 35–9.

22. See note L. Beria to J. Stalin, 12 March 1942, in Wojciech Materski (ed.), *Z archiwów Sowieckich tom II: Armia Polska w ZSRR 1941–1942* (Warsaw: ISP-PAN, 1992), pp. 49–73.
23. Grzelak, Stańczyk and Zwoliński, *Bez możliwości wyboru*, pp. 222–3.
24. See report of the State Security Commissar, G. Zhukov, Political Bureau, All-Union Communist Party (Bolsheviks) to the Chief Main Political Administration, Red Army, Col. Gen. A. Shcherbakov, 16 February 1944 and a similar report from V. Sokorski who served in the Polish Army in the USSR to Shcherbakov, 16 April 1944, in Józef Dawid and Aleksander Kochański (eds), *Polska-ZSRR Struktury Podległości: Dokumenty WKP(B) 1944–1949* (Warsaw: ISP-PAN, 1995), pp. 34–5, 52–5.
25. Edward Jan Nalepa, *Oficerowe Armii Radzieckiej w Wojsku Polskim 1943–1968* (Warsaw: Bellona, 1995), pp. 15–16.
26. *Ibid.*, p. 20.
27. *Ibid.*, pp. 21–2.
28. Kazimierz Kaczmarek, 'Wstawienie 2 armii WP Sierpień 1944 r.–styczeń 1945 r. Cz. I', *Wojskowy Przegląd Historyczny*, 4 (October–December 1971), pp. 40–1.
29. Tadeusz Rawski, 'Praca polityczno-wychowawcza w 1 armii Wojska Polskiego w końcowym okresie wojny', *Wojskowy Przegląd Historyczny*, 3 (July–September 1974), p. 56.
30. Grzelak, Stańczyk and Zwoliński, *Bez możliwości wyboru*, pp. 110–11.

# 4
# The Norwegian Army-in-Exile

*Christopher Mann*

This chapter examines the experience of the army of the Norwegian Government-in-Exile and their relationship with the British political and military authorities in the Second World War. It was a process that expanded and equipped the small number of defeated Norwegians that escaped to Britain in June 1940 into a force that could participate usefully in Norway's liberation in May 1945. Given the dire condition of what remained of Norway's military resources in the summer of 1940 this was a turn around of considerable proportions. Nonetheless the Army came low down on the list of the Norwegian Government's priorities, which preferred to concentrate on the navy and air force. Also the fact that Norway lay far from the route taken across the continent by the armies of the Western Allies, meant that the Army had few opportunities to make any significant contribution to the Allied victory. Therefore, the experience of the Second World War for the bulk of the Norwegian Army in exile was characterized accurately by one Norwegian soldier as 'sitting on my arse in Scotland and going on manoeuvres'.[1]

## King Haakon and the legitimacy of the exile government

Norway and Britain's military relationship did not start particularly well. Germany invaded Norway on 9 April 1940 and Britain pledged military assistance that day. Unfortunately British military intervention proved ill prepared, poorly organized and wholly inadequate. Disastrous defeat puts a strain on any partnership and this was not helped by the British and their French allies proving somewhat reticent in informing the Norwegians of their plans, particularly with regard to their intention to withdraw. For example, a Norwegian Colonel commanding Norwegian forces in the vicinity of Namsos, only discovered that his allies were evacuating the port on 2 May, five days after the order to withdraw had been given and hours after the bulk of Anglo-French forces had embarked.[2]

Nor did the Norwegian Army perform particularly well. Much of the reason stemmed from the long-term neglect of the armed forces generally over the preceding 20 years. There was an absolute paucity of modern weapons; one tank was bought in the mid-1930s 'so that the Norwegian soldiers could at least see one sample in their life time'.[3] This was not helped by the failure of the army to mobilize properly in the chaos of April 1940. Also contrary to popular myth, the largely road bound Norwegians often demonstrated less understanding of the local terrain and conditions than did the Germans. While the average Norwegian soldier possessed useful tactical skills such as skiing and marksmanship the inadequacy of training and the Army's poor doctrine and organization allowed the Germans to retain the initiative.[4] The exception was General Carl Fleischer's 6th Division based in northern Norway that was able to mobilize fully; the division more than proved itself in the fighting to capture Narvik.

Although Narvik was the only major Allied success of the campaign, the opening of the German offensive in France on 10 May distracted Anglo-French attention away from Norway. As the situation in France worsened, the British and French decided to end their commitment to Norway and evacuate their troops. The Norwegian Government, knowing that defeat was inevitable, decided to move into exile. So King Haakon VII, his prime minister, Johan Nygaardsvold, the Labour Government and elements of the Norwegian military left Norway aboard the British cruiser *HMS Devonshire* on 7 June 1940. The remaining Norwegian forces in Norway surrendered the following day.

Therefore, the dejected Norwegian Government, which arrived in Britain, had some cause to resent their hosts. Also the very real possibility of British defeat – which appeared apparent to everyone but the British – led elements of the Norwegian Government to urge caution in establishing formal ties with Britain which might damage the Norwegian position in a compromise peace with Germany.[5] Those in the cabinet advocating full partnership with Britain and a reversal of Norway's long held traditional policy of neutrality were much strengthened by the position taken by the King, the clear mandate of the Nygaardsvold Government and the failure of the German authorities in Norway to establish a new government by constitutional means.

On the night of the German invasion Vidkun Quisling, leader of the National Union (*Nasjonal Samling* – NS), the Norwegian equivalent to the Nazi Party, had attempted a coup d'état and proclaimed a government of national unity. Seeing how Quisling's action merely stiffened Norwegian resistance, the Germans appointed an administrative council to deal with civil affairs in areas under German occupation. This had the approval of the Supreme Court, the only constitutional authority left in the capital, Oslo.

After Norway's surrender, the German *Reichskommisar*, Josef Terboven, strove to transform the administrative council into a collaboration government. Naturally, the Germans wanted a stable regime in Norway and, in order to cause minimal upheaval, hoped that the new government could be established by legal means. Terboven's goal was to have the *Storting*, the Norwegian Parliament, meet to depose the King, set up a government that would cooperate with him and then dissolve itself. The Norwegian parliamentarians, given the situation prevailing in Europe in the summer of 1940, were surprisingly amenable. In June they appealed to the King to abdicate in favour a new council in the occupied country. Despite the King's refusal, they continued to negotiate with the Germans and on 10 September 1940 voted 75 to 55 to remove Haakon. However, the talks broke down that month and forced Terboven to establish a German commissarial government and return Quisling to a prominent role. Terboven's attempt to use the Norwegian legal system to produce a constitutional collaborationist administration had failed.[6]

The stance of King Haakon was of far greater importance than the machinations of Terboven and Quisling in Norway. He proved to be a focus of unity and inspiration for those Norwegians, both in exile and at home, determined to resist the German occupation. On 18 July Haakon rejected the June request to abdicate from the parliamentary leaders remaining in Norway. He emphasized the legitimacy of his Government and stated that it had received its mandate to continue the struggle in the last free parliament held on 9 April 1940. That day, at Eleverum, north of Oslo, the *Storting* had empowered the Government to carry out whatever measures necessary for Norway's security and future until the Government and President of the *Storting* could call an 'ordinary' meeting of the parliament. This was the *Storting*'s last free act and, according to Haakon, free was something that those proposing his deposition were most certainly not.[7]

Naturally, the Government-in-Exile's legitimacy was accepted by the Allied and neutral powers (Vichy France being the only exception). More importantly the majority of the Norwegian population under German occupation never seriously questioned it. One possible source of difficulty, the Norwegian resistance movement, never disputed the Government's authority and its military wing, *Milorg*, accepted the Norwegian High Command's control from February 1942. Thus when Nygaardsvold and his Government returned to Norway in May 1945 their legitimacy and authority were unquestioned. Although Nygaardsvold immediately stepped down, claiming that after ten years as prime minister he was looking forward to a holiday, he was replaced by another Labour politician, Einar Gerhardsen, whose caretaker government comprised both members of the Government-in-Exile and resistance leaders.[8] Gerhardsen remained Prime Minister until 1965 and the Labour Party has dominated post-war Norwegian politics.

## Birth of an exile army

Two days after King Haakon's 18 July broadcast, the Norwegian Ministry of Defence sent an *aide-mémoire* to their British counterparts stating that: 'It is the intention of the Norwegian Government to continue the fight outside Norway in collaboration with our allies and so far as our means will permit until final victory.'[9] In the formal treaty, eventually signed on 28 May 1941, the British and Norwegian Governments pledged to re-establish 'the freedom and independence of Norway' and to that end agreed that:

> The Norwegian Armed Forces in the United Kingdom...shall be employed either for the defence of the United Kingdom or for the purpose of regaining Norway. They shall be organised and employed under British command, in its character as the Allied High Command, as the Armed Forces of the Kingdom of Norway allied with the United Kingdom.[10]

The armed forces, however, at the disposal of 'the Kingdom of Norway' in the summer of 1940 were somewhat limited. While the Navy possessed the sizeable remnants of the Norwegian Fleet, the situation for the army was far grimmer. Although the British might have been able to embark a substantial proportion of the Norwegian Army's 6th Division from Narvik at the end of the campaign, they happily left them behind as a covering force for the evacuation. Furthermore, politically, the Norwegian Government felt that it could not order conscripts to leave Norway for exile.[11] They did, however, instruct a few professional officers to accompany them to Britain. These men formed the basis of the Norwegian staff set up in London. Major General Carl Fleischer was appointed commander-in-chief of Norwegian Forces. The former C-in-C,

General Otto Ruge, the only senior Norwegian officer to come out of the campaign with any credit, elected to stay behind and surrender with his troops. Fleischer established a training camp and staff at Dumfries and by July 1940 could muster just over a thousand men from various sources.

## Friction with Britain: Operations in occupied Norway

A small number of Norwegian troops, however, went into action earlier than most of their compatriots and were certainly the first members of the Norwegian Armed Forces to set foot on Norwegian soil again. Special Operations Executive (SOE), the British organization formed to support Europe's resistance movements, approached the Norwegian Army with a view to forming a unit of Norwegian volunteers which subsequently took part in a raid on the Lofoten Islands in March 1941. Although the raid met with no German resistance and was generally regarded as successful it caused some friction between the British and Norwegian Governments. Although British documents imply that the Norwegian military and foreign minister, Trygve Lie, had been consulted and proved enthusiastic, Lie claimed that 'the Norwegian Government was unacquainted with the preparations and execution of the raid'.[12] Therefore, he and the rest of the Government were angered by the use of their men on Norwegian territory without their sanction. This anger deepened when news of German reprisals against the Lofoten islanders filtered back to London.

The unit, however, expanded and was named Norwegian Independent Company 1 (*Kompani Linge* after its Norwegian founder, Captain Martin Linge, to its Norwegian members). The Norwegian Government's annoyance did not inhibit the British from using the Company again in December 1941 in two simultaneous raids, one against Vågsøy on the Norwegian west coast and the other on Lofoten Islands again. These raids brought to a head the Norwegian authorities' irritation at their exclusion from the decision-making process regarding operations in Norway. Lie ordered his Foreign Ministry to make it clear to the British that 'the Norwegian Government was one step away from publicly taking a stand against the British action'.[13] This would have caused a politically disastrous rift and been an excellent propaganda victory for the Germans and the puppet Quisling administration in Norway.

The issue caused a crisis of confidence in *Kompani Linge*. Much of the bitterness of their Government had been directed at them and they were left feeling isolated and resentful at the way that the British had used them. This was not helped by news of another round of German reprisals. On top of this Martin Linge was killed at Vågsøy, further shaking the company's morale. As the SOE Norwegian Section History recalled 'the Linge Company was full of dissatisfaction and its founder and leader was not there to put matters right'.[14] The discontent was manifested by 12 members who refused to continue without the assurance of the Norwegian Government's approval for their activities, claiming that they felt 'almost like mercenaries'.[15]

Sir Charles Hambro, Deputy Director of SOE, approached the new Norwegian Defence Minister Oscar Torp to arrange some sort of compromise because, as Hambro succinctly noted, the British could not operate in Norway without the Norwegians and the Norwegians needed British equipment, facilities and expertise.[16] Torp said that he hoped to maintain and improve the good relations between the Norwegian authorities and SOE but in return he made it clear to Hambro that 'he personally expected to be taken into our confidence absolutely'. Hambro had anticipated the problem before the December raids and, fearing the loss of SOE's Norwegian troops, he had pressed the British military authorities to agree to some sort of coordination with the Norwegian authorities, at the very least with Lie or Torp, in whom he had 'absolute confidence'.[17] He met considerable resistance. The opinion of much of the British military establishment was well summed up by an internal SOE memo which believed that 'of the races on earth there is surely none so indiscreet as the Norwegians'.[18] However, the refusal of Winston Churchill's chief of staff, General Hastings Ismay, is more telling. He felt that involving the Norwegian authorities, quite apart from anything else, would be a 'dangerous precedent' which 'would inevitably lead to the Dutch, the Belgians, the Free French – and possibly the Poles and Czechs – demanding a similar privilege when their territories are concerned'.[19]

A crisis point, however, in the relationship had developed and Hambro had to find a solution. He proposed to Torp that an 'Anglo-Norwegian Collaboration Committee' be set up and promised that SOE 'will not initiate any expedition to or against Norway without the knowledge and consent of the Norwegian members of the committee who will, of course, be at liberty to report direct to you'.[20] Although he could not make a similar commitment for the services, any request for use of SOE's specially trained troops by other departments – and operations in Norway would be impossible without them – would be submitted to the committee for the Norwegian members' and consequently Torp's approval. In return Torp appointed a successor to Linge and visited the company to steady their morale and reassure the commandos of their Government's approval.[21] The committee worked remarkably well, ensuring no repetition of the December 1941 incident, giving the Norwegians a hand in SOE's policy towards Norway and cementing a remarkably successful relationship between SOE, the Norwegian High Command and the Norwegian Resistance.

As part of a Norwegian desire to have a wider influence in military issues relating to Norway, Torp also reformed the Norwegian command system by establishing a unified Norwegian High Command. Quite apart from the military logic, creating a centralized military organization made sense given the limited number of staff officers at Torp's disposal. Although establishing a working relationship with the British took time, the High Command eventually assumed an integral role in the planning for Norway's liberation. General Fleischer disagreed with the reform, which did not envisage him in the role of supreme commander, and he therefore resigned. Fleischer was sent to Canada where he later committed suicide.

## Development of the exile army in Britain

The Norwegian Government was fortunate that its financial needs were met by their most important resource, the Norwegian merchant fleet, the fourth largest in the world, granting them a considerable degree of fiscal independence. It was also here that the Norwegians made their most important contribution to the Allied victory. As for Norway's armed forces the British were willing to provide equipment and places on training courses dependent on availability. The Norwegians, meanwhile, met the running costs of their establishments and paid and maintained their own men. However, finding those men was far more problematic. In expanding Norwegian forces the main difficulty, in common with most Governments-in-Exile, was the provision of manpower. A handful of the Norwegian military had left Norway with the Government and in the first year of the occupation many Norwegians escaped across the North Sea to Britain. This was never enough and the conscription of Norwegians in Britain began at the end of 1940 and an extensive recruiting campaign launched among the Norwegian emigrant communities in the United States.

The allocation of Norwegian military personnel illustrated the Government's belief as to where they could make the most useful contribution to the Allied cause. Keeping the Atlantic supply line open was probably the most important commitment that Britain faced, certainly in terms of mere survival. The Norwegian Government concurred and gave precedence to the Norwegian Navy. The Navy expanded rapidly, having the priority with regard to manpower, even drawing on the 30–35,000 sailors of the merchant fleet and transferring recruits from the army. The Norwegian Air Force came next and the process of creating four squadrons for service with the Royal Air Force inevitably used many of the best recruits available.

With the Navy and Air Force taking priority, particularly in manpower, the Army proved to be something of a 'Cinderella' service with regard to both personnel and equipment. Indeed, it often functioned as an emergency pool of manpower that was raided from time to time by the other two services and SOE's *Kompani Linge*. While admittedly the Army was working on a longer-term basis than the other services these deprivations caused a manpower crisis of serious proportions. The Army Command's demands that it required at least a degree of stability to build up a reasonable sized force were ignored for reasons of wartime expediency.

Nonetheless by early 1944 the Army had reached the size and composition the Army Command had envisaged. In view of the wide variety of specialized formations and nature of operations for which it was intended the Army can only really be characterized as Brigade Group size. It had been specifically trained to spearhead any return to Norway and consisted of three Independent Mountain Companies and smaller reconnaissance, artillery and logistical support sections. The Norwegian Command had been keen to keep abreast of military fads and therefore had gained War Office approval to form a parachute company in early 1942.[22] The Norwegian Army used standard British equipment, although not always the latest models. Despite their willingness to pay for new weaponry and vehicles, the small likelihood of the Norwegian Army being committed to battle for much of the war meant they were low in War Office allocation priorities. Indeed the Norwegians had at first been equipped with mules for transport as was appropriate to their intended role. They were not fully motorized until mid 1944.

The Norwegians also formed No 5 troop of No 10 (Inter Allied) Commando, who were somewhat more lavishly furnished. As there were so few opportunities for the Norwegians to see active service the unit had a high turn over of personnel to give as many soldiers as possible combat experience. The unit operated with the Norwegian Motor Torpedo Boat (MTB) flotilla along the Norwegian coast in the autumn and winter of 1942–43, acting as boat guards and undertaking small-scale raids in support of the MTBs. They also took part in the assault on

Walcheren Island on 1 November 1944. Here they supported 41 Commando in the clearing of Westkappel and were present throughout the battle for the island.

The Brigade was stationed in Scotland as part of 52 (Lowland) Division, Britain's only mountain warfare formation, training for the return to Norway. However, despite Winston Churchill's advocacy of such a project, the British military had considered and rejected the launching of an invasion of German occupied Norway. This was despite examining the possibility on numerous occasions from mid 1941 onwards. As Lieutenant General Morgan, responsible for the plan Operation Overlord accepted at Quebec in August 1943, said 'We went to Normandy or we stayed at home'.[23]

Therefore, the Army spent the greater part of the war running up and down hills in Scotland. Only their liaison officers accompanied the mountain-trained 52 Division when it was sent into the Netherlands in October 1944, proving remarkably useful as they were able to communicate with the local population.[24] The Norwegian Army was a resource, unlike the Navy and Air Force, which could only be committed once. The Norwegians did not have the manpower to create another and therefore the bulk of the Army had to be saved for operations on Norwegian soil.

A contingent of Norwegian troops was based in Iceland where they trained British and later American troops in Arctic warfare techniques. Also elements garrisoned various Norwegian possessions in the Arctic such as Jan Mayen and Spitzbergen where they established meteorological sections. Both were bleak and, in the case of Spitzbergen, dangerous postings. This was because the Germans had had a similar idea and also set up a weather station on Spitzbergen. Thus much of the Norwegians' time was spent hunting down the German weather observers. In response the Germans launched one their largest naval operations of the War. In one of the conflict's more mismatched actions the battleship *Tirpitz* and battlecruiser *Scharnhorst* with 10 fleet destroyers in attendance took on the 152 Norwegians armed with small arms and a couple of 40 mm anti-aircraft guns. While the Germans killed six Norwegians and captured 41 they withdrew after six hours leaving the hundred or so survivors to re-establish themselves quickly.[25]

## Exile 'police troops' in Sweden

The Norwegian Government also had another source of trained and equipped manpower, but the use and control of these men was heavily restricted. As the war progressed despite large-scale German forces remaining in Scandinavia, neutral Sweden began to take a tougher attitude towards Germany and pursue an approach far more amenable to the Allies. Taking advantage of the more sympathetic Swedish attitude, thousands of Norwegians fled into Sweden along well-organized escape routes. The Swedish police chief, Harry Sönderman, organized the training and equipment of 13,000 young Norwegian men as 'police troops', or more accurately light infantry, on Swedish soil. In October 1944 Trygve Lie visited Stockholm to ask if it was possible 'to move the police troops to the places where we [the Norwegian Government] wanted them'.[26]

It was not as simple as it sounded; the Swedish position was that the police troops could not be sent into Norway while the war continued. They agreed with Lie that the police troops should be used first and foremost to 'establish law and order in liberated areas' although they might just have to take on other tasks.[27] Fortunately, to quote Jacob Sverdrup's official history of Norwegian foreign policy, they 'chose to give a liberal interpretation to their neutral policy'.[28] These men played key roles in both Finnmark and the liberation in May 1945.

## The Exile Army in the liberation of Norway

In October 1944 the Red Army entered the northernmost Norwegian province of Finnmark in the pursuit of the retreating Germans. The Army could at last make a contribution. The cooperative attitude of the Norwegian High Command meant that they had been heavily involved in British planning for Norway's liberation since late 1943. However, the entry of the Soviet Army into Norway caused a serious reconsideration of the situation. There was no question of British troops entering a Soviet zone of operations but the Norwegian High Command managed to gain both British and Soviet approval for their proposal to send a token force of a Mountain Company of the Norwegian Brigade, roughly 200 men, into Finnmark. Churchill felt this was an inadequate response as this was 'their chance to go back to their country'.[29] However, this was about a third of Norwegian first line infantry strength and the rest had to be retained in Britain in enough force to carry out their role under the contingency plans for Norway's liberation. The Mountain Company entered Norway on 10 November 1944.

Their commander, Colonel Dahl, soon discovered that the Russians had halted their advance and the Germans were continuing to withdraw while carrying out a scorched earth policy. He pushed his limited force forward into the no-mans land in the wake of the withdrawing Germans and wondered what to do with the local population that remained in the area. He was, however, reinforced by 1,300 Norwegian police troops from Sweden flown in by American Dakotas. Fortunately the Swedes agreed that Finnmark was a liberated area rather than a zone of operations and thus the troops could be sent there. The Norwegian High Command proposed sending an expanded Norwegian expedition to Finnmark to facilitate the relief of the civilian population. Ironically considering Churchill's opinion, the British turned down the proposal because the Norwegian resources requested were deemed too vital to the overall Allied war effort.[30] It took the direct intervention of Norwegian Commander-in-Chief Crown Prince Olav at the highest levels in Washington to get the decision reversed but by then the war was almost over and preparation for the liberation of Norway in the wake of the German surrender had begun.

The smooth and bloodless liberation of Norway garrisoned by almost 400,000 Germans was a fitting and satisfactory conclusion to the war for the Norwegian armed forces. Norwegian paratroops were the first substantive Allied force to enter Oslo on 9 May 1945. There can be no doubting the tactical skills of the Norwegian Army; in the little fighting that they saw – the operations of *Kompani Linge*, Norwegian troops in Finnmark and the commandos along the Norwegian coast and on Walcheren Island – they acquitted themselves well. General Sir Andrew Thorne who commanded the Brigade when it was part of Scottish Command and also when it returned home as part of the Allied Forces that liberated Norway considered that 'the individual young Norwegian [as] about the finest material which could be found in any army'. Thorne was not so impressed by the standard of Norwegian senior officers, nor did he have much regard for the Norwegian command and staff system. Thorne had studied the 'administration of quite a number of Armies other than my own' and in his opinion the Norwegian system came out below that of the Americans, Germans, Swedes, French and Danes.[31]

Given such limited forces at their disposal, it was hardly surprising that the Norwegian military concentrated its manpower in front line roles and devoted particular energy to acquiring tactical expertise. This led to a neglect of the more mundane administrative and organizational skills so vital to modern warfare. This problem manifested itself during the liberation when command, control and logistics collapsed in the northern sector around Tromsø which was the responsibility of the Norwegian Brigade. Thorne was forced to replace the Norwegian zone commander with a British officer because of what one of Thorne's staff described as 'the chaos that occurs in Norwegian administration through lack of trained officers'.[32] While this was partially the fault of the British for so willingly undertaking so much of the support functions of Norwegian units, it did not bode well for the long term success of any independent Norwegian operations.

Thus the Norwegian Army returned home to Norway victors. Yet Norway had been a very minor part of great coalition and largely subordinated their efforts to those of their Great Power partners, particularly Britain. The Norwegians accepted that they were very much a junior partner and could have very little influence on the overall direction of Allied strategy. Norway also chose to concentrate on the contribution its merchant shipping, Navy and Air Forces could make. The Army's opportunities to take an active part in the struggle were limited purely by the shape that Allied Grand Strategy took. All that can be said is that when they achieved a high level of competency in tactical if not administrate skill and when they did see action they acquitted themselves well.

## Notes


1. Leif Andreasson in BBC Documentary, *Icemen*, 1998. See also Mick Conefrey and Tim Jordan, *Icemen: A History of the Arctic and Its Explorers* (Bassingston: Boxtree, 1998), pp. 132–46.
2. François Kersaudy, *Norway: 1940* (London: Arrow, 1990), pp. 179–81.
3. Ministère des Affairs Étrangères, Brussels, 11075/Oslo 35/40, J. U. de Schooten to Spaak, no 84–59, 27 January 1938 in *Ibid.*, p. 11.
4. David Thompson, 'Norwegian Military Policy, 1905–40: A Critical Appraisal and Review of the Literature', *The Journal of Military History*, 61(3), (1997), p. 517.
5. Olav Riste, 'Relations Between the Norwegian Government in Exile and the British Government', in Patrick Salmon (ed.), *Britain and Norway in the Second World War* (London: HMSO, 1995), pp. 40–1.
6. Hans Fredrik Dahl, *Quisling: A Study in Treachery* (Cambridge: Cambridge University Press, 1999), pp. 180, 190–1.
7. Johannes Andenæs, Olav Riste and Magne Skodvin, *Norway and the Second World War* (Oslo: Aschehoug, 1966), pp. 96–7.
8. Johan Nygaardsvold, *Norge i Krig: London 1940–45* (Oslo: Tiden, 1982), p. 228.
9. Aide-Mémoire from the Royal Norwegian Ministry of Defence, 10 July 1940, Public Record Office (PRO), FO 371/24838, No 297.
10. *Agreement of the 28 May 1941 between the Government of the United Kingdom and the Royal Norwegian Government concerning the organisation and employment of the Norwegian Armed Forces in the United Kingdom*, 7 April 1942, Riksarkivet (RA – Norwegian National Archives), SOK 291, Mappe:70.1 Regjeringen Avtaler, SOK 704,0/TP/EP.
11. David Thompson, 'Controversial Aspects of Norwegian Military History' (unpublished 1995), p. 20. A much revised version of this article appeared as 'Norwegian Military Policy, 1905–1940: A Critical Appraisal and Review of the Literature', *Journal of Military History*, 61(3), (1997), pp. 503–20.

12. *Tip and Run Raids on Fishing Ports in the Lofoten Islands*, 2 January 1941, PRO, DEFE 2/141, and Trygve Lie, *Kampen for Norges Frihet 1940–45* (Oslo: Borregaard, 1958), p. 220.
13. Lie, *Kampen for Norges Frihet 1940–45*, p. 253.
14. J. S. Wilson, *Norwegian Section History 1940–45* (unpublished, 1945), p. 17, Norges Hjemmefrontmuseum (NHM – Norwegian Resistance Museum).
15. NHM, Diary of Birger Fjelstad cited by Arnfinn Moland, 'Milorg and SOE' in Salmon (ed.), *Britain and Norway in the Second World War*, p. 144.
16. *Anglo-Norwegian Collaboration Regarding the Military Organisation in Norway*, 24 November 1941, enclosure to CH/88, Hambro to Torp, 25 November 1941, PRO, HS 2/127.
17. Hambro to Ismay, 30 November 1941, PRO, HS 2/127, CH/NO/150.
18. *Operation Claymore*, 3 February 1941, PRO, HS 2/224.
19. Ismay to Hambro, 8 December 1941, PRO, HS 2/127.
20. Hambro to Torp, 14 January 1942, PRO, CH/660.
21. Olav Riste, *London-regjeringa, I. 1940–42: Prøvetid*, 2nd edition (Oslo: Det Norske Samlaget, 1995), p. 177.
22. Petersen to Carlisle, 23 March 1942, RA, Militærattasjeen i London 35, Mappe 355: Parachute Jumping, MA/355.
23. Sir Frederick Morgan, *Peace and War* (London: Hodder and Stoughton, 1961), p. 175.
24. *Report on study period for the Norwegian Operational Liaison Officer January 1945*, Lt Col Pran, Liaison Inspector, 31 January 1945, RA, SOK 291, Mappe H 722.3: Admralstaben krigsoppsetnings planer.
25. For a reasonable account of the Norwegian Army's role on the Atlantic islands see (anon.) *Arctic War: Norway's Role on the Northern Front* (London: HMSO, 1945).
26. Lie, *Kampen for Norges Frihet 1940–45*, p. 327.
27. *Möte mellom utenriksminster Trygve Lie og utenriksminster Chr. Günther i Stockholm*, 30 October 1944, RA, FO 61, Mappe: Forhandlingene i Stockholm 1944–45.
28. Jakob Sverdrup, *Inn i storpolitikken, 1940–49* (Oslo: Universitetsforlaget, 1996), p. 169.
29. Churchill to Ismay for COS, 26 October 1944, PRO, PREM 3/328/8.
30. COS (45) 31st Meeting, 29 January 1945, PRO, CAB 119/107.
31. Thorne to Ruge, 9 September 1945 and GON 73, Thorne to Brooke, 20 September 1945, PRO, WO 106/1984.
32. Col. Garner Smith to Col. Stockdale, 26 May 1945, PRO, WO 106/1985, GON 111/1.

# 5
# *Jai Hind!*[1]: The Indian National Army, 1942–45

*Robin Havers*[2]

## Introduction

The Indian National Army (INA) was an Indian military formation that fought on the side of the Japanese, against the British, between 1942 and 1945. The INA was the result of an informal alliance between the radical expatriate Indian political leaders of the Indian Independence League (IIL) and the Imperial Japanese Army (IJA). The INA existed in two distinct incarnations. It was raised and led initially by a disillusioned British-Indian Army Officer, Captain Mohan Singh, who had been captured in the opening stages of the Japanese invasion of Malaya. After the British surrender at Singapore in February 1942, Singh recruited Indian troops of the British-Army from Japanese Prisoner of War (POW) camps with a view to eventually fighting the British in India. Disagreements between Singh and the Japanese, over both the intended size and the specific role of the INA, led to Singh's dismissal. His replacement in June 1943 was a well-known political figure in the Indian independence movement, Subhas Chandra Bose. This second life of the INA proved to be far more robust and substantial than the first. Pre-war, Bose had established an international reputation as a nationalist politician, although his belief in the best way to achieve independence increasingly brought him into conflict with other leaders of the Congress Party. Following periods in various British prisons, and after serving as President of Congress for a year in 1938, Bose fled India. He spent time in exile in Nazi Germany and there raised a small force from among Indian POWs but with little hope of actually fighting in India. With the defeat of British arms at Singapore, Bose saw that the best chance of winning Indian independence lay with the Japanese and the fledgling INA. Before he could journey to Singapore, however, the first INA had already fallen apart. When Bose eventually arrived in June 1943 he was required both to rebuild the INA as well as lead it.

Bose changed the scale of the INA and overcame many of the problems that had defeated Mohan Singh. Bose recruited extensively among Indian civilians in Malaya as well as the POW constituency established by Singh. More significantly, Bose was instrumental in providing a wider, political, context for the INA to operate in. He created a Japanese-sponsored Indian 'Provisional Government' and the INA became, in effect, the military organization of what Bose considered a legitimate government-in-exile. The INA, at Bose's insistence, accompanied the IJA in the assault on Burma and fought in the Arakan and at Imphal. Minor exceptions notwithstanding, the INA was generally undistinguished in combat although the extent to which this was due to external factors, such as poor logistical support, rather than lack of fighting spirit is debatable. As the Japanese army was defeated in Burma so the INA crumbled without ever securing the mass defections from the British-Indian Army that Bose had confidently predicted.

Despite Bose's success the INA, arguably, achieved far more after his death. When, in November 1945, the British publicly tried former INA men in the Red Fort at Delhi the INA phenomenon, which had been carefully kept from the public domain during the war years, was thrust upon an unsuspecting Indian population that was more ready than ever for independence. The trials and the associate publicity helped ensure that the activities of the INA were now well known. In the volatile political climate of post-war, but pre-independence, India the trials did little to either to calm the mood of militancy among Indian nationalists nor to result in the widespread vilification of the accused, as the British had hoped. They ended in farce with the main accused released after being found guilty, their sentences suspended.

## The origins of the Indian National Army

The immediate origins of the INA lay with the alliance of the Imperial Japanese Army's General Headquarters and the Indian Independence League.[3] The IJA in the personage of an Intelligence Corps Major, Iwaichi Fujiwara, and the IIL, under Pritam Singh and Rash Behari Bose (neither related to the two leaders of the INA).[4] Both organizations had longstanding plans for some form of Indian independence army although, as will be seen, their aims in doing so were not necessarily coterminous. The IIL was active across South East Asia and was a descendent of the First World War vintage *Ghadr* party that had openly agitated for Indian independence. Its members were intent on capitalizing on Britain's problems in the European conflagration and threw in their lot with the Japanese. On 1 December 1941 Fujiwara, the 'midwife of the INA'[5], drew up an agreement that provided the basis of cooperation between the Japanese and the IIL. The agreement was aimed at 'the establishment of peace in Greater East Asia by co-operation between Indians and Japanese' and to this end the Japanese promised to render 'all possible support' to the ambitions of Indian nationalists.[6] The Japanese also reassured the Indians that they had no 'political, economic, cultural or religious' ambitions in India itself and that they would respect the property and freedom of Indians in territory that came under the sway of Japan.[7] The Indians had no wish to exchange British Imperial rule for the Japanese variety. The agreement also provided for IIL members to accompany the IJA into areas such as Malaya where they would endeavour to win over local Indian communities. In Malaya alone the Indian Diaspora amounted to c.800,000 people.[8] Most significantly, for the formation of the INA, was the clause that related to the creation of an Indian Voluntary Army to 'fight for Indian independence'.

## The First INA

Originally, the INA was drawn exclusively from Indian POWs of the Japanese. For many, their experiences in Malaya, whether examples of overt racism or of seeing the previously undefeated British vanquished in such a convincing fashion, proved to be the vital catalyst in their willingness to join. Few on the Allied side, whether British, Indian or Australian, covered themselves with glory in Malaya and Singapore and disillusionment and recrimination was widespread following the surrender.[9] Indian army soldiers were considered to be largely apolitical and great efforts were made to insulate the troops from political ideas. Recruits were traditionally drawn from the 'martial races' of India that were considered indifferent to political matters. However, with the ongoing agitation for Indian independence, many Indian officers had given considerable thought to the future of India. For these men the INA was merely the logical extension of previously held political feelings. Indeed the loyalty of Indian officers was under suspicion well before the outbreak of war and well before either the IIL or the disasters in Malaya and Singapore had a chance to politicize them further. The programme of 'Indianization' of the Indian Army Officer corps also had a role to play. In 1942 a secret report informed Lord Wavell, that 'we have… bred a new class of officer who may be loyal to India and perhaps to

Congress, but is not necessarily loyal to us'.[10] As early as 1939 British intelligence was raising concerns about the activities of Japanese nationals in Malaya:

> There are indications that the local Japanese are anxious to effect rapprochement with the newly arrived Indian troops. Indian officers have been entertained by Japanese and more prominence to Indian matters is evident in the 'Singapore Herald', a Japanese newspaper printed in English.[11]

The strength of the Indian Army also resided in the high degree of regimental pride and a tradition of service that often existed through several generations of the same families. British officers frequently stayed with their unit from subaltern up to Lieutenant Colonel. The coming of the European war necessitated the expansion of the Indian army and the consequent dilution of many of these strengths. Existing Indian Army battalions were milked of the more seasoned NCOs and officers and replaced by those with little or no experience. Many of the new officers and NCOs often could not speak Urdu.[12] The IIL and the Japanese skilfully exploited all these weaknesses.

The prime mover in the initial INA formation was Captain Mohan Singh, a professional soldier with 1/14th Punjab regiment. Singh's own political consciousness appears to have been already developing by the time of his arrival in Malaya. He noted that there is 'a difference between the soldiers of a free nation and soldiers of a subject nation' and that: 'The soldiers of a free nation fight because it is their duty to fight national wars right or wrong, we fight because we are ordered to by our alien rulers'.[13] Singh believed that 'there was not the slightest doubt that we were being exploited by the British for their own ends. The war was not our war. Not a single Indian was consulted before plunging our entire nation into the most destructive struggle'.[14] His disenchantment had grown in Malaya and many Indian officers complained of discrimination from British civilians.[15] While these incidents were not the reason for the formation of the INA, they seemed to many to be indicative of a fundamentally inequitable system.

After being captured by the Japanese in the opening days of the Malayan campaign, Mohan Singh met an IIL activist, Pritam Singh. Pritam persuaded Mohan to form the INA with Japanese help. Mohan Singh did not agree immediately but eventually he was prepared to act. On 30 December 1941 he proposed five main points to the Japanese:

1.  The Japanese Army (IJA) should give full cooperation for raising a liberation army for India.
2.  The IIL and the INA should run independently.
3.  The IJA should allow Indian POWs to be controlled by Singh.
4.  These Indian POWs who would join the army should be freed from 'concentration camps'. Those who would not would also remain POWs under Singh.
5.  The Japanese army should give the liberation army the status of an allied army.[16]

The agreement gave Singh effective authority over all Indian POWs captured by the Japanese. It was conflict over Japanese infringement of these principals that prompted Singh's fall from grace with the Japanese.

Singh's motivation to recruit Indian POWs may well have had non-political reasons as well and he was certainly keen to keep Indian troops out of Japanese hands as far as possible. There was also an element of compulsion underlying the first INA. Many Indian soldiers were forced to join as a result of either coercion or the threat of severe punishment. The extent to which Singh himself was aware of this is debatable.[17] Singh's own methods of recruitment varied. Frequently officers who spoke out against the INA were confined in what was termed an 'Officers' separation camp' where they were persuaded through ridicule, propaganda and discomfort to bring them around to the INA way of thinking. The close, familial nature of the British-Indian Army meant that Indian troops generally looked to their officers for guidance on a range of matters and many joined the INA because their officers told them to. Some joined simply to avoid spending the war as POWs. Of those recruited for 'espionage' work, many, after being inserted into Burma or Indian ostensibly to spy on the British, simply gave themselves up, pleased at having used the pretence of the INA to escape captivity.

After the British defeat at Singapore in February 1942, Singh appealed to Indian POWs at their camp in Farrar Park to join him. The camp held only Indian troops, officers and other ranks, and was a direct result of the Japanese segregation of Indians from their British officers. Approximately 40,000 Indian POWs pledged their support and from this total Singh planned to raise two divisions. Despite their initial, apparent, enthusiasm the Japanese proved to be reluctant to move the INA idea much beyond the sphere of political propaganda. Certainly, the Japanese were unconvinced of the merit of such a large force as Singh proposed.

Eventually, after much discussion, Singh was granted permission to raise one division and, in September 1942, the INA 1st Division was formed. This formation was c. 14,000 strong, with 9,000 men organized into three guerrilla regiments each named after an Indian nationalist leader (Ghandi, Nehru and Azad). The remaining 5,000 comprised the 1st *Hind* Field Force Group and a further 3,000 INA fulfilled support roles such as intelligence and training.[18]

Bolstered by the recruitment of the 1st INA Division, Singh attempted to raise additional forces. The Japanese steadfastly refused to sanction an increase in trained INA soldiers and also refused to supply equipment beyond poorly maintained ex-British weapons. The Japanese compounded the tension by ordering INA units to the Indo-Burmese front without consulting Singh. This was a clear infringement of the INA's autonomy as set out in the 'Five Principals'.[19] The final straw for Singh was the employment of Indian POWs who had not joined the INA as labourers.[20] This together with political disagreements between the soldier Singh and the politicians of the IIL as to the exact role of the INA , led to the Japanese arrest of Singh with the explicit connivance of Rash Bose. Singh concluded that the Japanese 'wanted the army [INA] and the organisation to be just a show piece and a convenient puppet, but not a strong and powerful reality which may become a problem for them later on thwart their secret designs on India'.[21] Before he could be arrested Mohan Singh dissolved the INA and its men, all of whom had sworn a personal oath of allegiance to him, complied with the order.

## Subhas Chandra Bose and the second INA

Despite the disappointments of Mohan Singh the Japanese were still keen to see an INA of some description, for propaganda reasons if nothing else. The new leader of the INA was to be Subhas Chandra Bose. Bose was born on 23 January 1897 at Cuttack in the state of Orissa, He attended the Scottish Church College and was an 'enthusiastic' member of its TA unit. Persuaded by his father to sit an examination for the Indian Civil Service (ICS), Bose went to England and Cambridge University. Despite finishing fourth in the examinations Bose declined an offer of a job with the ICS. Bose had become committed to the idea of an independent India but did not believe that this independence could be won via Ghandi's policy of civil disobedience. After serving time in prison Bose went to Europe in February 1933, spending time in Germany, Italy, Ireland and Austria among other countries. On his return to India, and following the publication of *The Indian Struggle* – banned in the UK and India – Bose faced another spell in gaol. After his release, on health grounds, Bose was elected as President of Congress in 1938. His belief, in 1939, that the war could lead to Indian Independence resulted in various meetings with Germans in India and subsequent imprisonment on charges of sedition. Bose escaped and headed to Berlin via Kabul. His sojourn in Germany saw the establishment of a 'Legion' of ex-POWs but Bose's hoped for declaration from the three Axis powers on the future of Indian never materialized. The British defeat at Singapore and news of the fledgling INA prompted Bose to return to the Far East. His arrival was delayed many months and he did not reach Singapore until June 1943.

Once there, however, Bose wasted little time in reorganizing both the INA and the IIL and announcing the formation of the Provisional Government. There is, however, a considerable degree of symbiosis apparent between Bose and his grandly titled 'Provisional Government' and the INA. The Provisional Government conferred on the INA the idea that it had both status and a role in the forefront of the struggle for Indian independence. Similarly, the impact of having a professionally trained army at his disposal, irrespective of the substantial reliance on Japanese support, helped to legitimize Bose's position and his claims to speak not only for Indians outside India but also within. Bose's frequent pronouncements to the effect that Indians would desert from the British when faced with the INA also served a similar aim. These claims suggested that Bose and his forces had a wider and a more significant relevance than simply being a rag-tag band of discontents on the margins, politically and geographically, of Indian attempts at independence.

The central unifying idea that underlay the creation of the INA was that of forcible Indian independence from the British. Under Mohan Singh's leadership this aspiration had been less explicit. With the arrival of Subhas Bose the role of the INA was far more obvious and more overtly political. One of Bose's first acts, on 21 October 1943, was to proclaim his 'Provisional Government of India' the *Azad Hind* – 'Free India' and to declare war on both Britain and the United States of America. Bose's announcement that 'The Provisional Government is entitled to and hereby claims the allegiance of every Indian' asserted a political authority that had significant ramifications for the INA.[22] The INA was now the armed force of a 'legitimate' Indian government. To legitimize his position further Bose pressured the Japanese to grant him some territory over which the Provisional Government might rule. In November 1943 the Japanese agreed to 'transfer' the Andaman and Nicobar Islands to Bose.[23] These islands, grandiosely renamed by Bose as respectively

'Shahid' (Martyr) and 'Swaraj' (Independence) were the only portions of Indian territory to be occupied by Japan during the Second World War. They also had a symbolic value as they were the traditional place of detention of Indian revolutionaries by the British.[24] Although Bose appointed a governor of the two islands, their importance to Japanese naval operations was significant and meant that the Japanese Naval authorities retained control over the territories. Despite these Japanese gestures, international recognition of Bose's regime was limited to the axis powers and their puppet client states.

Bose, however, was undeterred. He adopted the title of 'Netaji', which means 'leader' and has been interpreted as being akin to 'Führer'. Bose was aware of this and apparently unconcerned by its implications. Given the style of Bose's leadership it was not inapplicable. In a further effort both to build and legitimize the 'cult of the personality' that was growing around him Bose subsequently introduced 'Netaji week' in Singapore during July to emphasize further his central role in the developing Indian independence movement. Within the Provisional Government itself Bose held the positions of Head of State, Prime Minister and Minister of War and Foreign Affairs.[25] The INA under Bose also adopted a host of symbols to underline both its purpose and legitimacy. INA officers wore specially designed shoulder tabs with the initials INA prominently displayed and a new system of ranks was introduced along with decorations. Bose's practice of encouraging through promotion meant that, by August 1945, the INA was top-heavy with senior officers. Ironically, however, the INA's continued reliance on British Indian army equipment required them to dress in traditional khaki in contrast to the infinitely more concealing new jungle-green uniforms now sported by British (and indeed by Japanese) forces. The INA also adopted the 'Springing Tiger' as its official symbol together with a new flag, the Indian tricolour with the Tiger emblem super-imposed. The INA also began using the patriotic greeting, '*jai hind*' and there was also a 'national Anthem of Azad Hind'.

Whereas Mohan Singh had concentrated upon recruiting POWs, Bose cast the net rather wider and began actively to cultivate civilian recruits. This was partially due to the effect that the collapse of the First INA had on POW recruitment but also with an eye on widening the political appeal, and therefore the political power which could be wielded as a result when negotiating with the Japanese. The new INA boasted a similar number to the old, c.40,000 men of whom 15,000 were former POWs with most of the c.25,000 remainder being Tamils drawn from the labouring classes in Burma and Malaya.[26] Contemporary British intelligence reports and Japanese assessments indicate that units drawn from these latter groupings performed far better than their ex-POW comrades under combat conditions.[27] Unlike Singh, Bose successfully overcame Japanese reluctance and made plans to form three INA divisions. Only 1st INA Division was to comprise purely of ex-POWs; 2nd Division was a mixture of POWs and civilians and 3rd Division was to be civilians only.[28] One of Bose's most original contributions was the raising of a women's unit of the INA. The *Rani of Jhansi* unit was exclusively female and fought in Burma alongside its male counterparts.[29]

While Mohan Singh's attempts to gain additional Japanese support were largely unfruitful, Bose the seasoned politician was more successful. Bose continually harangued the Japanese for better training facilities and equipment and did manage to secure many of his requirements, notably a training base for his women's Regiment, despite Japanese difficulties in reconciling the idea of women as soldiers. Bose's successes were partially due, no doubt, to the critical mass that he himself had established for the INA and which the Japanese, consequently, were obliged to take more seriously. Bose's determination that the INA should fight in the forefront of the Japanese drive to India ensured that the 'Bose Brigade', comprising the INA's best troops, accompanied the IJA in February 1944 into the Arakan.

## Into battle

The level of military effectiveness demonstrated by the INA was generally low. Initial efforts by small groups of INA soldiers, in a reconnaissance and intelligence gathering role, had done little to change the Japanese impressions of their reliability or effectiveness. Many were captured without performing any useful task and many surrendered as soon as the opportunity presented itself. British Intelligence concluded that 'the INA was not to be feared as a fighting force' but purely because of the psychological effect it might have 'on a portion of the army as well as the civil population of this country'.[30] Ironically, this assessment was wholly accurate as far as the impact of the Red Fort trials went yet totally wrong in terms of what happened during the war proper. Bose's frequent claim that the mere presence of the INA would prompt mass desertions was proved false. When Bose met with the imprisoned Mohan Singh in December 1943 he was told that the much hoped for collapse of the Indian Army was seriously misplaced. Singh pointed out that many thousands of Indian POWs had refused to join the INA in the aftermath of the British defeat and the likelihood of whole units changing sides now that Japan herself was in trouble was slim indeed.[31] Bose was reluctantly forced to agree that 'there is some truth in what you have said'.[32] Despite this, Bose pressed on with his demands to see the INA join battle with the British. In the light of his claims and the nature of his 'Provisional Government' he had little choice.

The so-called 'Bose Brigade', consisting of three battalions each of five companies, drew the best men from the INA and participated in the Japanese attack in the Arakan in January–February 1944 and later in the attack on Imphal. The INA fought with mixed results and only a few Indian Army troops could be persuaded to cross over and join the INA. Despite his success in ensuring the INA's participation in the fighting, Bose was continually frustrated by Japanese reluctance to employ the INA in anything other than secondary roles.[33] Eventually, dispirited and with low morale the INA joined in the general retreat of the Japanese 15th Army. The INA had committed 10,000 troops into Rangoon in September 1944.

The effectiveness of the INA in battle was mixed. Some units such as the 1st Battalion, 2nd INA division performed well. The Japanese, who had maintained serious misgivings over the utility of the INA, considered that the aforementioned Tamil troops, recruited exclusively from Malaya, had generally performed well and done far better than their ex-Indian Army, ex-POW comrades. Despite Bose's assertions that the INA should be above all else a secular organization there is some evidence of conflict between Muslim and Sikh troops which went some way to undermining both the effectiveness and willingness of Muslim troops to fight on. As the war progressed and the Japanese position worsened so too did that of the INA. Desertions increased considerably and Bose was obliged to introduce capital punishment as a way of addressing the problem in March 1945. Sundaram considers that 'from April 1945... the INA's retreat, which had hitherto been orderly, became a rout and mass surrenders became frequent'.[34] Sundaram makes the following comments on the performance of the IJA in battle conditions: first that the Japanese at all levels of command did not think highly of the INA and that this consideration 'dictated INA–IJA relations for the whole period of the INA's existence'.[35] He believed that this coloured the INA's abilities by limiting its size, the quality of equipment it received and by logistical constraints. The INA originally received weapons from captured allied stocks, much of which was in a poor state of repair.[36] Rifles, for example, were 'old and rusty and had no oil bottles or pull-throughs for cleaning purposes'.[37] Other concerns included the diverse variety of weaponry supplied, including Lewis and Bren guns as well a general paucity of ammunition. While many of the logistical problems were similar for Japanese forces, the lack of faith in the INA meant that they were never a priority for the Japanese. Similarly, what the former Indian army troops considered to be adequate provisioning was vastly different to the levels that the IJA considered sufficient. This type of difference was obviously not a concern for civilians recruited directly to the INA and may also explain, in part, the at times stiffer resistance displayed by the former civilian elements of the INA. However, it may also be that had the Japanese had the confidence to deploy the INA as a more cohesive unit, rather than in the 'penny packet' fashion that they did then, as Sundaram suggests, the INA might have had the opportunity to live up to its emblem the 'Springing Tiger', rather than be dismissed as merely a paper one.[38]

## Conclusions

There were a number of contradictions within the INA–Japanese relationship. First, although a free and independent India was the ultimate and overriding goal for Bose himself, the Japanese never envisaged that India would fall into the wider design of the 'Greater East Asia Co-Prosperity Sphere'.[39] India, however, was important to the Japanese because of its strategic position and because it was the source of supplies to the Chinese and American forces in Chunking. Similarly, any anti-British sentiment to be accrued from the existence of the INA could only benefit the Japanese. The relationship between the INA and the Japanese is described follows:

> as Japan sought to expel British influence from India and the rest of Southeast Asia, so also Indian nationalists aspired to free India. Out of this common enemy arose the limited co-operation between Japan and India that focussed on the Indian National Army.[40]

The INA was 'British by conditioning and experience, partly Japanese in impetus and more Indian than the British Indian Army'.[41] On the Japanese side there were lingering concerns about the reliability as well military effectiveness of the INA. The Japanese, not unreasonably, did not place much store by the INA's ability to fight, principally because of the feeling that the regular British Indian Army did not generally distinguish itself in the fighting for Malaya. Events proved this feeling to have been misplaced but by then it was too late to do much to rescue the situation. These impressions on the part of the Japanese provided a double bind in that the Japanese were reluctant to provide much in the way of useful weaponry which in turn inhibited INA effectiveness in combat and so reinforced many of the Japanese prejudices.

Hugh Toye in his impressive and sober study of the INA written in 1956 wrote that, 'there can thus be little doubt that the Indian National Army, not in its unhappy career on the battlefield, but in its thunderous disintegration, hastened the end of British rule in India'.[42] Toye is discussing the impact of the Red Fort trials of INA figures on the Indian political landscape and no doubt he is right to emphasize the significance of the events in November 1945 and subsequently. Indian independence, however, was assured as soon as Clement Attlee and the Labour party took power in Britain in July 1945 and the popular support apparent for the INA was probably an effect of the realization that independence was inevitable rather than a cause. While it is beyond doubt that Bose wanted the INA to fight and be seen to be more than a 'paper tiger' it is doubtful whether he believed the INA would actually achieve much in a purely military sense. His conversation with Mohan Singh reveals some of the doubts in his mind over the likelihood of mass defections from the Indian Army. What Bose could most probably have expected from the successful participation of his troops in combat was a proportional increase in political capital rather than tangible military gains. The promise alone of the INA's effectiveness, in the teeth of obvious IJA doubts over what it might achieve, had secured Bose the support of Prime Minister Tojo himself. This support, at all levels of the Japanese military, had resulted in an army and government for Bose. Logically, any success at all on the battlefield might reasonably have been translated into even more Japanese aid and even more Japanese support in the future.

## Notes

1. Variously translated as 'India for ever!' and 'Glory to India'. *'Jai Hind'* was adopted as a familiar greeting amongst the INA at Subhas Bose's insistence.
2. The views expressed are those of the author and not necessarily those of the RMA Sandhurst or the UK Ministry of Defence.
3. Chandar Sundaram, 'A Paper Tiger', *War and Society*, 13(1), (May 1995), p. 35.
4. Bose had attempted to assassinate the then Viceroy of India, Baron Hardinge of Penhurst, in 1912 and had fled to Japan where he built up considerable support for his actions.
5. Gerard Corr, *War of the Springing Tiger* (London: Morrison and Gibb, 1975), p. 125.
6. T. R. Sareen, *Japan and The Indian National Army* (Delhi: Agam Prakashan, 1986), p. 22.
7. *Ibid.*

8. Hugh Toye, *The Springing Tiger* (London: Cassell, 1959), p. 7.

9. In January 1999 new files on Singapore were declassified for the first time, 'Proposals for a Public Inquiry into the Malaya Campaign-1942', cites the 'strain' on relations with India and Australia that such an inquiry would engender. See: CAB121/765, Public Record Office (PRO), London.

10. Peter Elphick, *Singapore: The Pregnable Fortress* (London: Hodder and Stoughton, 1995), p. 69.

11. See: WO208/1522, PRO, quoted in Elphick, p. 64.

12. *Ibid.*, p. 65.

13. Mohan Singh quoted in K. K. Ghosh, *The Indian National Army* (Meerut: Meenakshi Prakashan, 1969), p. 25.

14. Mohan Singh quoted in Ghosh, p. 25.

15. See Elphick, *The Pregnable Fortress*, pp. 45–77.

16. Mohan Singh quoted in Ghosh, p. 30

17. Toye, *The Springing Tiger*, p. 9.

18. Sundaram, *A Paper Tiger*, p. 37.

19. *Ibid.*

20. Sareen, *Japan and The Indian National Army*, p. 92.

21. Mohan Singh quoted in Sareen, p. 89.

22. Toye, *The Springing Tiger*, p. 77.

23. Joyce C. Lebra, *Japanese Trained Armies in Southeast Asia* (New York: Columbia University Press, 1977), p. 34.

24. *Ibid.*

25. Toye, *The Springing Tiger*, p. 206.

26. Sundaram, *A Paper Tiger*, p. 38.

27. Cited in Sundaram, *A Paper Tiger*, p. 53.

28. *Ibid.*, p. 40.

29. Peter Ward Fay, *The Forgotten Army 1942–45* (Ann Arbor: University of Michigan Press, 1993), pp. 215–22, 269–70.

30. Sareen, *Japan and The Indian National Army*, p. 103.

31. Gerard Corr, *War of the Springing Tigers* (London: Osprey, 1975), p. 148.

32. *Ibid.*

33. Sundaram, *A Paper Tiger*, p. 42.

34. *Ibid.*, p. 53.

35. *Ibid.*, p. 55.

36. *Ibid.*, p. 37.

37. Ghosh, *The Indian National Army*, p. 99.

38. Sundaram, *A Paper Tiger*, p. 54.

39. Lebra, *Japanese Trained Armies in Southeast Asia*, p. 20.

40. *Ibid.*

41. *Ibid.*, p. 25.

42. Toye, *War of the Springing Tiger*, p. 175.

# Part II
# Cold War and Beyond

# 6

## 'Things Were Bound to Happen'[1]: Cuban Exiles, the United States and the Bay of Pigs

*Martin A. Smith*[2]

'Fiasco' and 'disaster' are the two adjectives most commonly employed by analysts and commentators to describe the Bay of Pigs operation. It was an abortive attempt in April 1961 by a 'Cuban Brigade' (actually a force consisting of some 1,400 Cuban exiles), trained and armed by the United States' Central Intelligence Agency (CIA), to establish and hold several beachheads in and around the *Bahía de Cochinos* (Bay of Pigs) in Cuba. The objective of the exercise was to unseat Fidel Castro's government, though there were important differences within the political, clandestine and military branches of the US government as to how precisely this was to be achieved. In the event these differences proved academic, as the Brigade was defeated within three days by Castro's army, air force and militia. The vast majority of its surviving members were subsequently captured. They were to spend over 18 months in captivity before being returned to the US, in exchange for food and medicines, by Castro late in 1962.

The outcome of the operation subsequently generated three official inquiries in the US together with a growing academic literature. Much of this sought to assess the planning and execution of the operation in detail and to apportion blame for what Theodore Draper famously called 'one of those rare politico-military events – a perfect failure'.[3] The present chapter will not contribute directly to this debate. Rather, it will consider specific aspects of the concept, planning and execution of the Bay of Pigs operation.

Crucial among these was the role played by issues relating to *legitimacy*. This has two dimensions in relation to the Bay of Pigs. First, there is the question of the legitimacy of the Cuban exile movement in the eyes of people in the mother country. The assigned task of the invasion

Brigade was, in essence, to install a 'provisional government' to replace the Castro regime. The exiled political leaders were, therefore, staking an overt claim to rule Cuba. The legitimacy question also has, as noted, a second dimension. The exile political leadership and military Brigade were both brought together by an agency of the US government – the CIA. Yet the Chief Executive of that government, President John Kennedy, and some of his advisers, were concerned to a significant extent about the political and diplomatic consequences if the US was seen to be orchestrating a change to the government of Cuba. Indeed, most of those who blame Kennedy for the ultimate failure of the Bay of Pigs operation do so on the basis of his alleged caution induced by the desire to ensure that the US hand remained, as far as possible, hidden.

Following on from this attention is the question of the *military effectiveness* of the Cuban Brigade. In common with other issues connected to the Bay of Pigs, this has developed into something of a political football over the years. The view propagated by many Brigade veterans and their supporters has been one of gallant fighters who were ultimately let down by the hesitation and lack of effective support coming from the American government at crucial times. On the other hand, there were doubts at the time as to the likely military effectiveness of any force of Cuban exiles.

Finally, the overall *unity and cohesion of the Cuban exile movement* will be assessed. This is an important issue because disunity would weaken the credibility and effectiveness of the movement as a viable alternative to Castro. In addition, if profound and enduring divisions existed, they would lend substance to suggestions that there was in fact no authentic 'exile movement' at all and that its political and military wings were both mere inventions of the CIA, as Castro himself has always claimed.

## The legitimacy of the Cuban exile movement

The main issue to be explored in this section concerns the extent to which the Cuban exile movement in the United States, based mainly in Florida, could advance plausible claims to represent a legitimate alternative government to Castro's. In this context such legitimacy would depend upon the composition and nature of the exile movement and the extent to which it could credibly claim that its impetus and organization were coming from Cubans themselves rather than North Americans. The extent to which support for the Castro government within Cuba was likely to erode following a successful exile landing is also a relevant issue for consideration here.

In terms of the exile movement's composition, there has been a sense, both among contemporary participants and subsequent analysts, that claims to legitimacy were impaired by the involvement of 'old guard' figures in leadership roles on both the political and military side. Their presence undermined the credibility of attempts by the exile movement to appeal for the overthrow of Castro in order to make way for a new democratic system in Cuba or, as the Kennedy administration was fond of asserting from January 1961, 'rescuing the revolution' from being taken over by Communists. Especially controversial, therefore, was the inclusion in the exile Brigade of military officers who had served the former dictatorship of Fulgencio Batista whose regime had collapsed in January 1959, clearing the way for Castro's seizure of power.

The CIA tried to justify their involvement on the grounds that, while it might not be ideal, it was nevertheless essential because these were people with at least some experience in running the country. More particularly, the inclusion of former members of Batista's army in the Cuban Brigade, one of whom – José Peréz San Román – was appointed as the Brigade's overall commander, was justified on the grounds that they had received military training and thus had some fighting and operational skills. Herbert Matthews has argued that the CIA deliberately sought to use *Batistianos* in preference to disillusioned former Castro supporters and officials from the early months of his regime. This was because its operators instinctively distrusted anybody who had ever had anything to do with the revolutionary leader. In this way, the CIA in effect helped to undermine President Kennedy's approach to 'rescuing the revolution'. It instinctively disliked revolutions *per se* and was not interested in 'rescuing' one in Cuba.

According to Matthews and others, the most prominent casualty of this approach was Manuel Ray, who had been Minister of Public Works during Castro's first months in power but who had subsequently become disillusioned and ended up in the US.[4] Ray himself was highly critical of the extent to which the exile Brigade that went ashore at the Bay of Pigs had been manned and influenced by *Batistianos*. In secret testimony to the Taylor Committee, which Kennedy had established to investigate reasons for the failure of the operation in the spring of 1961, Ray argued that a key reason for failure was that 'the operation didn't go deep within the people in Cuba'. The main thrust of his criticism was over 'the fact that many of the elements in the invasion force represented the old army. We [i.e. Ray and other former Castro supporters in the exile movement] felt it was wrong to give the impression that the old army was coming back and we protested'.[5]

Moreover, Ray's experiences at the hands of the CIA lead directly to a second key issue – the CIA's failure to effectively support dissident and resistance movements *within* Cuba itself. From the standpoint of legitimacy, the absence of such activity compromised the credibility of claims that the invasion was being conducted on behalf of the Cuban people against an unpopular regime and that the exile army enjoyed widespread popular support. In retrospect it seems clear that the operation was almost bound to fail, for both political and military reasons, in the absence of effective indigenous supporting activity. As Draper noted in 1962, by themselves the exiles' leaders 'were hardly representative of Cuban society as a whole', consisting as they did mainly of *Batistianos*, other political and military throwbacks and middle class professionals.[6] Matthews is even more blunt on this key point:

> Anyone familiar with the psychology of nations under dictatorships, and with their exiles, knows that those who stay at home and stick it out are the ones the country turns to when the change comes. They do not want exiles to return to run the country which they have left – and particularly a country which will have changed enormously during their absence. The pathetic Cuban Revolutionary Council that Washington set up to form a provisional government in Cuba would not have been welcomed by the Cuban people, not even by the enemies of the Castro regime.[7]

Yet the CIA's operational approach in effect required the exile Brigade to succeed without any real support from inside Cuba. Richard Bissell, who as the CIA's Deputy Director (Plans) had overall responsibility for putting together the Bay of Pigs operation, subsequently asserted that 'we had made a major effort at infiltration and resupply, and those efforts had been unsuccessful. My conviction is that we simply would not be able to organize a secure movement in Cuba'.[8] It is true that there was, from the autumn of 1960, an American programme in operation to provide supplies for guerrilla groups inside Cuba by air and by sea, and that the programme was ultimately ineffective.[9] However there are good grounds for believing that the CIA was never more than half-hearted about this programme, for a number of reasons.

There were genuine concerns about the possibility of penetration of groups inside Cuba by Castro agents. Peter Wyden has suggested that this was the main reason why the CIA never seriously considered providing internal resistance groups with the means to communicate directly with the planes which were supposed to be dropping supplies to them; supplies which often went astray or were not recovered.[10] Partly also it was due to the prejudice against groups 'tainted' in the CIA's eyes by any former association with Castro or his government. Matthews once more cites the example of Manuel Ray:

> There were guerilla units operating inside Cuba, of which the most effective was the *Movimiento Revolucionario del Pueblo* (MRP) directed by ex-Minister of Public Works Manuel Ray. Frank Bender, the CIA operator, refused to give Ray and his associates money or help, and before the [Bay of Pigs] landing he had arranged to get Ray removed from the picture. The MRP – the only really efficient underground movement in Cuba – was not notified of the invasion date, and hence did not rise when the exiles landed.[11]

The question of control appeared to be paramount in the minds of CIA operatives and indeed the US government more generally. Before the CIA came up with its landing plan, there had been significant disquiet within the government about 'private' military actions against Cuba by exile groups based in Florida. These had occurred sporadically during 1959 and 1960. The US State Department was especially perturbed by them, because of concerns about damage to the political standing of the US in terms of public opinion in Latin America where many would believe that such activities enjoyed at least tacit US support. The Department also feared giving a propaganda boost to Castro.[12]

Once the CIA's landing plan was approved and began to develop in 1960, the 'control' issue manifested itself in an evident reluctance to trust the trained Cubans that it had inserted into Cuba supposedly in order to undertake acts of sabotage and link up with anti-Castro groups. They were, apparently, simply abandoned and did not learn of the invasion from the CIA until *after* the landings had taken place (by which time the news was common knowledge throughout Cuba).[13] Planning for the Bay of Pigs operation was, as Bissell admitted, 'unquestionably' influenced by the CIA operation in Guatemala seven years previously.[14] On that occasion, the reformist government of Jacobo Arbenz had been toppled, apparently by a CIA-sponsored exile force led by a dissident military officer called Castillo Armas. In reality, however, psychological operations (hostile US press coverage, dissident radio broadcasts and regular overflights by 'mysterious' aircraft) played the main role in inducing Arbenz to resign, as opposed to any real military success by the exile army. A number of the senior planners on the Bay of Pigs, including Bissell, had been involved in this earlier effort, code-named

*Operation PBSUCCESS.* One of the conclusions which they seem to have drawn from it was that internal resistance groups outside of direct US control were not required for (and may even impair the chances of) a successful outcome.[15]

In seeking inspiration for their Bay of Pigs planning, however, CIA officers seem to have assumed too blithely that military and popular support for Fidel Castro would prove to be as brittle as that which had existed for Arbenz in 1954. Colonel Jack Hawkins, one of Bissell's key point men on the Bay of Pigs project, had written an internal CIA memorandum at the beginning of 1961 in which he stated that 'it is expected that these operations will precipitate a general uprising throughout Cuba and cause the revolt of large segments of the Cuban Army and Militia'.[16] Bissell himself had, in February 1961, drafted a paper for President Kennedy in which he argued that:

> Any evaluation of the chances of success of the assault force should be realistic about the fighting qualities of the [Castro] militia. No definitive conclusions can be advanced but it must be remembered that the majority of the militia are not fighters by instinct or background and are not militiamen of their own choice. Their training has been slight and they have never been exposed to actual fire (particularly any heavy fire power) nor to air attack. *Moreover, the instabilities within Cuba are such that if the tide shifts against the regime, the chances are strong that substantial numbers will desert or change side.* [emphasis added][17]

The last sentence quoted bears the clearest imprint of the Guatemala experience. There was certainly a hope, if not an expectation, among the Bay of Pigs planners that Castro's military might refuse to fight in sufficiently large numbers so as to prompt the fall of his government.

Such *hubris* was reinforced by military assessments of the state of Castro's forces. A January 1961 evaluation prepared by the Department of Defense had concluded that the capabilities of Castro's military forces across-the-board were either 'low' or 'very low', although some change in this was anticipated once significant military aid began to arrive from the Soviet Union.[18] In the event, as the Taylor Report on the failure of the Bay of Pigs operation laconically noted, 'the effectiveness of the Castro military forces, as well as that of his police measures, was not entirely anticipated or foreseen'.[19] Twenty-three years later Richard Bissell admitted that 'Castro's ground forces moved more decisively, faster and in greater force than anyone [in the US] had anticipated', a development which he quixotically attributed mainly to 'bad luck'.[20]

It is not, of course, possible to determine definitively what would have happened to the loyalty and morale of Castro's forces if the exile Brigade had managed to maintain its beachheads. There are anecdotal accounts of desertions among the Castro forces that came into contact with Brigade troops, and of support for the invaders from local civilians.[21] Yet stories of micro-level defections offer scant basis upon which to support serious expectations of a mass collapse in popular and military support for Castro, as the CIA had anticipated and some exile leaders had predicted.[22] In any event, serious attempts to 'turn' the Cuban population and armed forces were never really tried. This was partly because of the CIA's high-handed contempt and disregard for dissidents within Cuba, as discussed above. Partly also it was because the invasion site itself militated against it, being as it was remote, inaccessible and thinly populated. As Hugh Thomas has noted, 'it would have been hard indeed to have found a region in Cuba in which a rebellion could have been less easily inspired among the local people'.[23]

## Support from the United States

In 1954, President Dwight Eisenhower had been of the view, as he famously put it, that 'if you at any time take the route of violence or support of violence...then you commit yourself to carry it through, and it's too late to have second thoughts...when you're mid-way in an operation'.[24] In 1961, President Kennedy would prove to be less committed, mainly due to legitimacy concerns. What was required in Cuba, Eisenhower felt, was an intervention that could be 'plausibly denied' by him on behalf of the US as a whole. The original 'Program of Covert Action against the Castro Regime', which he had approved in principle in March 1960, was premised on carrying out the action 'in such a manner as to avoid any appearance of US intervention'.[25] On the other hand, such considerations were constrained by his belief that once an operation was underway, then the US should be prepared to do whatever was necessary in order to ensure its success.

The CIA did not expect that the change in administration in 1960–61 would result in any great shift in this basic approach. In his internal memorandum, written during the transition from Eisenhower to Kennedy at the beginning of 1961, Colonel Jack Hawkins had argued that, even if the exile Brigade landings did not 'precipitate a general uprising' in Cuba, then:

> The lodgement established by our force can be used as the site for establishment of a provisional government which can be recognised

by the United States, and hopefully by other American states, and given overt military assistance. The way will then be paved for United States military intervention aimed at pacification of Cuba, and this will result in the prompt overthrow of the Castro Government.[26]

This attitude represented a misreading of the new President. According to Arthur Schlesinger, a young White House aide at the time of the Bay of Pigs operation, Kennedy's basic approach to the plans which he had inherited 'was to try to do *something*, but as little as possible. He wanted a neat little infiltration that was plausibly deniable, but which had some chance of success' [emphasis in the original].[27] Accordingly a March 1961 rewrite of the plan reflected this shift in the Kennedy Administration's view of the matter.[28]

Most significantly in retrospect, Kennedy decided to alter the CIA's plans for a campaign of air strikes to eliminate Castro's relatively few air assets in advance of the Cuban Brigade's landings. His main concern was to ensure that the United States should not be seen to be implicated in air attacks. To this end, an elaborate deception took place to explain the initial air attacks on Castro's planes, which took place 36 hours before the landings. Concurrently with the air strikes, a Cuban exile pilot was to land a B-26 aircraft, with Castro air force markings, in Miami and claim to be one of a number of defecting pilots who had decided to bomb their former colleagues on their way out of Cuba. This was accomplished but the cover story was quickly questioned, causing difficulties for the US delegation at the United Nations, which had presented the official version to the international community. This in turn led directly to Kennedy's decision to cancel follow-up air strikes and thus leave part of Castro's air force intact.[29] This was to prove a fateful decision as Castro's planes subsequently sank two of the exiles' supply ships causing the loss of essential ammunition and communications equipment. Indeed, the most popular alleged reason for the ultimate collapse of the operation was Kennedy's failure to authorize the prosecution of the air campaign until the whole of Castro's air force was destroyed.[30] John Ranelagh has written that, in contrast to the attitude expressed in Eisenhower's famous dictum quoted earlier, 'the lack of air support was the visible sign that Kennedy had lost his nerve and would not follow through'.[31]

The American ambassador to the UN, Adlai Stevenson, had been quick to make clear his displeasure at the initial air strikes. He cabled the State Department that he was 'greatly disturbed by clear indications received during day in process developing rebuttal material [sic] that bombing incidents in Cuba on Saturday were launched in part at least from outside Cuba' and could not 'understand how we could let such attack take place two days before debate on Cuban issue in [the UN] G[eneral] A[ssembly]'.[32] Ambassador Stevenson's displeasure was the proximate cause of the decision to cancel the follow-up air strikes. This was made clear in a memorandum drafted by the Deputy Director of the CIA, General Charles Cabell, and co-signed by Richard Bissell. According to their memorandum:

> The Secretary informed us that there were political considerations preventing the planned air strikes before the beachhead airfield was in our hands and useable. The air strikes on D-2 had been allowed because of military considerations. Political requirements at the present time were overriding. The main consideration involved the situation at the United Nations. The Secretary described Ambassador Stevenson's attitude in some detail. Ambassador Stevenson had insisted essentially that the air strikes would make it absolutely impossible for the US position to be sustained. The Secretary stated that such a result was unacceptable.[33]

The Secretary of State and the President were concerned to be seen to be 'playing by the rules', which the US had in theory accepted when it signed up to the United Nations and, on a regional basis, the Organization of American States (OAS). The UN had originally been created at American instigation in 1945. The extent to which the country's reputation within the UN and OAS mattered, particularly to the State Department, should not be underestimated. Some of the leading sceptics about the Bay of Pigs operation were senior State Department officials, with their doubts motivated largely by concerns about the impact of the operation on the US standing in the UN, OAS and international community generally.[34] In testimony to the Taylor Committee of inquiry into the failure of the operation in May 1961, Secretary of State Rusk stated that:

> When we talked about the possibility of failure we talked about far more disastrous results than actually occurred. For example, we had discussed the possibility of such things as being ousted from the OAS or censure by the UN, and lively and adverse reaction by our Allies in Europe. The results that developed were not as serious as those that we had considered.[35]

The doubts and hesitations in the minds of the President and his principal foreign policy adviser mattered. The US had become far more than a

benign but passive host country for the anti-Castro Cuban exile movement. It had chosen to involve itself as the creator and sponsor of an
exile army with the declared aim of provoking, through military action,
the downfall of the Castro regime. The operation's overall chances of
success were, therefore, adversely affected by what the CIA Inspector
General's report subsequently called 'the dangerous conflict between the
desire for political acceptability and the need for military effectiveness'.[36]
The CIA had been mistaken in its assumption that Kennedy, like
Eisenhower in Guatemala in 1954, would be prepared to authorize all
necessary means to achieve the desired objective once the operation
was underway.[37]

## The military effectiveness of the exile Brigade

The prevalent view among those who have considered the Bay of Pigs
affair has been that the exile Brigade fought with tenacity and courage
against superior Castro forces. Especially heroic deeds have been
ascribed to the Brigade's 2nd and 6th Battalions.[38] The main exception
to the statement that the Brigade forces on the beaches performed well
under pressure was the 5th Battalion. To begin with, this Battalion failed
to land as planned, as the Taylor Committee noted, 'partly because
of . . . boat troubles, partly because of lack of initiative on the part of the
Battalion commander'.[39] The 5th Battalion's troops were eventually forced
off their ship when it was hit by a Castro plane but when they reached
shore the disarray was such that the Battalion had already effectively
disintegrated as a coherent fighting unit.

Significant problems were also encountered with the Brigade's supporting forces. A planned diversionary landing elsewhere in Cuba, which
had been scheduled to take place two days in advance of the main
landings at the Bay of Pigs, never happened, 'probably because of weak
leadership on the part of the Cuban officer responsible for the landing';
one Nino Díaz.[40]

There were some problems with Cuban aircrew too. Their tasks were
twofold – to fly the sorties that were supposed to destroy Castro's air
force and to fly in supplies and evacuate casualties once the Brigade on
the ground had secured an airstrip. It is not the case that the overall air
campaign was seriously impaired by questionable morale among some
of these Cuban pilots. Nevertheless, there were criticisms made in the
official inquiries about the quality of the Cuban pilots and other aircrew.
The CIA Inspector General's report noted a history of problems with
Cubans failing to follow proper procedures dating back to the limited

attempts to supply internal resistance groups by air during 1960.[41] The Taylor Committee, meanwhile, heard testimony suggesting that Cuban pilots had been 'good until things started going wrong'.[42] Having said that, the Kirkpatrick Report at least was, in general, robust in its criticism of CIA failings and sympathetic to the role and agendas of Cuban participants in the operation.

At sea a major problem was the failure of the Brigade's supply ships to unload their full manifests of ammunition, communications and other essential supplies. Partly this was due to the sinking of two of these ships – the *Río Escondido* and the *Houston* – by Castro's air force. Following this, however, two sister ships – the *Atlántico* and the *Caribe* – effectively fled the scene with the consequence that they were unable to perform their essential resupply roles for the remainder of the operation.[43] In his own *post mortem* on the operation early in 1962, Richard Bissell conceded that there was 'no question' that 'trouble was experienced with the Cuban crews' of the ships. He attributed this to two factors: that the Cubans were expected to work under American skippers, and divisions among the Cubans themselves.[44]

The problems experienced with Cubans in the air and at sea may well have been due, at least in part, not to poor morale or simple cowardice, but rather to serious disenchantment with the lack of overt military support from the United States. As former CIA Inspector General Kirkpatrick recalled in 1972, 'the Cubans to a man:... expected that should the brigade falter, US Marines would pour out of Guantanamo, airborne units would be dropped, and it would be over about like that'.[45] In testimony to the Taylor Committee 11 years earlier, Bissell stated that Cuban pilots had become reluctant to fly when it became clear that they would not have support and protection from US naval aviation.[46]

The exile invasion forces were the creation of the US government; most especially the CIA. Under these circumstances it was only to be expected that the morale and combat effectiveness of the exiles in these forces would depend to a great extent on perceptions that the US was prepared if necessary to stand, not only behind, but shoulder-to-shoulder (in every sense) with participating Cubans. Once it became clear that this was not happening, significant problems began to develop.

## Divisions among the Cuban exiles

That the overall Cuban exile movement was seriously divided is accepted by all analysts of the Bay of Pigs operation. This was also apparent to the CIA and other US government officials at the time that the operation was being planned and put together. During the early stages CIA Director Allen Dulles reportedly told President Eisenhower that up to 184 different groups had been identified among the Cuban exiles living in the United States.[47] Disunity and its consequences were apparent in two important spheres during the planning and execution of the operation. First, it has been argued that it contributed to the extent to which the CIA dominated the whole enterprise. Second, there is evidence of a divide between the exile movement's political leadership and members of the Brigade that landed at the Bay of Pigs.

The CIA certainly used exile fractiousness in order to justify the extent to which the Agency had controlled and directed the operation. In his 1962 *post mortem*, Richard Bissell devoted a lengthy section to the argument that the CIA's original intention had been to 'encourage' Cuban exile leaders to come together and form a coherent and credible government-in-waiting. However, he stated that these efforts were constantly undermined by divisions, personality clashes and infighting.[48] Thus, as he had told the Taylor Committee nine months previously, during the 'creation of a political opposition ... it was found less and less possible to rely on the Cuban politicians'.[49] There was also a tendency among Americans involved at 'ground level' in the project, motivated by what was politely called 'ethnocentrism' at the time, to behave in a patronizing and condescending manner towards their Cuban interlocutors, or even to treat the latter 'like dirt' as the Kirkpatrick Report put it.[50]

CIA control of the operation extended to the maintenance of an effective barrier between its political and military components. In theory the Brigade was supposed to be fighting for the provisional government which the CIA had formed into what it called the 'Cuban Revolutionary Council' early in 1961. But there was strictly limited formal contact permitted between members of the Council and members of the Brigade in their training camps in Guatemala and Nicaragua, to the chagrin of prominent members of the exiles' political leadership.[51]

Bissell argued that two considerations had predisposed the CIA to restrict contacts between the political and military wings of the exile movement. First, there was concern that the factionalism that characterized the politicos would spill over into the Brigade's training camps and have a detrimental impact on morale and unit cohesion if greater contacts were permitted. Second, the CIA had been, he said, worried about word of the secret training programmes being leaked if outsiders were allowed in on a regular basis.[52] Bissell's first contention received some support from members of the exile Brigade themselves.

In testimony to the Taylor Committee, Roberto San Román, a member of the Brigade (and brother of its commander), hinted at the problems that had occurred when political leaders *had* been permitted to visit the Brigade in training:

> The different political groups in Miami all sent in representatives so that their men could try and gain control of the camp for them and thereby they would have influence in Cuba after the revolution. Furthermore, some of the big men in Miami when they arrived at the camp found they weren't big men anymore. They were soldiers just like everybody else. We military men were put in charge as we had more experience.[53]

Undercurrents of distrust by the Brigade of 'their' political leaders are also a feature of Haynes Johnson's 1964 account of the Bay of Pigs, which he wrote in collaboration with the four main leaders of the Brigade. While divisions among the Cuban exiles, both within the political community and between political leaders and Brigade members, were undoubtedly exploited by the CIA as a justification for its degree of control, they were evidently real enough.

## Conclusion: Things were bound to happen

CIA leaders and planners had confidently expected that 'things were bound to happen' as a result of the Bay of Pigs operation. In this they were right, although certainly not in ways in which they would have wanted. To begin with, it is difficult to argue with the view that an important consequence of the Brigade landings and their defeat in April 1961 was the strengthening of Fidel Castro's hold on power. In addition to being able to pose as the defender of Cuba against 'yankee imperialism' and its 'mercenary worms', the invasion gave him a pretext for clamping down on dissidents at home. Whether it also either precipitated or confirmed his adoption of Marxism-Leninism is disputed, but it is difficult to believe that it had no impact. In any event Castro remains in power; having outlasted Eisenhower, Kennedy and seven other American Presidents.

In the Soviet Union too, Nikita Khrushchev drew conclusions from the failed landings. First, that there was a threat to Castro who, from Khrushchev's perspective, was moving in a promising direction and represented the Soviet Union's best hope of developing a reliable ally in the United States' 'backyard'. Second, the Soviet leader in all probability saw Kennedy's failure to back the Brigade landings with direct US military intervention as a sign of weakness, suggesting that Kennedy could also be forced to accept a significant increase in Soviet military power in the region. These two factors, taken together, played an important role in precipitating the Cuban missile crisis 18 months after the Bay of Pigs operation.

The outcome of that crisis effectively ensured that there would be no further significant military action against Castro on the part of Cuban exiles living in the United States. Kennedy had given a 'no-invasion' pledge to Khrushchev as part of the diplomatic bargaining that settled the missile crisis; a pledge which the US has abided by ever since. Paramilitary raids on Cuba by exile groups acting on their own have reportedly continued right up to the present day.[54] Without official US sponsorship, however, they have been impotent. There is no contemporary Cuban exile army worth the name, nor has there been since 1961. The United States, acting through its CIA, had on that occasion invented one. It trained, equipped and armed it and then, as many Cuban exiles saw and still see things, the Kennedy Administration abandoned it on the beaches of the Bay of Pigs.

## Notes


 1. This title is taken from P. Gleijeses, 'Ships in the Night: The CIA, the White House and the Bay of Pigs', *Journal of Latin American Studies*, 27(1), (1995), p. 31.
 2. The author is grateful to the staff of the RMAS Central Library and the Information Resource Centre at the US Embassy in London for assistance in obtaining source material. The views expressed here are personal and should not be taken as representing the policy or views of the British Government, Ministry of Defence or RMAS.
 3. T. Draper, *Castro's Revolution: Myths and Realities* (London: Thames and Hudson, 1962), p. 59.
 4. H. Matthews, *Castro* (Harmondsworth: Pelican, 1970), pp. 210–11. See also Draper, *Castro's Revolution: Myths and Realities*, pp. 73ff.
 5. *Operation Zapata: The 'Ultrasensitive' Report and Testimony of the Board of Inquiry on the Bay of Pigs* (Frederick Maryland: Aletheia Books, 1981), pp. 338–41.
 6. Draper *Castro's Revolution: Myths and Realities*, p. 61.
 7. Matthews *Castro*, p. 212.
 8. Quoted in Gleijeses 'Ships in the Night: The CIA, the White House and the Bay of Pigs', p. 11.
 9. See the Kirkpatrick Report in P. Kornbluh (ed.), *Bay of Pigs Declassified: The Secret CIA Report on the Invasion of Cuba* (New York: The New Press, 1998), pp. 75–89.
10. P. Wyden, *Bay of Pigs: The Untold Story* (London: Jonathan Cape, 1979), pp. 55–6.
11. Matthews *Castro*, pp. 210–11.
12. For evidence of State Department disquiet about these activities see: *Foreign Relations of the United States 1958–1960 Volume VI Cuba* (Washington DC:

US Government Printing Office, 1991), pp. 632–5, 808–9. (Hereafter *FRUS 1958–60*.)

13. Wyden, *Bay of Pigs: The Untold Story*, pp. 245–8 and H. Johnson, *The Bay of Pigs* (London: Hutchinson, 1965), p. 120.

14. See *Bay of Pigs Declassified*, p. 152.

15. See S. Schlesinger and S. Kinzer, *Bitter Fruit: The Untold Story of the American Coup in Guatemala* (London: Sinclair Browne, 1982).

16. 'Memorandum From the Chief of WH/4/PM, Central Intelligence Agency (Hawkins) to the Chief of WH/4 of the Directorate for Plans (Esterline)', *Foreign Relations of the United States 1961–1963 Volume X Cuba 1961–1962* (Washington DC: US Government Printing Office, 1997), p. 11. (Hereafter *FRUS 1961–63*.)

17. Quoted in Gleijeses 'Ships in the Night: The CIA, the White House and the Bay of Pigs', p. 23.

18. *FRUS 1961–63*, pp. 36–7.

19. *Operation Zapata*, p. 41.

20. R. Bissell, 'Reflections on the Bay of Pigs', *Strategic Review*, 12(1), (1984), p. 69.

21. See *Operation Zapata*, p. 297 and Johnson, *The Bay of Pigs*, p. 116.

22. *Operation Zapata*, p. 338.

23. H. Thomas, *The Cuban Revolution* (London: Weidenfeld and Nicolson, 1986), p. 585.

24. Quoted in Schlesinger and Kinzer, *Bitter Fruit*, p. 178.

25. *FRUS 1958–60*, p. 850.

26. *FRUS 1961–63*, p. 11.

27. Schlesinger quoted in J. Blight and P. Kornbluh (eds), *Politics of Illusion: The Bay of Pigs Invasion Reconsidered* (Boulder: Lynne Rienner, 1998), p. 64.

28. See *Bay of Pigs Declassified*, p. 125.

29. See Wyden, *Bay of Pigs: The Untold Story*, chapter 5.

30. See A. Persons, *Bay of Pigs* (London: Mc Farland and Co., 1990), pp. 115–39; J. Ranelagh, *The Agency: The Rise and Decline of the CIA* (London: Weidenfeld and Nicolson, 1986), pp. 362, 368–9; R. Nixon, *RN: The Memoirs of Richard Nixon* (London: Book Club Associates, 1978), p. 233.

31. Ranelagh, *The Agency*, p. 369.

32. *FRUS 1961–63*, p. 230.

33. *Ibid.*, pp. 235–6.

34. *Ibid.*, pp. 95–9, 178–81.

35. *Operation Zapata*, pp. 219–20.

36. *Bay of Pigs Declassified*, p. 49.

37. See L. Vandenbroucke, 'The "Confessions" of Allen Dulles: New Evidence on the Bay of Pigs', *Diplomatic History*, 8(4), (1984), pp. 365–75.

38. See Johnson, *The Bay of Pigs*, pp. 163–72; Wyden, *Bay of Pigs: The Untold Story*, pp. 272–88; and Persons, *Bay of Pigs*, p. 83.

39. *Operation Zapata*, p. 23.

40. See Johnson, *The Bay of Pigs*, pp. 88, 95 and *Operation Zapata*, pp. 18, 97.

41. *Bay of Pigs Declassified*, pp. 78–80.

42. *Operation Zapata*, pp. 92, 121–2.

43. *Ibid.*, pp. 25, 191–2.

44. *Bay of Pigs Declassified*, p. 230.

45. L. Kirkpatrick, 'Paramilitary Case Study: The Bay of Pigs', *Naval War College Review* (November–December 1972), p. 37.

46. *Operation Zapata*, p. 91.
47. Gleijeses 'Ships in the Night: The CIA, the White House and the Bay of Pigs',
    p. 6.
48. *Bay of Pigs Declassified*, pp. 215ff.
49. *Operation Zapata*, p. 57.
50. *Bay of Pigs Declassified*, pp. 74–5.
51. See *FRUS 1961–63*, pp. 80–1.
52. *Bay of Pigs Declassified*, p. 136.
53. *Operation Zapata*, p. 295.
54. See 'Stingless Wasps', *The Economist*, 3 February 2001, p. 56.

# 7
# The Mukti Bahini – Midwife to a Nation?

*Keith Blackmore*

In 1971, Pakistan was torn apart by a political crisis under-pinned by economic grievance. An acceptable negotiated settlement proved impossible to achieve, and force was used to impose a solution. Pakistan's attempt to assert the authority of an increasingly discredited Military Government over the 73 million Bengali population of East Pakistan was a gamble. To attempt a 'security' solution depending for its successful implementation on only some 60,000 under-equipped troops considerably lengthened the odds. The presence of a powerful and unsympathetic neighbour able and willing to offer sanctuary, and more besides, to those resisting the 'occupation' of their homeland rendered Pakistan's regional position hopeless.

The approach adopted by the Pakistani Armed Forces and the para-military cohorts under their direction alienated the Bengali population. Direct Indian military intervention, when it came, was greeted as 'liberation'. Prominent in the reportage of the 16 day war of December were the 'People's Armed Forces', the Mukti Bahini, returning to join with other elements of the resistance to ensure the safe delivery of an independent Bangladesh. Was the main role of the Mukti Bahini to add a fig leaf of legitimacy to mask India's intervention in its neighbours business? Or did the Mukti Bahini make significant contribution to the outcome of that conflict? How did it cope with the challenges facing armies forced to conduct their campaign from exile?

## The political context

The attempt by Pakistan's President General Yahya Khan to move toward civilian rule ran up against the perennial problem in allowing the people to choose who governs them – what if they choose the 'wrong' person or party? In the elections for candidates to a new National Assembly eventually held on 7 December 1970 in East Pakistan the fiery and hugely ambitious Sheikh Mujib Rahman led the Awami League to spectacular success as they carried 160 of the 162 contested seats. While Mujib had been expected to do well success on this scale posed problems and it was asking a great deal of Khan, a self-styled 'simple soldier' and Mujib, a populist, gesture politician to resolve the issues fragmenting Pakistan. The Awami League had campaigned on the basis of a Six Point programme of reform appealing to a burgeoning sense of resentment in East Pakistan.[1] This programme would clearly establish a remarkable degree of autonomy. It is hardly surprising that when the Six Points were explained to Yahya he reacted that they amounted to an agenda for complete secession.[2]

The rebalancing envisaged by the Awami League amounted to Bengali domination over the whole of Pakistan, a prospect completely unacceptable to the ruling elite of Western Wing.[3] Yahya and the Pakistani Army were also deeply alarmed at the unexpected scale and scope of the electoral triumph of the populist Mujib. The commitment of the Bengali elite to confrontation of India over Kashmir was believed to be less than whole-hearted. Within the Six Points lay an implicit challenge, as future defence budgets would be subject to interference by those who might have different priorities. Moreover separate holdings of foreign exchange by the two 'Wings' could limit the ability of the Pakistani military to import expensive modern equipment. Not only the integrity of the state of Pakistan was at stake but also, in a worst-case scenario, a fatally weakened rump would find itself facing an India on one front only and lacking the resources to sustain a semblance of strategic balance. Other, more personal factors were also at work. 'The generals apprehended that Colonel M. A. G. Osmany would be the defence minister in an Awami League government and that he would revenge himself on the senior officers who had blocked his promotion and forced his retirement from the army.'[4]

Buoyed by his jubilant supporters' enthusiasm displayed at mass public meetings and demonstrations, Mujib pressed ahead with the Six Points so emphatically endorsed at the ballot. While the outcome of the election was clearly an endorsement of Bengali self-assertion it was interpreted by some of his supporters as a de facto referendum on self-determination and full independence for East Bengal. Mujib held off taking such a drastic step, concentrating on the political struggle over the disposition of power within Pakistan. Ayub's decision to delay the meeting of the newly elected Assembly resulted in a wave of mass demonstrations and politically motivated strikes.[5] Protracted negotiations between Mujib and the Head of State only produced an atmosphere of deepening mistrust. Yahya had posted General Tikka Khan to Dacca on 3 March to prepare the execution of a crackdown plan (Operation Blitz) that the Pakistani Military Staff had been revising throughout the year. For his part Mujib, as storm clouds gathered, sounded out Colonel Osmany as to the attitude of officers and men within the East Bengal Regiment (EBR) to which Osmany had very close links as its 'father'.[6]

After a nugatory round of last minute negotiations Yahya flew out of East Pakistan having authorized the implementation of Operation Blitz for midnight on the 25/26 March. The assumption was that a carefully prepared move against the political leadership and the disarming of 'suspect' Bengali elements of the Military, paramilitary East Pakistan Rifles (EPR) and Police would administer a short, sharp shock to the pretensions of the despised Bengali elite. The blow when it fell was not short, was of appalling ferocity and the shock effect, rather than paralysing, galvanized the opposition. The brutality of Tikka Khan's operation added important new strands to the quest for legitimacy by alienating any wavering Bengalis and encouraging political opponents to find common cause for the 'duration'. It also produced a flood of Bengali refugees into India, so transforming an 'internal' Pakistani affair into a regional and humanitarian crisis.

## The initial fighting

The Pakistani soldiers of 14th Division were tasked to disarm the EBR, EPR and Police and to secure important facilities such as airfields, main towns and Chittagong Naval Base. In Dacca they managed to secure key buildings, but efforts to seize the Police Armoury and the University encountered fierce resistance. This was subdued only by recourse to mortars and machine-guns inflicting heavy casualties. The cantonments of the EBR battalions and their Regimental induction centre saw scenes of confusion as, rather than allow themselves to be disarmed, the soldiers and recruits variously put up resistance or dispersed under their Junior Officers and NCOs taking with them the weapons and ammunition they could carry. In Chittagong the EBR shot non-Bengali Officers and under the leadership of Major Ziaur Rahman put up resistance for two weeks. Around this nucleus rallied the EPR, the Police and other volunteers. Eventually the Pakistanis, reinforced, were able to assert control and on 11 April the survivors withdrew to the Chittagong Hill Tracts. Such hasty, poorly coordinated yet spirited resistance marked the important first steps on the road toward the creation of a credible armed resistance. The Mukti Fouj, as the resistance were known at this early stage, escaped to the few, but extensive, forests and to the hill regions. From such terrain they could launch attacks against the 'occupiers', undermining their resolve and ensuring that their hold on the country remained tenuous. The passive civil resistance had indicated that the administration of East Pakistan could not continue in the face of the withdrawal of consent. The Mukti Fouj intended to demonstrate that the authority of the Pakistani government was confined to the ground the Army occupied and that even that was to be contested. Their ambition at this stage far exceeded their capability and taking on Pakistani Forces in stand up fights invited defeat in detail. Their motivation might have been high but their resources were limited.

At the time of the crackdown there were 6,000 regular Bengali troops in the five EBR battalions stationed in the East Wing and some 15,000 men in the EPR. The 45,000 police were mostly Bengali and the Pakistani Army, aware of their nationalist sympathies, attacked many of their posts. Survivors fled, taking refuge with the Mukti Fouj or decamping across the border. In addition the Razakars, a sort of Home Guard had also numbered 45,000. The non-Bengali element (mostly Biharis) had been given access to rifles and these 'Mujahids' remained loyal to the Pakistani authorities. The Bengali elements, armed with spears and lathis constituted the 'Ansaris' and this auxiliary force largely melted back into the civilian population.

## Bolstering legitimacy (India's reaction)

Although the Pakistani authorities managed to arrest Sheikh Mujib, the bulk of the Awami League leadership escaped to take refuge in India from where they were to form a Government in exile.[7] On 10 April, a broadcast announced the creation of a Republic of Bangladesh to be headed by President (in absentia) Mujib. A week later, in a ceremony held in view of representatives of the world press, a new administration was formed just across the border in liberated Bangladeshi territory. For all practical purposes the exiled Government operated out of Calcutta until the end of the crisis. However, important roots of legitimacy had been established. The democratic will of the Bengali people had been frustrated and they had been subjected to brutal repression under martial law imposed by an 'alien' military. That presence was being actively resisted now under the auspices of a duly constituted alternative government of National Liberation. Crucial to the fostering and broadening of this claimed legitimacy was the degree of recognition to be garnered in the wider international community, crucially by the government of India. The potential disintegration of Pakistan would obviously enhance India's strategic position. It would reduce, or even remove entirely the risk of a three front war against the two wings of Pakistan in concert with a belligerent China. There were strong pressures in Parliament on Prime Minister Indira Ghandi not only to recognize the new State of Bangladesh, but openly to commit Indian Forces to secure its liberation. Yet initially Ghandi delayed.

The refugees fleeing East Bengal at the rate of 60,000 a day were received into makeshift camps where their relief posed an increasing burden on India's strained resources. The influx of what was to exceed 7,000,000 displaced persons lent urgency to the need to find an acceptable outcome to the crisis. Apart from humanitarian relief for displaced Bengalis the Indian authorities limited their initial support to the Mukti Fouj. The Indian Border Security Force (BSF), containing many former soldiers, were permitted to offer safe havens to fighters pulling out of East Pakistan and to supply them with small arms and ammunition with which to re-enter the fray.

## Civil supremacy

The initial phase of resistance was not an unqualified success. In their favour the Mukti Fouj had a cadre of professionally trained Officers and men of the EBR and EPR. Indeed many had, like Major Khaled Musharraf, attended the Staff College at Quetta and had done the Special Service Group (Commando) course. They understood guerrilla methods and the counter-insurgency tactics their former colleagues were likely to use against them. Such was the nature of the internecine war taking place that individuals knew their adversaries personally and could seek to exploit perceived character traits accordingly.[8] In the right circumstances the guerrillas' skilful use of ground, exploiting readily available local knowledge, enabled them to mount successful ambushes, and to conduct protracted delaying operations including skilled demolitions. Yet their manpower resources were limited. In contrast the Pakistani Army steadily reinforced their position in the rebel province up to the strength of four divisions by drawing in formations from West Pakistan. As Indian airspace was at the time closed to Pakistan these reinforcements were routed via Sri Lanka. The presumed 'counter-insurgent' role for these troops and the need for 'soldiers on the ground' meant that these reinforcement divisions were deployed without their usual complement of supporting

Arms and Services. This was to rebound to their distinct disadvantage when the crisis later deepened into full-scale war. In the short term Tikka Khan and his successor Lt. Gen. Niazi were able to take the initiative. Having announced on 10 April that the crisis in East Pakistan was over with order restored in the main towns a new phase of the campaign to crush resistance was begun. By mid-May it was intended to secure all border towns and seal off the Mukti Fouj's supply and infiltration routes from India, to reopen road, rail and water communications in the province and to 'mop-up' any remaining centres of armed resistance.

Despite the dogged resolve of the Mukti Fouj the superior resources of the Pakistani Armed Forces prevailed. Although never successful in clearing the whole of the interior their ability to exploit an all arms combination told in their favour. With command of the air Sabre jets could strike in support of the ground forces with well prepared, methodical attacks. The willingness of lightly equipped guerrilla forces to try to hold ground in such circumstances was clearly misdirected enthusiasm. So the Mukti Fouj, in response to Osmany's guidance, having taken heavy casualties they could ill afford, dispersed into hiding or retreated back across the Indian border. A reappraisal of the methods and organization of Bangladeshi resistance was clearly in order if the armed struggle were not to degenerate into banditry cloaked in a flag recognized by no one. The Bangladeshi Defence Minister and C-in-C General Osmany had already begun the necessary reformation process.

## Bangladeshi response

Bangladesh was divided into sectors with local commanders appointed to conduct the guerrilla war that was to contest the 'occupation' through the coming monsoon season. This would oblige Pakistani forces to campaign in what was to most of the soldiers recruited in the West Wing would be distinctly unfamiliar and uncomfortable conditions. First there was a steady trickle of battle casualties from ambushes, sniping and mining attacks. Second, operating in a flooded landscape alive with leeches severely tested the health and morale of Pakistani Forces. General Osmany reorganized his forces for the long haul. The renamed the Mukti Bahini (Bengali for Freedom Forces) were to be recruited up to a target figure of 80,000. At its heart was the regular element, the Niyomito Bahini based on the remnants of the five EBR battalions. A further three or four battalions were to be raised and trained. These were to be formed into three weak Brigades named for the initial letters of their commanders (K Force, S Force and Z Force) supported by three 'Regiments' of artillery equipped with Indian-sourced light 105 mm guns.[9] Volunteers for the Mukti Bahini were not hard to find in the swelling refugee camps and many were of high calibre, such as well-educated student survivors of the attempted 'elitocide' of March.[10] 'Since most of the recruits were educated youths from schools and colleges, they were easy to train. The normal recruit's training period could be considerably shortened. Every six weeks 2,000 were being turned out for operational duty.'[11] Osmany also instituted a policy of vetting applicants. His intention was to maintain a semblance of the constitutional nicety that the armed forces should remain above party politics, and he was anxious to prevent the infiltration and subversion of the Mukti Bahini by the revolutionary left. This reduced the risk of internal division and factionalism while at the same time reassuring their Indian hosts that a newly emergent free Bangladesh was unlikely to foster pro-Beijing Maoist groups.

The sector troops were made up of EPR and Police augmented by locally recruited guerrillas known as Gono Bahini. In addition to perpetrating acts of sabotage they were well placed to gather intelligence, assist in the dissemination of propaganda and to exact revenge on 'collaborators' and their families. The Gono Bahini had rural and urban cells and were able to plant bombs to refute Pakistani claims that the Province had ever returned to normalcy after the initial violence. A small air component of transport and liaison aircraft loaned by the Indians was crewed and operated by Bengali ex-PAF personnel. This was of negligible combat value, although the air arm allowed Osmany to visit his widely dispersed command offering guidance and encouragement.[12] A naval arm was also formed around a tiny nucleus of Bengali NCOs who had defected to the Bangladeshi cause while on a technical training course abroad.[13] Some 500 recruits were trained in small boat work and specialist sabotage skills including planting limpet mines. This arm was well placed to exploit the vast network of inland water-courses in support of the economic war the Mukti Bahini engaged in as the other strand of their long term strategy to secure Bangladesh's liberation. The reorganized liberation armed forces, with relatively secure base areas in which to train, were well placed to embark on a dual pronged strategy. They harassed the forces of the Pakistanis and their locally recruited auxiliaries to erode their morale and ultimately their combat effectiveness. Simultaneously they aimed to disrupt the economy and damage the infrastructure of the territory.

Such a campaign was always likely to expose the civilian population to great hardship as the once flourishing tea and jute industries ground to a halt and, in retaliation for acts of resistance, residents of nearby villages were subjected to attacks of ferocity calculated to cow them into submission.[14] These acts of ruthless repression sharpened hatred on both sides. There was little remaining scope for a 'political' approach in the absence of a moderate middle ground. The nature of the repressive action made it increasingly difficult for the Pakistanis to gain any useful local intelligence upon which a counter insurgency strategy ultimately depends for success. In persisting in their campaign, and even escalating it during the monsoon season, the Mukti Bahini were making an important contribution toward the longer term goal by keeping the exiles' cause alive while encouraging the adversary to weaken his own case and capability.

## The conflict deepens

From late June, as the monsoon intensified, General Osmany increased the pace of the Mukti Bahini campaign. Secure training bases on Indian territory enabled the exiled army the luxury of a phased training programme wherein platoons and later company-strength units could be brought to a proficient level before being committed to action. Operating under their own officers and NCOs they could be used to add weight to operations being undertaken by guerrilla forces. For example, attacking detached border outposts provided important combat experience and, if all went well, boosted their own self-confidence. If, however, the opposition proved too difficult, the Mukti Bahini could re-cross the border to rest and recuperate under the cover of Indian guns. Indeed, an increasingly confident Ghandi Administration allowed the Indian Army to escalate support to include covering artillery fire.[15] This came from batteries in India directed by forward observers against Pakistani Forces seeking to close with Mukti Bahini formations. These cross-border activities proved an increasingly irksome issue for General Niazi.[16]

The Pakistani authorities perceived it a political imperative to maintain the integrity of the frontier in large part to deny the 'rebels' a firm base on the soil of East Pakistan in which to establish an alternative government. As well as drawing further reinforcement from West Pakistan, Niazi increased recruitment to the locally raised Razakars relying heavily on the Bihari community.[17] The aim of the Mukti Bahini during the Monsoon offensive was to try to weaken these Pakistani forces as much as possible so that when the rains ceased and the ground dried they would be poorly placed to mount a fully effective counter-attack. Attacks on vulnerable points such as electricity pylons and bridges encouraged the Pakistanis to disperse their forces into 'penny packets'. Their locally raised auxiliaries proved unable adequately to safeguard key points from Mukti Bahini assault without stiffening of Pakistani regulars. Even then, these mixed manned bases were subject to harassment. Their supplies were interrupted as road and rail links would be mined, often using devices lifted from Pakistani defences. When explosives were hard to come by, local villagers would be persuaded to turn out at night to dig up stretches of road or create barriers by felling trees. Such barriers always carried the risk for Pakistani forces of sniping by Gono Bahini or even a full-scale ambush sprung by Mukti Bahini operating with growing audacity deep into Bangladesh. Water transport was disrupted by sinking small country craft to block the channel or ambushing boats as they rounded bends in the rivers. Toward the end of September the Mukti Bahini offensive appeared to have achieved a considerable degree of success. Pakistani mobility had been greatly restricted. Some police stations could only be held by deploying in company strength with regular soldiers in support, and by constructing defensive positions, including bunkers, from which the Pakistanis emerged to mount limited patrols in daylight hours. In isolated and defensible enclaves around the borders the Mukti Bahini were even able to occupy and hold the ground. Certainly the Pakistanis were in an uncomfortable position, but they were not yet willing to admit defeat. Osmany's later assertion that the Mukti Bahini campaign alone would have produced victory in a matter of months is difficult to accept. However, the Pakistanis certainly faced the dilemma identified by Henry Kissinger that 'the guerrilla wins if he does not lose; the conventional army loses if it does not win'.[18]

## The government offensive

As the monsoon season drew to a close General Niazi intended to go on to the offensive. He needed to reassert control in the troublesome border regions even at the risk of stretching his forces rather too thinly. This strategy imperilled a conventional defence of East Pakistan should the situation deteriorate and war break out with India. From the end of September the battles between the Mukti Bahini and the Pakistani Army grew in intensity, but at this stage India was still reluctant to become directly involved by committing aircraft or armour, although Osmany pressed his case as strongly as he dared. General Niazi's frustration with the degree of support that India was already providing had prompted him to threaten to take the war on to Indian soil to attack Mukti Bahini safe havens.[19] Niazi's reinforced and reorganized forces were launched in a series of offensives throughout October and November aimed at

re-establishing control of areas and border outposts that had been relin-
quished during the Mukti Bahini monsoon offensive. On the frontier
near Jessore their successful attack was supported by armour and covered
by Sabre jets to which the sector guerrillas had no effective counter.
As the fighting on the border escalated, the risk of deliberate or accidental
cross-border incidents increased. After Niazi's October threat that if India
tried to force a war on Pakistan it would be fought on Indian territory,
direct firing across the Indian border by artillery and tanks became
more frequent.[20]

It was becoming increasingly clear that another Indo-Pakistani War
was in the offing, in which the status of the Eastern Wing of Pakistan
would be decided, unless international pressure could be brought to bear
to restrain the main protagonists. It is in this context that Bangladeshi
spokesmen declined to guarantee the safety of United Nations (UN)
personnel should they be deployed, as observers to the border region,
as the last thing they wanted was an internationally supervised status
quo.[21] From India's perspective the Mukti Bahini had performed a useful
role as part of a carefully orchestrated exercise in crisis manipulation.

## Indian intervention

From the very start of the crisis in March India had been under domestic
pressure to intervene directly but, 'Luckily, the Prime Minister and her
military advisers thought otherwise as war, being a serious business, could
not be waged just at the dictates of popular demand. A valid excuse, if
not a sound reason, was necessary to do so'.[22] The Mukti Bahini were
now well placed to help furnish just such a valid excuse. Intervention,
for which India had been making careful military preparation, would be
legitimized by the presence of Bangladeshis completing the liberation
of their homeland. Moreover, by escalating their attacks from refuges
close to the border and from the pockets of 'liberated' territory within
East Pakistan, the Mukti Bahini could act as a catalyst provoking retaliation. It would enable India to claim that its action was a reluctant resort
to self-defence and not a calculated act of aggression to wrest East
Bengal from Pakistan.

From the third week of November Mukti Bahini operations were
accordingly increased. In the new permissive environment they were
supported by Indian Army incursions, although this was still closely
limited in scope and depth. On 21 November, Mukti Bahini attacks were
launched all round the perimeter of East Pakistan with close Indian
cooperation. A pitched battle was fought at Boyra where elements of an

Indian Brigade with supporting armour became embroiled in the exchanges. Pakistani tanks were destroyed and two of the Sabre jets called in to provide close air support were shot down by the Indian Air Force. Although the Indians had withdrawn domestic and foreign correspondents, clashes of such intensity could not be hushed up and Mrs Ghandi announced to Parliament that the Indian posture was now one of 'constructive self-defence'.[23] Yahya responded the only way he could in the circumstances and declared a national State of Emergency. With a steady series of cross border clashes now occurring in the East as at Hilli and around Argatala, war seemed increasingly likely.

Pakistani strategy for defending the East had been based on a tenacious defence in depth to commit and hold sizeable Indian formations while mobile formations launched a crushing offensive from West Pakistan. In 1971, they appear to have greatly overestimated their ability to make headway in the West against a markedly improved Indian Army and Air Force. In the East the protracted struggle against the Mukti Bahini had left their available combat forces badly deployed. They were too widely dispersed, dug-in, lacking in depth and without an adequate reserve. General Niazi anticipated, or perhaps rather hoped, that Indian Forces would adopt a limited goal of gaining sufficient territory to which to return the Bangladeshi government in exile as a bargaining chip in a later round of internationally brokered negotiations.[24] Against the four Pakistani divisions the Indians had massed seven with three armoured regiments in support. Two of the armoured regiments were equipped with the Soviet PT-76 amphibious light tank.[25] Grouped into three Corps, the Indian forces were well provided with artillery compared with their adversaries. They had also made provision for engineer support to overcome the anticipated difficulties of sustaining offensive operations in a country criss-crossed by waterways, and in which those bridges not already demolished by the Mukti Bahini were likely to be dropped by a competent adversary. Although the balance of forces was clearly in India's favour it was deemed to be necessary to achieve a rapid victory before international pressure could deny India the strategic prize. Indeed, four days after war broke out the UN General Assembly adopted a resolution calling for a cease-fire and the immediate withdrawal of troops by both sides.[26] For India a swift conclusion was needed and the Mukti Bahini played a significant part in its delivery.

The Mukti Bahini were particularly useful in an intelligence-gathering role. Enjoying near universal popular support among the Bengalis information flooded in about the identity and strength of Pakistani formations. A cadre of professionally trained staff officers and well-educated volunteers working under their direction, was able to turn the wealth of detail into usable grade material to be passed up the chain of command to contribute to the development of the bigger picture. Drawing upon this invaluable network the Indians were able to develop a near complete picture of the Pakistani order of battle in the Eastern Pakistani Theatre.[27]

Once the war broke out on 3 December, the role of relatively lightly equipped Mukti Bahini formations was usually in support of the Indian divisions they accompanied in the advance. General Osmany had accepted that the Indians would be in overall command and that the Mukti Bahini would by-pass strong points, leaving them to be screened or reduced by the Indian Army with armour, artillery and air support.[28] To maintain the pace of the advance the Mukti Bahini worked closely with their sector forces and Gono Bahini to mobilize rapidly local resources to circumvent transport difficulties. Local craft arrived to ferry troops and supplies across rivers until such time as engineers could repair or replace damaged bridges. On land, bullock carts were assembled to help shift food, ammunition and ordnance toward the front.

Keeping up the tempo of the advance proved problematic. Conducting operations around the clock required solutions to night fighting without sophisticated technological aids. Night navigation was made greatly easier for the Indians by the availability of knowledgeable, enthusiastic local guides. The guerrilla's intelligence networks were able to pass on information about ambushes set by the Pakistanis and give advice on how the positions might be turned or avoided.

If the Indians were to avoid a protracted fight for Dacca it was important to disrupt and hinder the withdrawal of Pakistani forces toward the Capital with its naturally strong defensive position.[29] The Mukti Bahini often acted to form blocking positions behind Pakistani formations due to be assaulted frontally by the Indians. Success was variable, although they continued to mount ambushes against the increasingly demoralized retreating soldiers. Scenting victory in the days shortly before the final Pakistani surrender, some 35,000 guerrillas converged on the capital to play their part in its liberation, but General Niazi surrendered to the Indians on 16 December 1971. To avoid rubbing salt into Niazi's wounds the Mukti Bahini and General Osmany were denied a formal part in the surrender ceremony.[30]

## Conclusion

With the birth of a new state of Bangladesh the army formed in exile could return home to become its duly constituted army. Sheikh Mujib also returned to lead the country. Mindful of the role the military had played in Pakistan's political history Mujib was determined to keep Bangladesh's army small and under-equipped in the hope of ensuring that they could pose no threat to the Bangladesh's internal settlement.[31] The Mukti Bahini was a successful army of national liberation. Despite its dependency on Indian support, it derived its legitimacy in the first instance from the popular aspiration for self-determination expressed by the Bengalis at the ballot box. The brutal and clumsily executed repression added a further layer of legitimacy, bolstered by the successful formation of alternative state structures in exile around which resistance could coalesce. With numerous volunteers of high calibre it faced no difficulty in sustaining its strength until the victory was achieved in a relatively short time. The support and assistance offered by India was crucial and its direct intervention proved decisive on the battlefield. Yet the contribution made by the Mukti Bahini to the speed of that success deserves to be acknowledged. Its sanctuary in neighbouring India proved not so much an 'exile' than a springboard to success.

## Notes

1. For the Six Points in full see Appendix 1 in R. Jackson, *South Asian Crisis* (London: Chatto and Windus 1975), pp. 166–7. Reform had brought about the electoral system adopted for 1970 with 162 elected seats for the East and 138 for the West.
2. General Yahya Khan, C-in-C Pakistan Army, had taken power in March 1969. Jackson, *South Asian Crisis*, p. 22.
3. H. Zaheer, *The Separation of East Pakistan* (Oxford, Oxford University Press, 1994), p. 131.
4. *Ibid.*, p. 130.
5. On 1 March Pakistan Radio announced the postponement of the National Assembly sine die. On 6 March Yahya announced that he had decided to call the National Assembly into session on 25 March. See Jackson, *South Asian Crisis*, p. 29.
6. A confirmed bachelor, sporting a formidable moustache, Colonel Osmany had taken a paternalistic interest in selection and career development of EBR personnel even after his retirement.
7. Zaheer, *The Separation of East Pakistan*, p. 178.
8. This was also true for the previous wars between India and Pakistan of those who had served and trained together before Partition.
9. Major Khalid Musharraf, Major Safiuallah and Major Ziaur Rahman. S. Singh, *The Liberation of Bangladesh* (New Delhi: Vikas, 1980), p. 31.
10. Major General D. K. Pallit, *The Lightning Campaign* (New Delhi: Thomson Press [India], 1972), pp. 54–5.
11. *Ibid.*, p. 57.
12. The Alouette helicopters were capable of being fitted with rockets and machine-guns. Singh, *The Liberation of Bangladesh*, p. 37.

13. Pallit, *The Lightning Campaign*, p. 59.
14. *Ibid.*, pp. 35–6.
15. Jackson, *South Asian Crisis*, p. 101.
16. General Niazi had taken over from General Tikka Khan on 3 September, *Ibid.*, p. 80. Interesting assessments of the Generals' characters are to be found in the works of Singh, *The Liberation of Bangladesh* and Zaheer, *The Separation of East Pakistan, passim.*
17. These reinforcements included paramilitary and police formations. See Jackson, *South Asian Crisis*, p. 132. The Bihari community was to suffer dreadful retribution and persecution after the conflict.
18. Henry Kissinger quoted in Roy Linklider, *Stopping the Killing: How Civil Wars End* (New York: New York University Press, 1993), p. 25.
19. Pallit, *The Lightning Campaign*, p. 71. Also, on cross border incidents in November see Zaheer, *The Separation of East Pakistan*, p. 354.
20. M. Ayoob and K. Subrahmanyan, *The Liberation War* (New Delhi: Chand, 1972), p. 208.
21. Jackson, *South Asian Crisis*, p. 67.
22. Singh, *The Liberation of Bangladesh*, p. 93.
23. Zaheer, *The Separation of East Pakistan*, p. 356.
24. Singh, *The Liberation of Bangladesh*, p. 65. See also Palit, *The Lightning Campaign*, p. 99.
25. The PT-76 was reported to be prone to overheating when 'swimming' wide, strongly flowing rivers.
26. With the Security Council blocked by the veto power, a resolution was passed in General Assembly 104 to 11.
27. Pallit, *The Lightning Campaign*, p. 154.
28. *Ibid.*, p. 155.
29. Singh, *The Liberation of Bangladesh*, p. 216.
30. The surrender ceremony took place at the Race Course. The instrument of surrender was duly signed by General Niazi and by Lt. General Jagjit Singh Aurora in his capacity as GOC-in-C Indian and Bangla Desh Forces in the Eastern Theatre. Jackson, *South Asian Crisis*, p. 144.
31. An account of the unhappy early course of civil–military relations in Bangladesh is to be found in A. Mascarenhas, *Bangladesh: A Legacy of Blood* (Sevenoaks: Hodder and Stoughton, 1986).

# 8
# African Exile Armies: ZANLA, ZIPRA and the Politics of Disunity

*Edmund Yorke*[1]

Zimbabwe African National Liberation Army (ZANLA) and Zimbabwe Peoples Revolutionary Army (ZIPRA) comprised the official military wings of the two main parties opposed to the white supremacist Rhodesian Front regime led by Prime Minister Ian Smith. Smith's government had consistently refused to accept the principle of black majority rule and, under British and international pressure, had finally rebelled against British rule in November 1965.[2] ZANLA was attached to the political party ZANU (Zimbabwe African National Union) ultimately led by Robert Mugabe, and ZIPRA comprised the military wing of the Joshua Nkomo's ZAPU party (Zimbabwe African Peoples Union). Both movements fought a protracted nearly 15 year bush war against the Rhodesian Security Forces drawing support largely from the adjacent African host countries of Mozambique, Zambia, Tanzania, Botswana and Angola (commonly referred to as the *Front Line States*).[3] They also received limited support from two other African liberation groups the African National Congress (ANC) and Front for the Liberation of Mozambique (FRELIMO).

Before 1972 their military performance had proved somewhat ineffective but strategic changes in the form of the collapse or retreat of Rhodesia's two key allies, Portugal and South Africa, combined with better training, equipment, and more experience meant, that, after that date their military effectiveness rapidly improved. Their growing threat was graphically illustrated by Rhodesian intelligence figures. Between 1974 the date of the final withdrawal of Portugal from Southern Africa and 1977, insurgent numbers had increased to more than five-fold from 400 to 2,350. Within two more years – by January 1979, combined ZIPRA and ZANLA numbers had reached over 11,000.[4] By then the severely over-stretched Rhodesian forces, defending hundreds of miles of border, besieged on all fronts and comprising or averaging at peak no more than 25,000 effectives, of whom only around 4,000 were white regulars or 'troopies', were facing military Armageddon. Only British Commonwealth and to a lesser extent American mediation, combined with pressure principally exerted by the war-ravaged Tanzania, Mozambique and Zambia on both ZANLA and ZIPRA, forced all warring parties together to end the war at the 1979 Lancaster House Summit meeting in London.[5] This war of attrition had cost up to 30,000 lives, the vast majority of them comprising guerrilla fighters and civilians but including 1,000 dead amongst the Rhodesian Forces.

## Political perspectives: Legitimacy and internal group rivalries

To establish a credible basis for legitimacy is a vital necessity or pre-requisite for any guerrilla or insurgent group seeking to successfully overthrow or replace an established regime. As David Burns confirms, there are two aspects of legitimacy – international and domestic, 'both of which may overlap and frequently interact'.[6] The former is best defined by Martin Wight as 'the collective judgement of international society about the rightful membership of the family of nations; our sovereignty may be transferred and how state of succession is to be regulated when large states break up into smaller or several states combine into one'.[7] Moreover, as Guelke observes, international legitimacy is quite distinct from domestic legitimacy – 'the opinions of the inhabitants of a territory as to the rightfulness of the state under which they live',[8] though as Burns succinctly points out, 'this may be a factor influencing international opinion'.[9]

The refusal of the Smith Regime to grant or facilitate black majority rule culminating in the illegal 'Unilateral Declaration of Independence' (UDI) in November 1965, ensured that both ZANU and ZAPU and their military wings ZANLA and ZIPRA enjoyed a position of almost universal global legitimacy. The British Government's 'six principles', initiated by Prime Minister Harold Wilson were designed to ensure the return to liberal democracy in the rebellious Rhodesian Colony. These were:

1.  its unimpeded progress to majority rule;
2.  guarantees against retrogressive amendments to the constitution;
3.  an immediate improvement in the political status of the black population;
4.  progress towards ending racial discrimination;

5.  constitutional proposals that were acceptable to the people of Rhodesia as a whole; and

6.  no oppression of the majority by the minority or the minority by the majority.

This approach was later fully endorsed by the United Nations.[10] Only a few isolated states such as South Africa then practising apartheid and the Portuguese Government, upholding colonial rule by force until 1974 in Angola and Mozambique, were exceptions to this rule.

Such political support did not of course by any means guarantee early military success. As early as 1966, one year after UDI, ZAPU, then the dominant nationalist organization, realized that, for both logistical and 'kith and kin' reasons, Britain, the mother country was not prepared to intervene militarily. In the words of J. Cilliers, 'the major task of the insurgent forces at this early stage was therefore to convince the Organisation of African Unity and the world at large that the forces to overthrow the regime of Ian Smith really did exist. This was vitally important if financial and political support was to be forthcoming.'[11] It was a problem shared by many other embryonic national liberation movements and their attached exile armies.

Acquiring domestic legitimacy was equally fraught with problems. To win and retain the support of the indigenous population, the exile party or government needs to offer a viable alternative government or at least introduce a counter political culture. The latter was certainly achieved by the predominantly Shona supported ZANU/ZANLA who skilfully invoked Chaminuka, the spirit of the Shona national prophet of the 1896 resistance era. He was allegedly reached through a medium claiming to be the reincarnation of Nehanda, a powerful priest of the period. ZANLA guerrillas, by cultivating this alliance of traditional and new authority, sharing similar goals, seeking the 'retrieval of lost lands and lost autonomy' and by 'observing the ancestral prohibitions' were transferred from '"strangers" into "royals", from members of lineages resident in other parts of Zimbabwe into descendants of the local Mhondoro with rights to land'.[12] By these means, 'the authority of the ancestors was tapped to provide legitimacy to armed resistance and violent insurrection and the pact between guerrillas and peasants was struck at such great depth that the peasants began invariably and unthinkingly to refer to the guerrillas as *vasikana* and *vakomana*, our "daughters" and our "sons".'[13] Similarly, but arguably less successfully, ZIPRA with its high proportion of urban-based Ndebele personnel, were able to exploit the memory of the last Ndebele independent ruler, Lobengula, as a potent symbol of resistance. Both parties and armies in exile could therefore claim *unbroken* resistance to colonial/white domination. This strategy was also the result of facing an initially powerful settler state and one which certainly helped to account for the guerrillas' reliance on cultural nationalist appeals and their scant utilitarian appeals.[14]

For ZANLA, this platform could be further used to demolish the chiefly elite, who acted as internal props of and collaborators with the Smith Regime. Under this new mantle of legitimacy, ZANLA cadres progressively undermined the functions of the chiefs, most of whom were at least passive supporters of the illegal Salisbury government. Land allocation and local taxation powers were commandeered and, the guerrillas successfully infiltrated and controlled the local administration of law. They 'demanded that all disputes should be brought to them for arbitration. In this way they challenged the authority of the state-controlled chiefly courts to resolve the disruption brought about by war as well as by the less exceptional calamities of everyday life.'[15] With this progressive undermining of chiefly authority ZANLA were able to push for the elimination or assassination of chiefs. It was a campaign that successfully disrupted high policy making within the Smith regime. In March 1975, Chief Chirau, a key collaborator and later one of the architects of the Internal Settlement of 1978, reported to Prime Minister Smith, he had been receiving 'threatening letters' and 'one of his strongest supporters had been killed by terrorists'.[16]

Into this growing political vacuum new ideologies could be inserted as part of the process of establishing legitimization. Mugabe's ZAPU/ZANLA movement headed by the Chimurenga (War Council) pursued an unrelenting Chinese-influenced Marxist strategy during the liberation war seeking primarily a radical redistribution of land from the ruling white minority classes and communal property ownership. In 1979, as Rhodesia's security forces were fatally over-stretched, Mugabe expressed his confidence for a rapid political and military victory:

> Our liberation struggle had progressed to where we believed we had more than 2/3 of the country...we had the rural areas in our grip ...the end of 1979, with the coming of the rains, was going to see the development of the *urban* guerrilla struggle...we felt that we needed yet another thrust in order to bring the fight home to where the whites had their citadels.[17]

Similarly ZAPU and ZIPRA, heavily influenced by Soviet, Vietnamese and Cuban revolutionary experiences and aware of the growing weaknesses of the Rhodesian security forces, took steps to set up a 'Revolutionary' Council in 1976, the key executive of this 'party and army in exile'. This Council included a 'War Council' of five permanent members headed by Joshua Nkomo and a 'Congress of Militants', in effect 'an ad hoc party congress of soldiers and workers with limited powers and duties'.[18] The War Council had the responsibility to develop and implement the political and military strategy of the party and to issue general policy directives. Thus both armies in exile endeavoured 'to construct a shadow state of parallel state of government'[19] in the specific regions over which they claimed and sought control.

## Factional rivalries and disputes

The prolonged detention of the ZAPU and ZANU leaders, Joshua Nkomo and Robert Mugabe by the Rhodesian authorities ensured that, before their release in 1974, both movements suffered to some extent from a power vacuum. The uncertainties of power attainment inevitably encouraged factional rivalries or challenges both within and between the insurgent groups. Despite the eventual formation of the unified Patriotic Front in 1976, deep ethnic rivalries persisted between the predominantly Ndebele supported ZIPRA and the predominately Shona supported ZANLA exile armies. At a tactical level for instance, ZANU criticized ZAPU's links with the ANC and their Soviet confrontational, partisan-style action before proper political preparation and the formation of cadres. There was friction and occasional clashes between both groups over recruitment from each other's designated areas. The differing scale of effort also affected their relationship. The 1967 Mbeya Accord between ZAPU and ZANU, designed to unite their two military wings, soon collapsed because ZAPU leaders (notably James Chikerema), opposed being forced to join hands with ZANU at a time when ZANU had deployed only a very small number of trained ZANLA men and apparently had little obvious popular support inside Rhodesia.[20]

Arguably internal rivalries within the two exile armies were much more damaging. There were several cases of disappeared personages on both sides but the most notorious incident concerned the killing of one prominent ZANU leader, Herbert Chitepo, by means of a car bomb attack in Lusaka, Zambia. Up to 150 ZANLA guerrillas were killed in the subsequent internecine purge.[21] ZIPRA suffered severe internal splits during the early 1970s particularly in 1970 and 1971 and notably when ZAPU began to appraise the record of its disastrous 1965–69 campaigns. This self-examination exercise triggered severe problems within ZAPU's and ZIPRA's organization, especially when Jay Moyo, ZAPU's political leader, issued a paper, 'On the Observations of our Struggle' which was blatantly critical of a rival ZIPRA military leader, James Chikerema. Chikerema angrily refuted the allegations arguing that the political leadership ,'had no right to decide on a military matter which was an issue to be resolved by himself alone as head of ZAPU's Department of Special Affairs.'[22] Chikerema proceeded to organize a rival group led by Walter Mthimkhulu with the authority to safeguard his own interests. Mthimkhulu's group itself later mutinied against Chikerema and arrested both political and military leaders such as Moyo and T. C. Silundika but they significantly failed to arrest Chikerema himself and another leading Chikerema supporter George Nyondoro, however. The result was a dangerous three-way split within ZAPU:

1.  the Front for the Liberation of Zimbabwe (FROLIZI) led by Chikerema which had a military wing;
2.  the Mthimkhulu group which claimed to be neutral and independent; and
3.  the rest of ZAPU led by Moyo.

A far more potent rival group to both the mainstream ZAPU and ZANU movements emerged in the form of the breakaway Zimbabwe Peoples Army (ZIPA) which originated in November 1975 as an alternative strategy group, drawing disaffected members from both ZANLA and ZIPRA. The political and military vacuum created by these constant internecine clashes 'all contributed to a situation ripe for ZIPA's assumption of leadership and for their construction of the foundations necessary for the execution of the struggle based on the postulates' socialist transformation'.[23] Comprising predominantly younger ZANLA operatives, ZIPA strategy was more radical, energetic and fast track and was designed to establish rapidly fully liberated zones in Zimbabwe using, in this case, Vietnam-style tactics based on the military philosophy of General Ngyuen Giap. As one ZIPA commander put it: 'the first stage was to chase the enemy out of what would have been the future base areas so our main task was to politicise the masses. You'd organise them, you'd chase out the enemy, you'd consolidate in this base area. What we are now in Tanzania or Mozambique should be in Zimbabwe, after we'd liberated some zones. That was the strategic thinking'.[24] This fledgling ZIPA group, enjoying better military training than their ZANLA/ZIPRA counterparts, took the field in January 1976 when a new offensive was launched in northeast Rhodesia. However, this relatively small 100-strong group achieved little militarily and, with early infiltration by Rhodesian intelligence, their attacks further south were easily contained. By early 1977, moreover, ZIPA had been rejected by both Nkomo, head of ZAPU/ZIPRA as a ZANU creation and by President Machel and FRELIMO leaders as a maverick movement, which dared to a attack FRELIMO's own guerrilla strategies. It was the 'final nail in the coffin' for ZIPA. ZIPA's overtly hostile attitude even to ZANLA's use of traditional religious symbols also helped to ensure that under such all-round pressure it was eventually dispersed and subsumed by ZANLA.[25] Nevertheless, it remains the outstanding example of the extreme vulnerability of exile armies to internal dissension.

## Relations with host or sponsor states

At a local level the Front Line states comprising Zambia, Tanzania, Mozambique, Angola and Botswana provided crucial moral and material support to both liberation movements. The outwardly benign role of such states as providers of political havens, military bases, food and supplies actually concealed immense tensions. These tensions can be defined in both external and internal security terms. National liberation exile armies are, of course, primarily motivated in creating war machines capable of defeating the security forces of the target regimes, in this case Rhodesia. In the words of Kenneth Grundy, 'as such they represent concentrations of organised trained and armed men, concentrations that could become a problem in internal security for the host government'.[26] In this respect Zambia was probably the host state which suffered most. On the 24 April 1970, the *Times of Zambia*, reported a ferocious gun battle between rival ZAPU factions in which four were wounded and six missing. Again, in March 1971, over 20 leading ZAPU officials were kidnapped by dissident elements of their military wing who were apparently disgruntled with the conditions of service and pay. The Zambian government, in order to keep law and order, was forced to intervene and large numbers of ZAPU military and administrative staff were detained and transferred to a special camp at Mbaloma in the Central Province. It was eventually reported that 163 ZAPU members were held at Mbaloma, 34 at Kasama and eight were held at Chipata.[27] On occasions guerrilla fighters were suspected of supporting opposition groups within their host states with the added potential danger of selling their weapons to them. In July and August 1971, 129 members of exiled nationalist organizations in Zambia surrendered to Rhodesian security forces at various border posts. Their erstwhile host President Kaunda had ordered them out. He bluntly explained: 'We wish to ensure against any coup in which these liberation movements might be involved.' Elements from these nationalist groups were alleged to be fomenting unrest, particularly on the university campus. Again in Kaundas' words: 'Of late a group of disgruntled politicians have resorted to gun-running and sending out our people for military training to countries hostile to Zambia with a view to subverting the tranquillity of the Republic'.[28]

Four years later, the Zambian authorities, dismayed at the increasing anarchy arising from constant infighting within ZANLA units, again cracked down after the Chitepo murder by arresting 1,300 or more guerrilla fighters. In both the front line states of Zambia and Mozambique, housing increasingly large numbers of both armies in exile, crime levels particularly around guerrilla bases arose dramatically as deserters linked up with local criminals. By the later stages of the war even the major urban centres of Lusaka and Maputo were experiencing this phenomenon.[29]

Equally devastating for the host states was the fact that their willingness to receive refugees and host guerrilla factions made them a ready and vulnerable target for retribution or retaliatory raids by the target regime. Four of the front line states: Zambia, Mozambique, Angola and Botswana became particular targets of the Rhodesian revenge raids mainly carried out by Rhodesian special forces such as the Selous Scouts and the Rhodesian SAS. An outstanding example was a daring raid by 84 Selous Scouts launched against the ZANLA base at Nyadzonia in the Manica Province of Mozambique. Dressed as Mozambique Army soldiers, the Scouts entered the camp via a circular route during muster parade killing about 300 ZANLA and Mozambique troops. A subsequent Mozambique Army Board of Enquiry estimated there was over 1,000 fatalities.[30] During the November 1977, Chimoio and Tembue raids by a composite SAS and Rhodesia Light Infantry force, not only were an estimated 2,000 ZANLA recruits killed but also many local Mozambique civilians also perished in significant numbers with severe damage to local infrastructure. The earlier Mapai raid of May–June 1977 had already finally destroyed what remained of the Mozambique railway system in the Gaza Province.[31] An equally daring raid into Zambia also in 1977 conducted by mainly Rhodesian SAS commandos and primarily aimed at killing the ZAPU/ZIPRA leader Joshua Nkomo, resulted in both Zambian Army and civilian deaths in Lusaka and culminated in the sinking of the Kasangula ferry, a major trade link between Zambia and Botswana. Similarly, the sabotage and closure of the Benguela railway line, by Rhodesian and South African-backed UNITA guerrillas, further paralysed Zambia's trade. In the last year of the war (1979) in angry response to the shooting down of a Rhodesian airliner, the Rhodesian Air Force even launched a raid into Angola 'circumventing both the British maintained Zambian air defence and the Soviet radar tracking system, and killing over 160 insurgents'.[32]

These incursions in the later 1970s had enormous political repercussions for the two exile armies. At the 1979 Havana Summit, desperate to avoid further punishing raids, President Machel of Mozambique and Presidents Kaunda of Zambia and Nyerere of Tanzania put immense pressure on a deeply reluctant Mugabe and Nkomo, leaders of ZIPRA and ZANLA, literally to force them to the peace table at Lancaster House, London. As Kaunda later recalled, both exile army leaders were subjected to massive pressure and even verbal threats.

> We had a job to convince both Robert Mugabe and Joshua Nkomo to go to London. They were saying 'No'. They were going to continue to fight. We then said to them No! No! You must go...otherwise we will take very strong steps against you. In fact, it is not too much to say we *turned* on the freedom fighters in Cuba...they were dependent on us in order to continue that fighting. If we said 'No' to the fighting, it would be 'No'. There would *be* no fighting.[33]

At Lancaster House similarly extreme pressures was placed on both men by all the Patriotic Front host states. President Machel 'virtually ordered Mugabe to sign, indicating that, if he did not, the most he could expect back in Mozambique was political asylum or a "villa on the coast"'.[34]

This is not to say that the presence of the exile armies was entirely detrimental to the host states or wholly parasitic by nature. Both host states and ZIPRA and ZANLA obviously benefited from a mutual interaction or cross-over of political and military ideas and experience. FRELIMO and ZANLA who frequently trained together benefitted from this cooperation and were a common regular target for Rhodesian security force attacks. Similarly, guerrilla wages and spending power could clearly stimulate local economies, especially in the immediate vicinity of their military bases.

## Military perspectives: Tactics and recruitment

The geopolitical position of both exile armies, in particular the physical distance they shared from the locus of power in their home country, certainly influenced the shape and style of their respective military cultures. The small but highly focused Rhodesian war machine was based on centralized government recruitment and deployed a more conventional and cohesive, if dated, armed force. In contrast both ZANLA and ZIPRA, initially denied these advantages, were forced into more irregular or unorthodox modes of warfare with less centralized control mechanisms. For ZANLA this military necessity led to the rapid adoption by the Chimurenga of a Maoist-style covert and protracted attritional war,[35] designed to wear down the Rhodesian Government's economic and human resource base and, ultimately, the morale of the ruling white elite. These tactics relied predominantly on terror campaigns in rural areas, thus progressively overstretching depleted Rhodesian forces and ultimately restricting them to an inherently defensive and demoralizing strategy of forcing local Africans into protected villages and of securing white urban areas.[36] Rhodesian intelligence records reveal how this attritional strategy ultimately succeeded as, by late 1978, predictions were made of imminent collapse and even last stands restricted to major white urban settlement areas.[37] Similarly, ZIPRA, although the bulk of its forces were trained by Soviet, East European and Cuban instructors in Zambia and Angola for a Soviet style conventional assault at the critical moment, also had to resort to largely attritional tactics until 1979, the last year of the war. Only then as Rhodesia lay militarily prostrate could ZIPRA, using Soviet light vehicles and a few obsolete tanks, contemplate a full-scale conventional assault from Zambia.[38]

The detached and more isolated position of these armies in exile inevitably influenced the techniques or pattern of recruitment, which they deployed in their respective ethnic tribal areas situated across the borders of Zambia and Mozambique. Clearly lacking the local advantages of the well-oiled and highly organized Rhodesian recruitment and propaganda machine, both ZANLA and ZIPRA felt obliged to deploy higher levels of coercion in securing recruits. This culminated in numerous cross border raids in the mid-to late-1970s, which often included the mass abduction of village mission or school youths. They were also necessarily forced to participate in more covert and unorthodox activities such as the extensive use of *Mujibas* (boys) and *Chibwidos* (girls) to supply food, intelligence and general porterage.[39] For both ZIPRA and ZANLA there was also a marked tendency to use a proportionately high number of women,[40] both as combatants and non-combatants, but again particularly as providers of food and intelligence to their 'boys in the bush'. The looser, more dispersed military structures of both ZIPRA and ZANLA led to armed bands scattered over thousands of square miles in Rhodesia. This resulted in an excessive use of terror tactics. The Elim Mission massacre in 1978 saw several British missionaries, their wives and a three-month baby beaten, raped and bayoneted to death.[41] There were allegations of continuing physical abuse of male recruits and sexual abuse of their own female fighters. The Rhodesian units were also often guilty of excesses in their often ruthlessly conducted containment strategies.

## The legacy of exile armies in post-independence politics

The end of the liberation war, the negotiated settlement at Lancaster House and the veritable triumph of the exile armies signified only limited internal peace for the new Zimbabwe state. The barely concealed tensions between the two exile armies spilled over into the post-independence period and significantly undermined the stability of the new Zimbabwean state during the early 1980s and again in the late 1990s. The simmering animosity between ZAPU/ZIPRA and ZANU/ZANLA reached its peak with an explosion of bitter internecine violence at the Entumbane Barracks, Bulawayo, in February 1981, where scores of demobilized guerrillas and local civilians were killed. As Abiodan Alao observes, these clashes were inevitable:

> By the end of 1980, only 15,000 of the estimated 65,000 guerrillas had been re-trained. The remainder were still in the assembly points – and they still had their weapons. Towards the end of 1980 the Joint High Command decided to transfer them...to...already overcrowded townships where pre-independence ethnic and political differences had not been completely resolved...what ignited the tension in Entumbane was that the ZANLA and ZIPRA troops were obliged to live next to each other. These clashes were to have a fundamental impact upon the early development of the ZNA (Zimbabwean National Army).[42]

The majority Shona-speaking ZANU-PF government of Robert Mugabe later took swift revenge using both these disturbances and the alleged discovery of ZIPRA armed cachés to launch a major crackdown in Matabeleland, the main ethnic support base of ZIPRA. Deploying the infamous North Korean trained 5th Brigade, comprising many ZANLA veterans, a wave of terror was launched against Ndebele civilians and ZIPRA veterans alike resulting in widespread torture, imprisonment without trial and even mass executions. An estimated 3,000 people were killed. The scale of such disruption was immense with wide areas of rural Matabeleland de-populated and many male ZAPU ZIPRA veterans literally forced to flee to work on the South African mines in order to escape further persecution. This internecine strife was no means over. The 1981–3 purges in Matabeleland left a legacy of bitter memories and added to it was a general disenchantment felt among all exile army veterans over the lack of government reward for their services to the liberation struggle. On returning home many veterans were further castigated by local villagers for themselves not fulfilling their wartime promises of land redistribution.[43] The exile army veteran issue has thus engendered a profound impact on post-independence Zimbabwe politics.

## Conclusion

This chapter has analysed and discussed some of the distinctive political, social military characteristics and dynamics of two southern African exile armies both of whom sought to overthrow the illegal government of Rhodesia. Both ZANLA and ZIPRA clearly demonstrated unusual military characteristics, some of which were possibly unique to Africa, especially in regard to their military cultures and overall recruitment strategies. The initial military dominance of Rhodesia, the target state and the often precarious nature of their existence within the territories of increasingly reluctant host governments (notably Zambia and Mozambique) forced them to engage in a far more intimate level of relations with their indigenous supporters compared to other exile armies. The skilful use of potent religious and historical symbolism, particularly by ZAPU/ZANLA in order to legitimize its cause, served a 'deeper purpose, to confer on the movement the respectability of age and challenge the existing regime as an alien imposition and historical aberration, as well as building a new "national myth" for the emergent state'.[44] Furthermore, the ethnic diversity of these two exile armies and the enforced absence of their leadership during the early crucial stages of the liberation struggle contributed to factional rivalries both within and between ZANLA and ZIPRA. The brief emergence of a third rival exile army, ZIPA was a major testament to the depth of their internal dissension. Yet both exile armies proved able to sustain domestic and international legitimacy over one and a half decades, and to fight an increasingly successful bush war, culminating in the final negotiated peace settlement at Lancaster House.

### Notes

1. The views expressed are those of the author and not necessarily those of the RMA Sandhurst or the UK Ministry of Defence.
2. For the political background to the 'Rhodesian Crisis' see for instance, R. Blake, *A History of Rhodesia* (London: Eyre Methuen, 1977) and D. Martin and C. Johnson, *The Struggle for Zimbabwe* (Harare: Faber and Faber, 1981).

3. For comprehensive treatments of the military events of the war see, principally, J. Cilliers, *Counter-Insurgency in Rhodesia* (London: Croom Helm, 1985), K. Flower, *Serving Secretly* (London: John Murray, 1987) and L. H. Gann and T. H. Henriksen, *The Struggle for Zimbabwe: Battle in the Bush* (New York: Praeger, 1981). For a historical background to these guerrilla war tactics see E. J. Yorke, 'Irregular War 1900–1990', in *100 Years of Conflict* (Gloucestershire: Sutton Books, 2000).

4. A. Clayton, *Frontiersmen: Warfare in Africa since 1950* (UCC Press 1999), p. 67. This figure did not include an estimated further trained 16,000 ZIPRA and 3,500 ZANLA based across the border and 2,900 ZIPRA and 14,000 ZANLA training externally.

5. See especially E. J. Yorke, 'A Family Affair, The Lancaster House Agreement 1979', in D. H. Dunn (ed.), *Diplomacy at the Highest Level* (London: MacMillan – new Palgrave Macmillan, 1996), pp. 200–20 and M. Charlton, *The Last Colony in Africa* (Oxford: Oxford University Press, 1990) *passim*.

6. D. Burns, 'Insurgency as a Struggle for Legitimation: The Case of Southern Africa', *Small Wars and Insurgencies*, 1(5) (Spring 1994), 33.

7. M. Wight, *Systems of States* (Leicester: Leicester University Press, 1977). Encl. in Burns, 'Insurgency as a Struggle for Legitimation: The Case of Southern Africa', p. 33.

8. A. Guelke, 'International Legitimacy, Self-determination and Northern Ireland', *Review of International Studies*, 2(1) (January 1984), 38.

9. Burns, 'Insurgency as a Struggle for Legitimation', p. 34.

10. See Yorke, 'A Family Affair', pp. 201–2.

11. Cilliers, *Counter-Insurgency in Rhodesia*, p. 6.

12. D. Lan, *Guns and Rain* (London: James Currey, 1985), p. 164.

13. *Ibid.*

14. N. J. Kriger, *Zimbabwe's Guerilla War* (Cambridge: Cambridge University Press, 1992), p. 242.

15. Lan, *Guns and Rain*, p. 167.

16. I. Smith, *The Great Betrayal* (London: Blake Publishing, 1997), p. 247.

17. Interview with Robert Mugabe, in Charlton, *Last Colony in Africa*, p. 52–3. See also Yorke, 'A Family Affair', p. 206.

18. J. Brickhill, 'Daring to Storm the Heavens; The Military Strategy of ZAPU 1976 to 1979', in N. Bhebe and T. Ranger (eds), *Soldiers in Zimbabwe's Liberation War* (Oxford: James Currey, 1995), p. 54.

19. Burns, 'Insurgency as a Struggle for Legitimation: The Case of Southern Africa', p. 37.

20. D. Dabengwa, 'ZIPRA in the Zimbabwe War of National Liberation', in Bhebe and Ranger (eds), *Soldiers in Zimbabwe's Liberation War*, p. 29.

21. Clayton, *Frontiersmen*, p. 64 and Moore, 'The Zimbabwe People's Army: Strategic Innovation or more of the same?', in Bhebe and Ranger (eds), *Soldiers in Zimbabwe's Liberation War*, p. 74.

22. Dabengwa, 'ZIPRA in the Zimbabwe War of National Liberation', p. 31.

23. Moore, 'Zimbabwe People's Army', p. 77.

24. *Ibid.*, p. 78.

25. N. Bhebe and T. Ranger (eds), *Society in Zimbabwe's Liberation War* (Oxford: James Currey, 1996), p. 178.

26. K. Grundy, 'Host Countries and the Southern African Liberation Struggle', *Africa Quarterly*, 12(2) (April–June 1970), 20.

27. A. R. Wilkinson, 'Insurgency in Rhodesia, 1957–1973: An Account and Assessment', *Adelphi Papers*, no. 100 (London: 1973), p. 21.

28. *Ibid.*

29. The author was himself the victim of an armed robbery conducted by a mixed gang of local Lusaka criminals and demobilized ZIPRA guerillas in Lusaka in February 1980. The gang, guilty of many other residential raids was the subject of a major manhunt by the Zambian Police.

30. See Cilliers, *Counter Insurgency in Rhodesia*, p. 170.

31. *Ibid.*

32. Clayton, *Frontiersmen*, p. 67.

33. Interview with Kenneth Kaunda, in Charlton, *Last Colony in Africa*, p. 68.

34. K. Flower, *Serving Secretly*, p. 247.

35. For background to these tactics and irregular war in general see Yorke, 'Irregular Warfare 1900–1990'.

36. Cilliers, *Counter Insurgency in Rhodesia*, pp. 243–54 This conclusion is an erudite analysis of this critical military situation.

37. See Brickhill, 'Daring to Storm the Heavens; The Military Strategy of ZAPU 1976 to 1979', in Bhebe and Ranger (eds), *Soldiers in Zimbabwe's Liberation War*, pp. 48–72 for details of preparations for the final 'Zero Hour Plan'.

38. See principally, Lan, *Guns and Rain*; Kriger, *Zimbabwe's Guerrilla War*; and T. O. Ranger, *Peasant Consciousness and Guerilla War in Zimbabwe* (London: James Currey, 1985) for numerous references to the role and importance of African youths for both exile armies.

39. For an erudite discussion see L Scott, 'Women and the Armed Struggle for Independence in Zimbabwe (1964–1979)', *Occasional paper no. 25*, Centre of African Studies, University of Edinburgh, 1990.

40. For a harrowing analysis of this horrific incident perhaps only matched by the shooting down of two Rhodesian airliners (in one of these incidents it resulted in the massacre of surviving passengers) see D. J. Maxwell, 'Christianity and the War in Eastern Zimbabwe: The Case of the Elim Mission', in Bhebe and Ranger (eds), *Society in Zimbabwe's Liberation War*, pp. 58–90.

41. A. Alao, 'The Metamorphosis of the "Unorthodox": The Zimbabwe National Army', in Bhebe and Ranger (eds), *Society in Zimbabwe's Liberation War*, p. 109.

42. *Ibid.*, especially, pp. 125–38.

43. Burns, 'Insurgency as a Struggle for Legitimation: The Case of Southern Africa', p. 49.

# 9

# South African Exile Armies: *Spear of the Nation* and Other Weapons in the Anti-Apartheid Movement[1]

*James Higgs[2]*

## South Africans in exile: Armies, groups and guerrillas

A striking feature of South African history is the diversity of its military antecedents. One of the most celebrated of these is that of the Zulu people who visited such a crushing defeat on the forces of the British Empire in the battle of Isandhlwana in 1879.[3] Within a few years those same forces were being opposed by an even more tenacious and tactically astute foe: that of the Boer commando.[4,5] When the Union Defence Force was created in 1912, it was formed out of eight military traditions. Coincidentally, it would also be eight military units, which would eventually form the South African National Defence Force (SANDF) when it eventually came into being in the democratic South Africa.

A number of organizations and disparate groups can claim to have been associated with the armed struggle to end the South African apartheid regime. Far fewer can establish that they operated extensive operations from outside the homeland. Perhaps the most prominent in exile was the African National Congress (ANC) and it, along with the South African Communist Party (SACP) supported the formation of *Umkhonto weSizwe*, (known as MK and meaning 'Spear of the nation'). MK formally declared war on the Republic of South Africa on 16 December 1961.[6] Not the least of the ANC's significance is the fact that after the fall of apartheid, it formed the first majority-rule government in South Africa in 1994 under the leadership of President Nelson Mandela.

The Pan Africanist Congress (PAC) was formed in 1959 as a result of a division from the ANC and also developed a military wing in September 1961; *Poqo* which, in exile, was later to become the Azanian Peoples

Liberation Army (APLA). For the scope of this chapter, the ANC and MK will be considered as the principal 'army' in exile and therefore the main focus of attention. While other organizations such as the PAC did have organizations outside South Africa, their network of international contacts was less extensive and these will be considered only to set the context in which the ANC and MK operated.

Another potential confusion in the South African context could arise over the issue of the whether the apartheid regime's declaration of so-called homelands should be allowed to influence the interpretation of 'exile'. In the following considerations, Transkei, Bophuthatswana, Venda and Ciskei will be assumed to be part of South Africa, so that while important resistance took place in these regions, they, like much of the domestically generated liberation struggle, are left for consideration elsewhere.[7]

## Ideology

MK derived its ideology from a number of sources, including the liberation struggle to free South Africa from white-dominated Apartheid rule, the opposition to colonial rule and, for some, from its developing association with the communist Soviet Union. The armed component of the liberation struggle began in earnest after the ruling National Party banned the ANC and the PAC following the Sharpeville massacre and the attempted assassination of Prime Minister Hendrik Verwoerd in April 1960. For the PAC, the characterization of the enemy was itself a matter of race. One APLA commander was to say to the Truth and Reconciliation Commission (TRC):

> The enemy of the liberation movement of South Africa and of its people was always the settler colonial regime of South Africa. Reduced to its simplest form, the apartheid regime meant white domination, not leadership, but control and supremacy . . . The pillars of apartheid protecting white South Africa from the black danger, were the military and the process of arming the entire white South African society. This militarisation, therefore, of necessity, made every white citizen a member of the security establishment.[8]

## Legitimacy

The legitimacy or degree of popular support of an armed force in exile rests on a number of pillars.[9] These can be summarized as:

- political authority – the extent to which the fighting forces act under the political guidance of a body with democratic credentials;
- custom – the extent to which a 'reserve' of popular trust has been generated by the actions of the military forces and their perceived intentions;
- effectiveness – the degree of success in achieving assigned objectives;
- efficiency – the economical use of resources and their use for appropriate (e.g. uncorrupted) purposes;
- participation – the extent to which the fighting units broadly represent the people they are charged with defending; and
- symbolism – the degree to which the fighters are regarded as 'ours' by the civil population and are prepared to make material sacrifices in order to support them.

The liberation struggle claimed legitimacy from the position that apartheid was identified as a crime against humanity in international law and that its principal and internationally recognized opponents were the ANC and PAC. Perhaps more difficult to establish, is the basis of authority on which the ANC and PAC acted on behalf of a large number of South Africans. Of course, to be able to call elections or communicate easily with the mass of people would have meant the achievement of the aims of their struggle.

## Internal repression and the emergence of MK and the PAC: 1960–64

The initial period of activity is marked at the beginning by the banning of the ANC on 8 April 1960 following the Sharpeville killings of 21 March. It was marked at the end by the imprisonment in November 1964 of the leadership of MK after the Rivonia trials. During this period MK was formed, theoretically separate from the ANC but in practice subject to its political guidance. The membership of the High Command of MK is revealing in that it was made up of three members of the ANC and three of the SACP; Nelson Mandela (as chairman), Walter Sisulu and Andrew Mlangeni from the former and Joe Slovo, Govan Mbeki and Raymond Mhlaba from the communists.[10] The first actions of MK were carried out on 15 and 16 December 1961. These were essentially acts of sabotage against fixed installations, as this form of target would minimize the risk of civilian casualties. Having only just moved away from a strategy of non-violence, the ANC was at this stage still developing its ideas on armed struggle and was not to regard itself as having formally begun the armed struggle campaign until 1967.

More significant than these acts of sabotage was the beginning of a recruitment drive to send fighters abroad for military training. Groups numbering between 25 and 35 were sent to Morocco, Algeria, Egypt and Ethiopia via Tanzania, Sudan and Kenya (to name but a few). Seven activists were trained in Czechoslovakia, among them Joe Modise and four received instruction in the use of explosives in Cyprus. After initial training many went on to the Soviet Union and at least one group to China. The destination for those heading to the Soviet Union was to be Odessa, where training was to be carried out in a climate that was as close as could be found in the Soviet Union to African conditions. One of the reasons for MK entering into this form of voluntary exile was the increasing difficulty that was being experienced in training within South Africa. In all, some 23 states would host the training of what would later become known as 'Non Statutory Forces'.[11] This was a remarkable testament to the legitimacy of the liberation struggle in the eyes of the international community and, at the same time, a potential problem. The need to maintain political contact with and the support of the people at home would be an enduring issue.

During this period, the leadership of MK was working on a plan for revolutionary warfare that was revealed when in 1963 MK's leadership was arrested in Rivonia together with documents that referred to 'Operation Mayibuye'. This was an ambitious plan for the international isolation of South Africa, the mobilization of African and socialist countries in material support of the ANC and the recruitment of 7,000 people into MK to initiate a guerrilla war intended to mobilize the local population. The arrests at Rivonia together with the repressive measures increasingly employed by the South Africa authorities (notably the torture of detainees), marked the end of this stage of effective internal resistance and the shift in responsibility for the leadership of the leadership struggle to its organizations in exile.

The arrest of the High Command of MK at Rivonia was evidence both of its inexperience with covert operations and of its failure to organize appropriately. The reliance on a leadership of known individuals allowed the South Africa security forces to identify them quickly.[12] It may be that Nelson Mandela was not unaware of this danger, but recognized that in order to establish his authority and the legitimacy of the ANC and MK he knew that he had to put himself into the 'firing line'. In a sense, Mandela was to become an icon for the resistance movement, not because of his military activities but as a result of the personal sacrifice he and others were to make in prison. The tactical failure of the capture of the MK high command was to be turned into the strategic inspiration on which countless revolutionaries at home and sympathizers abroad would base their faith on the liberation cause. Ultimately, the long-term imprisonment of senior members of the ANC and MK would achieve a form of living martyrdom, a very useful tool in the armoury of the liberation struggle.

## Resistance leadership moves to the ANC in exile: 1965–73

Vladimir Shubin estimates that by the mid 1960s MK had about 500 trained fighters at its disposal, but that those infiltrated back into South Africa were quickly being arrested. The strategic situation shifted on 11 November 1965 with the Unilateral Declaration of Independence (UDI) from the Commonwealth by the white minority government of Ian Smith in Rhodesia. This act of self-imposed isolationism enabled governments sympathetic to the liberation struggle to act against Rhodesia without risking British and western disfavour.

The ANC authorized joint military action with The Zimbabwe African People's Union (ZAPU) in June 1967 and the result was what became known as the Wankie operation, the first stage of which lasted from mid August to mid September. A second stage in March 1968 resulted in the capture and death of a number of MK fighters and the withdrawal of others to Botswana where they were captured. The aim was to open up a channel for the infiltration of MK fighters into South Africa, however, the route was not established and no incursions had penetrated the homeland without capture; the operation was deemed a military failure even by the ANC. However, tactical success for an irregular formation like that of MK would never be the most important measure of its strategic significance or its legitimacy. As long as MK fighters were seen to be taking on the might of the state forces of apartheid, their actions would be the basis for building a political movement which, in the eyes of many parts of the international community, would have unimpeachable authority.

Nevertheless, following the disastrous operation in Zimbabwe, a very high level of dissatisfaction was expressed from within MK about the leadership from the ANC, notably in a paper signed by Chris Hani. The paper outlines a number of concerns in very strong language, among them; that ANC officials were receiving salaries and benefits not available to MK, that the 'internally directed activities' of the ANC's 'so-called Department of Security' were 'notorious', while being unable to analyse the lessons of the costly failures in Zimbabwe.[13] These events can be seen as a challenge to the legitimacy of the ANC leadership by the fighters on the ground and indeed the harsh discipline imposed on Chris Hani subsequently confirms that it was perceived in this way by some senior figures.

Initially, the ANC in exile was based in Tanzania, but had been required to move its headquarters in July 1969 from Dar es Salaam to the outlying town of Morogoro, signalling the nervousness of host governments at harbouring revolutionary movements with even the most impeccable credentials in their capital cities. For the ANC, this meant increasing difficulty in maintaining international communication channels.

In 1969 the ANC held its first conference in exile in Morogoro, Tanzania and discussed the Hani document and another entitled 'Strategy and Tactics of the South African Revolution'. This new approach recognized the problems experienced in Rhodesia and outlined a move towards the mass mobilization of the people in South Africa through enhanced and consolidated underground ANC machinery. Perhaps its most important function, however, was to ensure that there was no enduring split between the ANC and MK. In this sense, the challenge to the legitimacy of the leadership by the Hani paper had been turned into a determination to strengthen its claim to legitimate democratic authority. Other decisions implemented as a result of Morogoro included the confirmation that non-Africans could serve in the ANC in exile, another example of its increasing claim to act as legitimate authority for the broadest constituency of anti-apartheid politics. As a result of the increasing difficulties of maintaining a presence in Morogoro, most of the MK fighters were transported to the Soviet Union, many to a camp which had been set up to specialize in guerrilla fighting in the Crimea at Perevalnoye, near Simferopol. Many would not return to South Africa before 1972.

One other operation during this period is worthy of note; the attempt to land fighters by sea known as 'Operation J'. After extensive training in the Soviet Union, the Politburo authorized the operation in October 1970 and an MK crew set out from a naval base in Somalia in the attempt to open a sea route into South Africa. They were driven back by engine trouble and the attempt was abandoned. Some of those trained for this operation were subsequently infiltrated into South Africa having been flown to Botswana and Swaziland; the South African authorities also captured these fighters.

These operational failures, particularly those of the Wankie campaign, indicate not only the difficulties inherent in taking on the organized and well-funded forces of opposing states but also the insufficient grasp of how to play to the strengths of an irregular military force. The ANC and MK had not given enough attention to the development of sympathetic hearts and supportive minds of the civilian people who might assist them while on operations. This failure to reinforce the symbolic aspects of the legitimacy of MK needs to be set in the context of operating beyond South Africa's borders. MK needed to generate support from local populations, not on the basis of narrowly defined nationalist solidarity but on the less certain loyalties of anti-colonialism and anti-racism.

## The collapse of South Africa's buffer zone and the revitalization of internal resistance: 1974–78

The collapse of authoritarian rule in Portugal on 25 April 1974, paved the way for the independence of its colonies in Southern Africa, Angola and Mozambique. When Mozambique gained independence in June 1975, the ANC already had personnel in place in Moputo and Swaziland and were working to re-establish communication channels to South Africa. By this time the PAC were also conducting training in Swaziland; but in 1977 the Swaziland authorities banned the PAC, arrested its members, and eventually deported them away from the reach of the apartheid regime through the offices of the UN.

In the event, the uprising that began in South Africa on 6 June 1976, owed more to the spontaneous reactions of repressed students and locally based activists such, as the Black Consciousness Movement, than to the work of the ANC. Although it is true that the PAC may have contributed some guidance once it was under way. 'The Soweto Uprising', as it became known, was of enormous significance as a manifestation of the spirit of the people from which the ANC could draw both inspiration and, more problematically, recruits.

The TRC reports that MK were able to raise their second battalion from those who volunteered after Soweto and many were sent for training to camps in Angola, while others were able to pursue studies in Moscow. Two sections of MK fighters had completed their training under Cuban instruction in Angola before 1977 was over.[14] At the beginning of the following year the strength of MK outside South Africa was 1,167.[15] By 1979, Soviet instructors were replacing the Cubans[16]. However, it is also clear that the circumstances of the urgent flight from South Africa allowed many to claim educational qualifications which they did not possess and the discipline and commitment of some to the ANC was not of the highest order.[17]

## Politicization and the setback of the Nkomati Accord: 1979–84

In 1978, senior members of the SACP, the ANC and MK had under-taken a fact finding mission to Vietnam with the aim of learning the lessons that had led to the defeat of the United States by the technologically inferior, but highly motivated North Vietnamese Army. The report was completed in March 1979 and was known as 'The Green Book'. Its effect was to lead to the overhaul of the ANC/MK strategy at a meeting between the National Executive Committee of the ANC and the Revolutionary Council. In particular, there was to be a move away from rural guerrilla warfare towards an emphasis on urban activity. A closer connection between military and political objectives was also envisaged, so that the public profile of MK would be raised and support for the ANC increased.

Perhaps the most well known example of an MK attack which fitted the requirement of raising the notoriety of the ANC came in May 1983 when a car bomb killed 19 people and injured 217 in Pretoria's Church Street. 1983 was significant for two other reasons; the development in South Africa of the United Democratic Front (UDF) and the deterioration of relations between the ANC and Mozambique. An understanding had been reached between South Africa and Mozambique that would put the ANC into a very difficult position. In exchange for the cessation of South African military assistance to Renamo, President Samora Machel of Mozambique had agreed to limit military aid to the ANC. Formalized as the Nkomati Accord of 16 March 1984, it was to ban all supplies of arms to the ANC and limit the number of ANC activists in Maputo to ten. Taken together with a similar agreement that had already been reached between South Africa and Swaziland, this was to severely limit ANC/MK logistic and communications activity.

This period also saw two groups of events that represented very serious threats to the reputation and legitimate status of the ANC in exile.[18] The fact that they are well documented is due in large part to the frankness of the ANC in submitting representations on the subject. The first was concerned with the events surrounding the unmasking in 1981 of a number of spies who were suspected of working undercover for the South African security police.[19] Ad hoc military tribunals heard the evidence and passed sentence and a number of suspects were executed and at least one was tortured under interrogation.

During 1984, there was a mutiny in the MK camps in Angola which was motivated by a combination of frustration at the inability to infiltrate fighters into South Africa and a reaction against the severe disciplinary methods of the ANC's own Department of Intelligence and Security. Ronnie Kasrils described how at Viana, outside of Luanda, mutineers took control before they were persuaded to return to order.

When, three months later, there was another insurrection at Pango, killing several of their comrades, MK imposed order and executed seven ringleaders and imprisoned others at Quattro Camp. Many of these individuals were detained for years without trial.

Oliver Tambo was later to refer to some of the individuals concerned as having made 'terrible mistakes' in the methods that were being applied in the camps. The number of enquiries set up into these events are testimony to the seriousness with which a movement claiming to be fighting for the establishment of liberation and the end to undemocratic rule viewed its own shortcomings. To have reacted with any less frankness could have damaged the long-term credibility of the ANC and the legitimacy of its subsequent authority to govern.

## The struggle intensifies at home: 1985–89

A decision by the National Executive Committee of the ANC in 1986 initiated a process that became known as Operation Vula (meaning 'open'). Recognizing that the prospects of a successful resistance movement would depend crucially on the quality of its leadership, it was resolved to move senior members of the ANC into South Africa, notwithstanding the risks of capture. As well as creating an effective underground movement, the aim was also to supply it with weapons. Having received extensive training and technical support in Moscow, in 1988, MK's Deputy Commander (and subsequently the first African commander of the South African National Defence Force) Siphiwe Nyanda and Mac Maharaj were inserted into Durban. Ronnie Kasrils (subsequently Deputy Defence Minister in the administration of President Nelson Mandela) arrived in South Africa in 1989.

During this period it had also become clear that there was an increasing possibility of a negotiated political settlement. Operation Vula, then, would be run in parallel both so as to serve as an alternative strategy if the discussions failed and also to provide the ANC with a stronger political bargaining position if they were to succeed. The negotiations process came into the open when South African President P. W. Botha entertained Nelson Mandela in July 1989.

The TRC report categorizes MK's military operations after 1985 into four areas: bomb attacks on urban targets, the landmine campaign of 1985–86, engagement of members of the South African security establishment and the killing of individuals perceived as enemy agents or traitors.[20] While the urban bomb attacks were intended to be targeted at the security establishment, in fact more civilians were killed, indicating both intentional mis-targeting by MK as well as the inevitable mistakes and confusions arising from the pressures under which they were working.

The land mine campaign in the Transvaal was intended to target the South African Defence Force (SADF) and white farmers who formed the commando reserve forces. In fact the main victims were black farmers and their families. Had this activity been allowed to continue it would have represented a dangerous threat to the legitimacy of the ANC and MK actions as the casualties amongst non-combatants and potential supporters increased. The discontinuation of the operation when this became apparent was an important recognition of this fact. When MK engaged the South African security members directly the attrition rate for the guerrillas was high, particularly in the urban areas. The casualties for the apartheid regime were, by contrast, not of great military significance. Once again, it is possible to raise questions over the military effectiveness of this aspect of the MK campaign. Attacks on 'enemy agents' were routinely broadened to include black members of the police force and leaders of locally organized groups who operated vigilante style tactics. The danger to the ANC of this type of operation was that it could threaten the authority and legitimacy of the campaign if violence undertaken in the name of the struggle were to be poorly targeted or personally motivated. One MK commander assesses the operations during this time as follows:

> MK operations rose to over 300 a year for 1987 and 1988, the highest in our history. Over a third of these attacks were on the police and army. Reported security force captures of MK combatants decreased after 1987. In 1989, with MK operations still running high, the number killed and captured was 75. This figure, at a time when infiltration had increased, was an indication of the safer routes home, the improved capacity of the underground, growing links with the rural people and of more security-conscious support for MK operations... The armed struggle, as waged by MK, was promising to become more effective in the 1990s. This was one of the factors that effected the thinking of the regime, when the country's rulers decided to opt for a negotiated settlement.[21]

Whether MK would have fulfilled the potential being foretold for it by Ronnie Kasrils is not a question that can be easily settled. However, the fact remains that MK had established that it would not be eliminated by the South African authorities in the foreseeable future: that in itself was an incentive to move towards a process of political negotiation.

## The transition to democracy: From 'Spear of the Nation' to national defence: 1990–94

Following the election of F. W. de Klerk as state President in September 1989, he announced the unbanning of the ANC, PAC and SACP in February 1990 as well as the decision to free Mr Nelson Mandela and all political prisoners and the measures for the return of those in exile. What followed was one of the most confused and confusing periods in the struggle. Although the ANC announced the 'unilateral suspension of armed actions and related hostilities' in an agreement with Pretoria in August 1990, the level of violence within South Africa was actually set to rise. This was due in large part to the changing political balance within the country and the increasing rivalry between the ANC, the Inkatha Freedom Party (IFP; drawing its support from the Zulu peoples), the PAC and other groups of informally associated with these parties (sometimes called Self Defence Units) or self-appointed vigilante movements. A considerable amount of evidence supplied to the TRC links the supply of weapons to the IFP in the 1990s to the South African authorities.

Now began a crucial phase for MK – its transition from guerrilla army in exile to integrated component of the regular forces of a democratic state. What was being proposed was a breath-taking leap for all the parties involved. It would attempt to place together in one organization individuals who just a matter of months before had been engaged in a vicious and determined attempt to annihilate each other. For MK the preparation for this process began after 1990 with an increased external training programme, with additional emphasis on the skills of conventional forces. When these were added to existing strength, it put the total available for integration at 26,000. These figures indicate how large numbers of volunteers who had not been trained abroad were added to the ferce and also how existing MK guerillas would become 'diluted' by those whose experience in the struggle was not necessarily under MK discipline. Table 9.1 shows the make-up of the integrated South African National Defence Force.

The process of bargaining about the future form of the defence force of democratic South Africa was initiated in 1993 by the SADF. That the SADF was allowed to engage in discussions directly was a reflection both of the power of the organization in the regime and a recognition that if the democratization of South Africa was to progress smoothly it had to be with the collaboration of those in the SADF who might otherwise attempt disruptive measures (evidence of the emergence of a 'third force' in South Africa is well documented).[23]

*Table 9.1*   South African National Defence Force Integration[22]

| Force | Numbers |
| --- | --- |
| South African Defence Force (SADF) | 110,000 |
| TBVC ('Homeland' forces) | 6,000 |
| MK (ANC) | 26,000 |
| APLA (PAC) | 6,000 |
| Kwa Zulu Self Protection Force | 2,000 |

The key issue for MK was to be whether it would be 'absorbed' into the SADF (overwhelmed not only by the SADF's numerical superiority but also by its culture, traditions and values) or whether there would be more of a marriage of interests with compromises and concessions on both sides. The formal meeting between the SADF and MK took place between in Simon's Town in April 1993, where the substance of the discussions comprised a briefing by the SADF on its disposition of forces. MK declined an invitation to reciprocate in this manner, no doubt not only because it was not prepared for this eventuality but also because it was not yet secure enough to make itself vulnerable to the forces of the old regime.

## Conclusion: Legitimacy and struggle

While for much of the international community the legitimacy of the ANC and MK was not much questioned, for South Africans as a whole the issue was contentious and potentially extremely damaging. In the event, the democratic elections of 1994 were marked by a great deal of violence, but the greater part of it was between supporters of the Inkhata Freedom Party and those of the ANC. The emphatic victory for the ANC was an affirmation of the judgement of the majority of South Africans that the liberation struggle was justified in general even if some actions were to be assessed as violations of human rights by the Truth and Reconciliation Commission.

The military effectiveness of the campaign by MK was deeply flawed at the tactical level for much of the struggle. However, its real strength lay in the recognition that armed struggle continued to manifest the resistance of the liberation struggle and the will to continue against the might of the Apartheid State despite heavy losses of personnel. The fact that there was no shortage of volunteers for MK operations despite the prospect of death or, sometimes worse, capture, was another powerful symbol of the strength of the liberation movement.

The beginnings of the integration process that would form the South African National Defence Force marked a remarkable recognition that the leadership of the SADF had accepted the legitimacy of MK and others as the as the rightful participants in the formation of democratically sanctioned defence forces. For their part, the ANC and MK fighters recognized that the expertise of the SADF in the operation of regular armed forces could, if properly 'transformed', provide a remarkable symbol of the newly unified South Africa.

## Notes

1. The views expressed are those of the author and not necessarily those of the RMA Sandhurst or the UK Ministry of Defence.
2. I am grateful to Mark Shaw of the South African Institute of International Affairs for suggestions made during discussions at Jan Smuts House in March 2001.
3. For a contemporary account consider D. C. F. Moodie, *Moodie's Zulu War* (Cape Town: North and South Press, 1988).
4. See T. Pakenham, *The Boer War* (London: Abacus, 1979).
5. A remarkable insight into this conflict is offered by F. Pretorius, *Life on Commando During the Anglo-Boer War 1899–1902* (Cape Town: Human and Rousseau, 1999).
6. The declaration of war has symbolic significance, but no force in international law which stipulates that only states can declare war.
7. See for example H. Suzman, *In No Uncertain Terms* (Johannesburg: Jonathan Ball, 1993).
8. *Truth and Reconciliation Commission Final Report*, vol. 2, chapter 1, paragraph 21.
9. For a full exploration of this subject see J. Higgs, *Conditions of Legitimacy of Armed Forces as a Social Institution*, unpublished dissertation (University of Lancaster, 1983).
10. For insight into Mandela's perspective see A. Sampson, *Mandela The Authorised Biography* (London: Harper Collins, 1999).
11. Figures supplied by the Johannesburg Military History Museum.
12. A point made by Rocky Williams in 'The Other Armies: Writing the History of MK', in I. Liebenberg *et al.* (eds), *The Long March* (Pretoria: Haum, 1994).
13. Cited in Vladimir Shubin, *ANC: A View from Moscow* (Belville: Mayibuye Books, 1999).
14. *Truth and Reconciliation Commission Final Report*, vol. 2, chapter 1, paragraph 102.
15. Shubim, *ANC: A View from Moscow*, p. 196.
16. *Ibid.*, p. 187.
17. *Ibid.*, p. 172.
18. It should be noted that there is not the opportunity in this chapter to examine the extent of human rights atrocities committed by the forces of apartheid. For further studies on these activities see not only the five volumes *Truth and Reconciliation Commission Final Report*, also, for example, Eugene de Kock, *A Long Night's Damage* (Saxonwold: Contra, 1998).
19. These events have been the subject of a number of investigations; see report of the Skweyiya Commission of Enquiry (Centre for Development Studies,

UWC, 1992), an Amnesty International Report of 2 December 1992 and the Motsuenyane Commission of Enquiry of 1993.
20. *Truth and Reconciliation Commission Final Report*, vol. 2, chapter 1, paragraphs 144–7.
21. R. Kasrils, *Armed and Dangerous* (London: Heinemann, 1993).
22. Cited in G. Mills, 'The South African National Defence Force: Between Downsizing and New Capabilities?', Paper delivered at the Australian National University, 15 January 1988.
23. See *Truth and Reconciliation Commission Final Report*, vol. 2, chapter 7, paragraphs 497–510.

# 10
# Hopeless Gestures: Iraqi Exile Forces Since the 1968 Revolution

*Sean McKnight*[1]

'Exiled armies' is an expression that can cover a wide variety of circumstances. In the case of Iraq – unlike the armies examined elsewhere in this book – a foreign occupier has not driven an existing military force into exile. Indeed, one of the major armed alliances opposing Baghdad is only Iraqi by force of political necessity and both alliances operate armed forces inside Iraq. It is even questionable whether the terms 'army' and 'exile' are appropriate for the armed Iraqi opposition.

To describe a military force as 'exiled' implies that it still owes its loyalties primarily to the state that it has left. However, the Iraqi opposition has not really left, as it controls areas within Iraq, uneasily in the Kurdish north and very tenuously in the southern marshlands. These enclaves really represent a type of internal exile. In the case of the north, Iraq's fear of the United States has 'semi-detached' the area from Iraq. More importantly, armed Kurdish groups owe loyalty to a theoretical Kurdish state and the loyalties of many of the Shi'a Arab opposition groups are partly determined by their religion. Despite owing loyalties that detract from loyalty to Iraq, the main political groupings of Iraqi Kurds – the most inclined of the opposition to reject the Iraqi state – still couch their opposition to the Ba'thist state in terms of changing Iraq rather than breaking it up. The Patriotic Union of Kurdistan (PUK), for instance, declares that it, 'strives for the right of self-determination for the Kurdish people within a united democratic Iraq'.[2] Similarly, Massaud Barzani, leader of the Kurdish Democratic Party (KDP) declares their aim to be democracy for Iraq and autonomy from Iraq'.[3] It thus seems reasonable, cautiously, to label the armed Iraqi opposition as 'exiles', while accepting that they lack the simple loyalty to a homeland of some exiled movements.

But if the situation of the armed Iraqi opposition is complex, only a minority of states in the modern world command uncomplicated loyalty from their citizens, and few exiled forces have the opportunity to form a completely conventional army. Most of the eleven million Iraqis – 11 per cent of the population – who have fled their country have done so for political reasons; providing a large pool from which the opposition can recruit.[4] It is also possible to question whether the armed Iraqi opposition is an army. It is certainly the case that – with the exception of some Kurdish forces – they did not constitute an army prior to exile. The label 'army' implies some of the qualities of a conventional force, as opposed to an insurgent, rioter or bandit, and much of the military activity of the Iraqi opposition is unconventional. However, the persistence, and at times quasi-conventional nature, of opposition operations against the Iraqi regime, make it appropriate to use the label 'army'.

## Iraqi exile armies: Fertile soil, poor crops

At first glance Iraq appears to offer a good place to grow exiled armies. Since the creation of the Iraqi state there have been armed groups that have challenged the regime of the day, and large numbers of Iraqis have been alienated from their various governments. It is also fairly easy for Iraqis to obtain weaponry, particularly small arms. Several of Iraq's neighbours are willing to host anti-regime Iraqis, and Iran is willing to provide substantial military support for such groups. Indeed, given the unpopularity of the Ba'thist regime it not surprising that many outside observers have predicted its imminent demise at several times in the past decade. There are numerous Iraqi opposition groups – the US State Department counted 82 in 1988. However, many are small; the Free Iraqi Council (FIC) apparently only has one member, others are internally divided and several are suspected of being controlled from Baghdad.[5] The view from Baghdad that, 'this opposition has no roots or existence in Iraq and that its elements have no activity outside the hotels, restaurants and intelligence centres of London, Washington and other Western capitals'[6] only echoes western reservations about the opposition.

Not all the Iraqi opposition can be so lightly dismissed; the main Kurdish group are the Kurdish Democratic Party (KDP), founded in 1946, and the rival PUK founded in 1975, both possess thousands of armed supporters. Smaller groups such as the Iraqi Communist Party are fairly well organized and practised at conspiratorial politics. Finally, there are the Islamic groups (principally Shi'a) such as *al-Dawa Islamiya* (Islamic Call) and the *al Majlis al-A'la lil Thawra al Islamiya fi al'Iraq*

(Supreme Assembly for the Islamic Revolution in Iraq – SAIRI) who potentially command even more armed supporters than the Kurdish groups. Unfortunately for the opposition, Kurdish, Marxist and Shi'a resistance movements are not natural recipients of Western support, indeed, they are often overtly hostile to Western interests. The 'respectable' face of the Iraqi opposition is the Iraqi National Congress (INC) that forms only part of the opposition and has little in the way of its own armed forces. The armed opposition is concentrated in three areas, the Kurdish north, the marshes of the south and inside Iran. In the north, opposition forces are dominated by the Kurds, but there are smaller armed groups representing Iraq's other ethnic minorities such as the Assyrians and Turkomans, and there are some Arab forces who in the main are deserters from the Iraqi Army. In the south a dwindling group of armed Ma'dan (marsh Arabs), and Iraqi Army deserters hold out in the marshes. A larger force of armed mainly Shi'a Arabs are based in Iran. It is the Arab Shi'a and the Kurds – operating in exile and in internal exile – who constitute the bulk of the armed forces of the Iraqi resistance.

## The Kurds: Iraq's internal exile army

With the exception of General Qasim (1958–63) Iraqi governments since 1958 have been intensely Pan-Arab, making it harder to accommodate all the Kurds within Iraq's political structure. This culminated in the Ba'th's fusion of Arab nationalism, 'socialism' and totalitarianism – a fusion made all the more effective by the massive increase in oil revenues available to the government. It is thus unsurprising that since 1961 Baghdad has been unable to resolve its Kurdish problem. Kurdish resistance to Baghdad takes three broad forms; armed Kurds across the border, mainly sheltering in Iran; Kurdish guerrillas in the mountains of northern Iraq; and, when things were going very well for the Kurds, quasi-conventional forces in control of a liberated zone.

When the Iraqi monarchy was overthrown in 1958, the Kurds saw themselves as partners in the new Iraqi Republic – much as the current Kurdish leadership envisages its role in a post-Saddam Iraq. Several prominent Kurdish exiles were allowed to return, including Mustafa Barzani who in his 11 years of exile, had been involved in the short-lived Kurdish Mahabad Republic in Iran and while in the Soviet Union held the rank of General in the Red Army.[7] However, the Qasim regime broke its promises of Kurdish autonomy, fearing it would lead to independence and distrusting the powerful Iraqi Communist Party in which the Kurds were influential. Fighting erupted when Qasim enticed the Zibaris, a rival Kurdish tribe, to attack the Barzanis. This proved ill-advised, as the Barzani victory over the Zibaris, and the increasing military activity of the Iraqi Army in the north, persuaded the KDP to join the fighting, so that what could have been dismissed as a tribal conflict now had a legitimate claim to being a national uprising. The defeat of an Iraqi brigade in October 1961[8] gave further impetus to the rebellion. The forces loyal to Barzani grew rapidly from 600 in 1961 to 5,000 the following year, with a further 5,000–15,000 armed Kurds from other tribes also taking up arms against the Baghdad government.[9]

Since 1961 the Kurds have continuously maintained their own armed forces, although their war with Baghdad has been punctuated by periods of truce. The main type of Kurdish military activity against Baghdad has been guerrilla warfare. However, on at least four occasions anti-government Kurdish forces have temporarily waged a more conventional style of warfare. These peaks of the Kurdish struggle against Baghdad have seen guerrilla forces within Iraq joining with armed Kurds from across the border and attracting defections from Kurdish forces serving Baghdad. The Kurds claim several victories in battle over the Iraqi Army, and military successes such as the 1966 'Battle' of Handrin[10] that have often been followed by temporary political gains. In the middle 1960s and 1970s and again during the 1980–88 Iran–Iraq War and most recently in the aftermath of the 1991 Gulf War, Kurdish military activity appeared on the verge of winning major concessions from Baghdad, but in all these cases high hopes have eventually been frustrated.

By far the best chance for the Iraqi Kurds to achieve a measure of autonomy came in the aftermath of the Gulf War. Indeed, for a few days in 1991 it seemed as though the Kurds would be instrumental in overthrowing the Ba'thist regime. Although these hopes were not realized, the Western military threat was sufficient to force Iraq to accept the creation of the Kurdish safe haven as a kind of mini-state. Until 1996 it provided the INC with the opportunity to establish something that resembled an Iraqi government in exile.

In 1991 the *intifada* in southern Iraq triggered a spontaneous rising in the Kurdish north. This in turn led to large-scale defections from the 250,000 strong force *Salah al-Din*, a force of Kurds ostensibly loyal to Baghdad and known derisively as the *Jahsh* (a play on the similarity of the words for army and donkey) by anti-government Kurds. These events persuaded the KDP, led by Masaud Barzani (Mustafa's son) and the PUK lead by Jalal Talabani, to commit their experienced *Peshmergas* guerrillas to the uprising. Despite the rivalry between the KDP and PUK, which has driven both parties to ally with Baghdad at various times, the two parties genuinely cooperated in 1991. Saddam's humiliating defeat in the Gulf War, the uprising in southern Iraq and rumours that the United States would intervene on behalf of the opposition, appeared to give the Kurds their window of opportunity.

Within days Kurdish optimism appeared justified, swelled by the *Jahsh* there were possibly 400,000 Kurds in arms against Baghdad, and, having taken an estimated 100,000 Iraqi troops prisoner, the Kurds had access to substantial amounts of military equipment.[11] Hitherto the KDP and PUK had drawn their strength largely from the mountainous rural areas, but in 1991 they made a big, and fairly successful, effort to win over the urban Kurds – hitherto reasonably quiescent Iraqi citizens. Ironically the fiercest resistance faced by Kurdish forces in the first few days was from the exiled Iranian National Liberation Army, the armed wing of the *Mojahideen e Khalq*.[12] When on 20 March the major northern city of Kirkuk fell into Kurdish rebel hands it appeared that the Ba'thist regime was on the verge of collapse.

The collapse of the Kurdish revolt was, if anything, even more spectacular than its initial success. Indeed, so rapid was the collapse that it is hard to analyse why the Kurdish military failure was so spectacular. The forces of neither the KDP, nor the PUK, were able to make the transition from unconventional to conventional warfare. Kurdish forces proved incapable of using the substantial arsenal of ex-Iraqi Army heavy equipment they acquired; artillery pieces lay idle for lack of firing pins and the Kurdish rebels proved to be incapable of matching ordnance to weaponry.[13] Factional division within the Kurdish movement also produced poor command and control.

The speed of the Kurdish retreat into the mountains was, in part, a result of the Kurd's decision to avoid any last ditch stands in the face of the Iraqi Army's offensive. However, the military failings of the Kurdish uprising make it clear it is difficult to develop a conventional army in exile, and that the transition from unconventional guerrilla warfare to the set-piece battles required in conventional warfare is not an easy one to make. In the absence of whole hearted and long-term support from a host state – even Iran's support for the Kurds was spasmodic and half-hearted – the Kurds were always going to find it difficult to meet the demands of conventional warfare.

The fact that the Kurds lack a reliable cross border state sponsor is an important factor preventing their armed movement from being more effective. Turkey and Iran are the two most logical sponsors of a Kurdish movement, in terms of their self-interest and the guerrilla-friendly mountain ranges contiguous with their borders. However, there are substantial Kurdish minorities in both Turkey and Iran, and both states have had to fight against Kurdish separatists. Understandably neither Turkey nor Iran is willing to give whole-hearted support to the Iraqi Kurds. Arab nationalist Syria has been less supportive, and in 1997 it even turned against Arab opponents of Baghdad when it suppressed the Radio Voice of Iraq.[14] Turkish and Iranian ambivalence to the Iraqi Kurdish struggle in turn makes the United States cautious in its support of the Kurds.

Another major problem for the Kurds is the factionalized nature of Kurdish politics. Indeed, it could be argued that the Iraqi Kurdish movement is little more than a collection of warring tribes with very parochial, and often very conservative, agendas.[15] Significant numbers of Iraqi Kurds are prepared to support Baghdad and in every conflict with the Iraqi government there have been Kurdish forces fighting with the government forces. One of the factors that lead to the collapse of the 1991 uprising was the arrival of suitcases full of cash that persuaded several *Jahsh* leaders to stay loyal to Baghdad and others to defect.[16] Other Kurds have more worthy motives for supporting Baghdad. 'Ubaidullah Barzani, Mustafa's son, joined the Ba'thist National Front in 1974 because of the Ba'ths commitment to "socialist" objectives.'[17]

There are also sharp divisions between the Kurdish groups that oppose Baghdad dating from before 1961. Within the KDP, which Mustafa Barzani had helped found in 1947, there was a major schism between the Barzanis, who had a very conservative agenda and those like Jalal Talabani who advocated social reforms. A major factor driving Mustafa Barzani into confrontation with the Iraqi government was Qasim's favourable reception of rival Kurdish tribes such as the Herki, Surchi and Zibari.[18] When fighting started in 1961, the KDP initially held aloof regarding it as an inter-tribal dispute and, perhaps, hoping to see Barzani cut down to size.[19] In July 1964 Barzani set up a rival KDP and this division was formalized in 1975 when Talabani formed the PUK. Unfortunately for Kurdish aspirations, these two factions have fought other Kurds, including each other, at least as often as Iraqi government forces. In the 1980s the KDP was obliged by its Iranian sponsors to fight against Kurds struggling for autonomy in Iran. Currently the PUK is engaged in a feud against the Turkish Kurdish Workers Party (PKK). Most traumatically in 1996 the KDP allied with Baghdad to defeat its PUK rivals. With this sorry history of internecine dispute and self-interest it is tempting to conclude that there is in reality no Kurdish movement.

However, the circumstances of the Iraqi Kurds make it hard for them to create a united movement; unreliable sponsors, limited resources and above all the strength of Baghdad conspire to promote the parochial and divisive. Over the years the Ba'thist regime's response has been ruthless and brutal. It made no attempt to distinguish between Kurds and anti-government Kurds in its genocidal anti-Kurdish *Anfal* campaign. The *Anfal* campaign of 1987–88 was the first of several large-scale exercises in ethnic cleansing. Chemical weapons were used against Kurdish towns, there were mass executions and forcible relocation; according to Kurdish sources over 180,000 died.[20] The events of 1991 make it clear that unified action is possible, but they also make it clear that this can happen only in very unusual circumstances. The prognosis is not very favourable for Kurdish aspirations.

## The Shi'a: The reluctant exile army

Over the past 40 years the Kurds have appeared the more formidable of the various groups of the armed Iraqi opposition. Yet in many ways it is the Islamist groups who are better placed to challenge seriously the Ba'thist regime. The majority of the Iraqi population is Shi'a Muslim. Moreover, Islamist groups attract considerable support from Iraq's alienated Shi'a. However, these groups also draw support from outside this Arab Shi'a core. *Al-Da'wa* claims to be 10 per cent Sunni and there are over 1,000 armed Kurdish supporters of SAIRI.[21] Whereas the idea of a Kurdish led government of Iraq seems inherently unlikely, the vast majority of Iraqi Islamists are ethnically Arab, which makes them credible claimants for power.

The origins of the modern Shi'a-dominated Islamist movement in Iraq can be traced to the 1950s, when, far from being a threat to the Baghdad government, Islam was in decline. Modern secular movements, such as Arab nationalism and communism, had substantial appeal and young Iraqis, particularly the educated, were turning away from religion. Symptomatic of the decline of Islam was the dramatic decrease in the numbers of religious scholars studying at the Shi's shrine cities of southern Iraq.[22] That this decline was arrested was partly due to the charismatic Shi'a cleric, Sayyid Muhammad Baqir al-Sadr, who preached that Islam needed to embrace modern political and social possibilities. This campaign of Islamic renewal was supported by the Ayatollah Mushin al-Hakim, the most widely respected senior Shi'a cleric of Iraq in the 1960s, who provided the funds to establish new Islamic libraries, schools and religious centres. However, *al-Da'wa*, which al-Sadr helped found in 1968, was initially not a revolutionary movement. The Shi'a tradition of quietism – acquiescence to the authority of the (Sunni) state – inclined most Iraqi clerics to adopt peaceful tactics even when they reluctantly entered the political arena. Indeed, in 1965, Ayatollah al-Hakim, and most of the Iraqi Shi'a clergy, gave a frosty reception to the revolutionary ideas of a fiery clerical exile from Iran: the Ayatollah Ruhullah Khomeini. That the Islamist movement became increasingly revolutionary and violent was largely a result of the policies pursued by the Ba'thist regime after 1968.

From the early days the Ba'th regime has followed a policy of 'religious cleansing'. In 1969 an estimated 20,000 Shi'a were expelled from Iraq followed by 40,000 Fayliya Kurds in 1971 – their Shi'a beliefs making them doubly suspect.[23] These substantial expulsions were dwarfed in the 1980s when an estimated one million Iraqis, almost all of them Shi'a, were deported.[24] These mass expulsions were given a veneer of legitimacy since over two million Iraqi citizens are described as of Iranian origin on their citizenship documents.

The Ba'thist government has also attacked the independence of the Shi'a clergy, by removing their independent incomes and confiscating the funds of their religious foundations, since they believed clerics who depended on a government salary would be more compliant. During the 1970s, Islamic schools were abolished, instruction in Islam was removed from government schools and recitations from the Koran were no longer given on radio and television.[25] There has also been a systematic attack by Baghdad against senior clerics who are critical of the regime. Several clerics have been executed, most notably the Ayatollah al-Sadr in 1980, and many more have disappeared into custody or have just been murdered. Typical of these murders was the 1999 killing of the al-Sadr's cousin, Ayatollah Muhammad al-Sadr, and his two sons, two weeks after his sermon calling for the release of political prisoners.[26] Since 1980 at least 11 Ayatollahs have almost certainly been killed by the regime and hundreds of clerics have disappeared.[27] The family of the Ayatollah Mushin al-Hakim has suffered from the particular venom of the regime. In May 1983 alone over 100 were arrested of which six were immediately executed, followed by ten more in early 1985.[28] The execution in May 2000 of the Imam of the Al-Mushin mosque, Shaykh Ali al-Ka'bi, demonstrates that the systematic killing of senior Shi'a clerics continues.[29]

Given Ba'thist policy it is not surprising that Shi'a opposition to the regime became increasingly violent during the 1970s. The Ayatollah Sayyid Muhammad Baqir al-Sadr, already under house arrest, made a special tape for followers urging that, 'In the present situation Islam needs not reform, but revolution.'[30] The formal recognition of Saddam Hussein's pre-eminence in the regime in 1979 only confirmed that the choice was war against the regime or total acquiescence.

However, many of Iraq's Shi'a citizens did not allow their religion to define their politics – the appeal of more secular loyalties that helped spark the Islamic revival of the 1950s still remains strong. Even Iraqis who are revolutionary Islamists are not united in one movement; they are divided into different groups reflecting local affiliations and the Shi'a tradition of adherence to individual senior clerics. For example residents of Karbala are more likely to join the Islamic Task Organization (*Munazzamat al-'Amal al Islami*), but in Najaf it is *al-Da'wa* that the activists join. Despite the aspirations of SAIRI to bring these groups under its aegis the Islamists remain divided. There are even some senior Shi'a clerics who cooperate with the government, for instance in 1983 the prominent Najafi cleric, Sheikh Ali Kashifa Ghita chaired the government sponsored Popular Islamic Conference and branded the Ayatollah Khomeini a heretic.[31] A significant proportion of Iraq's Shi'a still follow the quietist approach. The Grand Ayatollah Abolqassim al-Khoei continued to eschew involvement in politics until he became reluctantly involved in the 1991 *intifada*, dying while in government custody in 1992. However, unlike the Kurds, the Shi'a element actively supporting Baghdad is relatively unimportant and the different groups in arms against the regime only attack each other verbally.

Since the 1970s the various Shi'a movements have waged a guerrilla war against the Ba'thist regime. The relative lack of publicity the Islamist struggle in Iraq has received in the West does not adequately reflect the serious nature of the challenge faced by the Ba'thist regime. The fatalities suffered by Islamist groups, 500 *al-Da'wa* activists up to 1980 and at a conservative estimate 5,000 by the mid-1980s,[32] suggest that their struggle has been intense. There have been numerous attempts to kill Saddam Hussein himself, the closest to success being an attack on the Presidential motorcade in 1983 near the village of al-Dujayl; the attack killed several bodyguards and pinned down the party for several hours.[33] There have also been attempts to kill other senior Ba'thists, for instance a grenade attack on the then Foreign Minister Tariq Aziz in 1980 and more recently SAIRI claims of attacks upon Tahah Yasin Ramadan and the deputy prime minister Muhammad Hamzah al-Zubayi.[34] Larger scale guerrilla activities have also been undertaken. The Islamist movement marked the twentieth anniversary of the execution of Ayatollah Baqir al-Sadr with several attacks, notably a rocket attack on the Republican Palace in Baghdad.[35]

## Iran and the Shi'a exile army

The Shi'a groups have also had the opportunity to create quasi-regular forces, largely because of the willingness of Iran to sponsor their struggle. While the Shah ruled Iran he was understandably ambivalent in offering support to Iraq's Islamists. However, the Islamic Republic of Iran could afford to be much more whole-hearted in its support, since Iraq's Shi'a neither threaten the integrity of the Iranian state nor its religious ideology. Iran already provided a refuge for large numbers of Iraqi exiles, but these numbers were to rise dramatically during the Iran–Iraq War (1980–88). The Islamists were able to recruit from Iraqi deserters and prisoners of war. The support of Iran has enabled SAIRI to move beyond possessing a formidable guerrilla force to attempting to create an army in exile.

The SAIRI armed forces inside Iran are organized into the *Basij*, who are lightly armed unpaid volunteers given a basic military training, and more formidable *Badr* Brigade. The *Badr* Brigade, which includes the *Hamza* force of ex-Iraqi prisoners of war, is trained by *Pasdaran* (the Iranian Revolutionary Guards) and has engaged in both conventional and guerrilla fighting. However, it lacks heavy weaponry and played a very modest role in conventional operations during the Iran–Iraq War. It is also very difficult to put an exact figure on the numbers of troops at SAIRI's disposal, even allowing for the fluctuations generated by the flow of events. Some experts suggest the figure is as low as 2,500.[36] Others talk of a Badr Corps organized into an Infantry Division, an Armoured Division and a guerrilla unit, which including Shi'a Kurds gives SAIRI an armed force of 40,000. At least 5,000 trained men from the Badr Brigade deployed into southern Iraq in 1991.[37] More recently SAIRI has talked about moving 20,000 fighters into Iraq.[38] The effort made in 1991 suggests that SAIRI command a substantial armed force, but that Iraq hopelessly outclasses it.

## The Badr Brigade and the 1991 uprising

The *intifada* in southern Iraq was sparked of by a spontaneous popular uprising which owed little to Iraqi opposition. The first anti-regime violence may well have been the rising on 28 February 1991 in the *Sunni* towns of Abu'l-Khasib and Zubair.[39] The revolt spread quickly to major urban centres of the south and for the first few days considerable numbers of Iraqi troops made common cause with the rebels. Indeed, it seemed as if the fall of the regime was imminent. Initially the *intifada* included Sunni and many Shi'a who hitherto had been uninvolved in any opposition activities, as well as the Islamist activists.

For the rebels to achieve a battlefield victory they needed either the support of an outside power, or for most of the Iraqi armed forces to make common cause with the rebels. However, the United States made it clear that it would not intervene in Iraq's civil war, not even to the extent of giving the rebels access to captured Iraqi arms dumps. American reluctance to intervene discouraged senior Iraqi commanders from changing sides, indeed the American administration rebuffed efforts of the opposition to put them in touch with senior officers who were considering making common cause with the rebels.[40]

The intervention of exiled Iraqi Islamist forces was to be equally disastrous for rebel hopes as that of American non-intervention. Within a couple of days of the commencement of the uprising up to 10,000 armed members of SAIRI's *Badr* Brigade crossed the border into Iraq. Their presence ensured that the rebellion in the south became increasingly stridently Islamic – this despite SAIRI's promises to other groups in the Iraqi opposition not to advocate an Islamic state.[41] However, the *Badr* Brigade, and the more zealous of the rebels, ensured the agenda in the south would be violent and intolerant. Symbolic of the attitude of SAIRI's army was their arrival brandishing a plentiful supply of spiritual ammunition – pictures of the Ayatollah Khomeini and other clerics – then going straight into decisive action against the bars and casinos of Basra.[42] So called Islamic courts sprung up and executions for *Kufr* (heresy) fanned the violence against any Iraqi complicit with the Ba'thist regime. The cry '*la sharqiyya, la gharbiyya, jumhouriyya Islamiyya*' (no east, no west, we want an Islamic republic) alienated many in southern Iraq and ensured that the United States would not abandon its policy of non-intervention. Only in the holy city of Najaf, where the Grand Ayatollah al-Khoei reluctantly assumed authority, did the uprising avoid the decent into extremism, although even here an estimated 500 members of the security apparatus were killed by the rebels.[43]

While the Shi'a extremists alienated potential rebels, Baghdad sought to conciliate its disaffected soldiers. The government announced a pardon for all deserters on 4 March, and went on to demobilize older conscripts and discharged the retired officers who had been called up during the Gulf War. Troops that remained loyal received cash bonuses and extra food rations.[44] Many well-armed and politically reliable sections of the Iraqi armed forces, in particular Republican Guard formations, had not been involved in the fighting in Kuwait while others deployed into the Kuwaiti theatre of operations survived the debacle. With a rapidity that startled the outside world Saddam assembled a force more than capable of crushing the rebellion in the south. This force, made up of Republican Guard formations, loyal Sunni and Yazeedi army formations, was immune from Shi'a clerics calls for fellow Muslims not to fire on fellow Muslims.

Facing this overwhelming force the rebels in the south nonetheless continued to resist. Government forces using armour, Scud missiles, heavy concentrations of artillery and helicopter gunships crushed the rebellion. Fighting was particularly fierce in the holy cities of Najaf and Kerbala, where rebel forces fought a last ditch stand from the precincts of both cities' holy shrines. The BBC journalist description of the retaking of Baghdad makes the ferocity of the conflict clear: 'Tanks moved in and cleared the opposition street by street. The damage was worse than anything suffered during the war with Iran or the Allied bombing. Dogs ate the bodies of the dead, left where they fell as a warning to the population. The executions began.'[45] It is hard to estimate the casualties of the uprising, 25,000 dead is a conservative figure. The intensity of the fighting indicates just how serious a challenge the uprising was to the Ba'thist regime.

Unlike the Kurds in the north anti-regime forces in the south have no real protection from government forces other than the extensive marshlands by the Iranian border or by going into exile. Indeed, since 1991 the Iraqi government has intensified its programme to eradicate the marshes. Iran provides a sanctuary for Iraq's defeated Islamists, but with Iran building bridges to the outside world the future of these exiles is uncertain. Although the armed Iraqi Islamists are not as divided as their Kurdish allies the 1991 uprising revealed some major weaknesses. Contrary to the popular picture of Shi'a Muslims in the West, many Iraqi Shi'a, while hostile to the Ba'thist regime, are unwilling to embrace a fundamentalist creed. Even if the rebellion had kept the support of most Iraqi Shi'a, the terrain of the south is very favourable for conventional operations. A successful rebellion either needs the support of a large part of the Iraqi armed forces or external intervention – the *Badr* Brigade was not an adequate substitute.

## Conclusion

It is tempting to conclude by reiterating the weaknesses of the Iraqi opposition, but this would be misleading, as the failure of the Iraqi opposition is more a comment on the Iraqi government's strengths than opposition failings. The Ba'thist regime, fully aware it is not popular, maintains an effective totalitarian apparatus. The Ba'thist regime's strength deprives the opposition of easy options and exacerbates their pre-existing fault lines. The very thing that gives the Kurds their strength in opposing the regime – their Kurdishness – makes it hard to forge bridges to other Iraqis and nearly impossible to attract defections from Saddam's loyalist core. In the long term the Arab Shi'a have to be seen as a more formidable threat to the regime. However, most Shi'a seeking to join internal exile forces in the dwindling remains of the marshes, or externally in Iran, are likely to be zealots whose Islamic agenda does not enjoy widespread support. The tendency to Shi'a extremism, which is in many ways foreign to the traditional attitude of the majority of Iraq's Shi'a, has been strengthened by exile in Iran. The Iraqi case brings out the problem of exiled armies, particular those facing a domestic rather than a foreign enemy. Being in exile may permit an opposition to arm and indeed to develop an army, but this very process makes it harder to attract wider support at home. This leaves the recourse to force; in Iraq it is only likely to succeed if an exiled force triggers mass defections from government forces. The armed Iraqi opposition has yet to solve this conundrum.

## Notes


1. The views expressed are those of the author and not necessarily those of the RMA Sandhurst or the UK Ministry of Defence.
2. *The Program and Political Platform of the Patriotic Union of Kurdistan: Adopted in the First PUK Congress 1992*, found at http://www.puk.org/aboutpuk.htm
3. BBC Mon ME1 MEPol from the *Al Khalij* (Sharjah) newspaper 2 September 1999, found on BBC World Monitoring Service, July–December 1999, CD Rom (BBC, 2000).
4. Rend Rahim Francke, 'The Opposition', Fran Hazelton (ed.), *Iraq Since the Gulf War* (London: Zed Books, 1994), p. 153.
5. Laurie Mylroie, 'The Administration, Congress and Iraqi Opposition', *Federation of American Scientists*, found at www.fas.org/news/iraq/1998/06/980618-in.htm
6. BBC Mon ME1 MEPol sm from an Iraqi TV broadcast of 3 December 1997, found on BBC World Monitoring Service, 1997, CD Rom (BBC, 1998).
7. Stephen C Pelletiere, *The Kurds and Their Agas* (Carlisle Barracks: Strategic Studies Institute, US Army War College, 1991), pp. 4–5.
8. Francois-Xavier Lovat, *Chronology of the KDP: Major Events of KDP History*, found at http://www.kdp.pp.se
9. Phoebe Marr, *The History of Modern Iraq* (Boulder: Westview Press, 1985), p. 170.
10. *Ibid.*, p. 200.
11. Peter W. Galbraith, *Civil War In Iraq* (Staff Report to the Committee on Foreign Relations United States Senate, May 1991), p. 3.
12. Kanan Makiya, *Cruelty and Silence* (London: Penguin, 1993), p. 85.
13. Galbraith, *Civil War In Iraq*, p. 4.

14. BBC Mon ME1 MEPol jw, the London based *Al-Sharq al-Aswat* newspaper 24 July 1997, found on BBC World Monitoring Service, 1997, CD Rom (BBC, 1998).
15. This line was argued very strongly by Stephen C. Pelletiere in his paper for the US Army War College.
16. Makiya, *Cruelty and Silence*, p. 86.
17. Peter Slugget 'The Kurds', in Deborah Corbett *et al.* (eds), *Saddam's Iraq: Revolution or Reaction* (Zed Books, London, 1989), p. 197.
18. *Ibid.*, p. 191.
19. *Ibid.*, p. 193.
20. Din Kakai, 'The Kurdish Parliament', in Fran Hazelton (ed.), *Iraq Since the Gulf War* (London: Zed Books, 1994), p. 131.
21. Joyce N. Wiley, *The Islamic Movement Of Iraqi Shi'as* (Boulder: Lynne Rienner Publishers, 1992), p. 3.
22. Figures given in Wiley, *The Islamic Movement Of Iraqi Shi'as*, p. 74 suggest a fall from over 12,000 pre 1914 to 1,954 in 1957 of whom only 326 were Iraqi.
23. *Ibid.*, p. 48.
24. *Dialogue*, (London: Public Affairs Committee for Shi'a Muslims, July 2000), p. 3.
25. Wiley, *The Islamic Movement Of Iraqi Shi'as*, p. 47.
26. *Dialogue* (London: Public Affairs Committee for Shi'a Muslims, March 1999), p. 1.
27. *Annual Report on International Religious Freedom for 1999*, 9 September 1999, United States Department of State, found at http://www.state.gov/www/global/human_rights/irf/irf/_rpt/1999/irf_iraq99.htm/
28. Wiley, *The Islamic Movement Of Iraqi Shi'as*, p. 60.
29. Iraq Report, vol. 3, no. 15 (22 May 2000), *Radio Free Europe/Radio Liberty*, found at http://www.rferl.org/iraq-report/index.html. Al-Ka'bi was the imam of the Al-Mushin Mosque in the shi'a al-Thawra suburb of Baghdad.
30. *Ibid.*, p. 64.
31. Dilip Hiro, *The Longest War* (London: Paladin, 1990), p. 107.
32. *Ibid.*, pp. 62–3.
33. Marr, *The History of Modern Iraq*, p. 303.
34. BBC Mon ME1 MEPol sad from *Al-Jazeera* TV, Doha 18 August 1999, found on BBC World Monitoring Service, July–December 1999, CD Rom (BBC, 2000).
35. Iraq Report, vol. 3, no. 15 (22 May 2000).
36. Anthony H. Cordesman, *Iran and Iraq* (Boulder: Westview Press, 1994), p. 226.
37. Makiya, *Cruelty and Silence*, p. 90.
38. BBC Mon ME1 MEPol lfjb/kam from the newspaper *Al-Ittihad* (Abu Dhabi), 19 February 1999, found on BBC World Monitoring Service, January–June 1999, CD Rom (BBC, 2000).
39. Abd al-Jabbar 'Why the Intifada Failed', in Fran Hazelton (ed.), *Iraq Since the Gulf War*, p. 106.
40. Galbraith, *Civil War In Iraq*, p. vii.
41. Makiya, *Cruelty and Silence*, p. 82.
42. *Ibid.*, p. 90.

43. Eric Goldstein, *Endless Torment: The 1991 Uprising in Iraq and its Aftermath* (New York: Human Rights Watch, June 1992), p. 50.
44. Dilip Hiro, *Desert Shield to Desert Storm* (London: Harper Collins, 1992), p. 400.
45. John Simpson, *From the House of War* (London: Arrow Books, 1991), p. 365.

# 11

# The Great Lakes: Crucible of Exiled Armies?

*Stuart Gordon*[1]

## Introduction

In the 1990s, much of the Great Lakes region was convulsed in violence with a death toll in excess of 2.75 million. Conflicts in Rwanda, Burundi, Zaire and Uganda, while not simply caused by, nevertheless share Hutu and Tutsi animosity as a common factor in their own unique conflict environments. The genocidal conflict between Hutu and Tutsi in Rwanda has also been a central factor in the creation of a variety of 'exiled' armies in the region.[2] This chapter examines the emergence of several of these exiled armies and considers the social and political processes at work in their creation. Moreover, it describes how the politics of internal political exclusion are a root cause of conflict within the region.

## The genesis of conflict in Rwanda

The hatred between Hutu and Tutsi is anything but primordial in nature. The pre-colonial relationship between Hutu and Tutsi was not defined simply in traditional 'ethnic' terms. It was a clientelistic and hierarchical relationship rather than a relationship built upon the more traditional tribal model of 'parallel existences' found in many other African states.[3] While the Tutsi clearly enjoyed the upper hand in this relationship, a common language, loyalty to the same feudal political structures, social mobility between ethnic groups and intermarriage created an unusual degree of normative and social cohesion between the two groups.[4] Belgian colonial rule in Rwanda and Burundi (Ruanda-Urundi) undermined this arrangement. Racial stereotyping of the Hutu (Bantu) as less intelligent and the Tutsi (Nilotic) as more sophisticated led to the Belgian colonial administration favouring the Tutsi both politically and socially. Tutsi pre-eminence in the colonial order hardened the social stratification by reinforcing the political, economic and social disadvantages of the Hutu despite the fact that they comprised 80 per cent of the population. The creation of a racial hierarchy, underpinned by administrative tools such as identity documents, proved a remarkably durable tool for ensuring social order and stratification. However, in the aftermath of the First World War the Belgians themselves undermined their instruments of control. The educational and evangelical zeal of Flemish missionaries served to erode Tutsi dominance. As the wave of decolonization broke upon central Africa, educationalists raised the consciousness of the Hutu people and showed them 'that they were a vanquished people ruled over by Ethiopians...who resented utterly the consequent humiliation and what seemed to them a progressive enslavement.'[5]

Decolonization in the 1950s accelerated the growth in Hutu political consciousness. The emerging Hutu elite agitated for change. In March 1957 they published the 'BaHutu manifesto', which demanded 'reforms in favour of the MuHutu (Hutu) population' subjected to a 'Hamite monopoly on other races which had inhabited the country earlier and in greater numbers.'[6] This new consciousness precipitated violence against the Tutsi population, further polarizing their respective senses of ethnic identity. After independence from Belgium, elections in 1961 led to a landslide victory by PARMEHUTU (the Hutu emancipation party). The ensuing violence against the Tutsi population led to over 20,000 deaths and the flight of another 200,000 Tutsi to neighbouring Uganda.[7] These refugees retained a desire to return to Rwanda, particularly in the face of persecution within Uganda, and were ultimately to form the Rwandan Patriotic Front (RPF).

Not surprisingly, the first Hutu Republic in Rwanda was founded upon a policy of ethnic exclusion and a belief that all Tutsi were subversives. Tutsi political leaders and all non-PARMEHUTU were suppressed or sent into exile and, by 1965, Rwanda was a single-party, Hutu-dominated state. A militarily coup in 1973 brought to power Juvenal Habyarimana, a Hutu officer, who continued in power until the eve of the genocide in 1994. Habyarimana's 'Second Republic' continued the policy of formal ethnic exclusion preventing Tutsi from entering government service, limiting their access to secondary and higher education and restricting their political representation. The politics of exclusion added to the grievances of the Tutsi population within and outside of Rwanda. However, these factors, while necessary, are not sufficient to explain fully the genocide of 1994. Endemic poverty and the impact of external manipulation were also major causal factors.

Rwanda is economically 'weak' in a variety of senses. It boasts Africa's highest population density per acre and is almost totally dependent upon the export of raw commodities – in particular coffee and tea – 99 per cent of its export revenue results from these exports. The structural weaknesses lay behind two critical sources of tension: poverty and competition for land. This is a particularly dangerous admixture in an ethnically divided land. During the 1980s Rwanda's economic problems were exacerbated by dramatic changes in the prices of Rwanda's principle export commodities. The 1990 *Economist Intelligence Unit* (EIU) country report for Rwanda points to a halving of Rwanda's earnings from exports between 1984 and 1989.[8] By the 1990s, the virtual collapse of the Rwandan economy increased competition for scarce economic resources, indirectly accentuating tension between ethnic groups.

The end of the Cold War saw the active promotion of liberal economic and political values by external actors particularly by the US. This provided a means for stemming what John Pender describes as Africa's own 'moral malaise-reflected in dictatorship, corruption and state intervention'.[9] While it is questionable as to whether the US was genuinely committed, both in terms of political will and the application of real resources to this policy, it is clear that Rwanda's poverty made it exceptionally, and perhaps *uniquely*, vulnerable to *any* pressure from the US. The Hutu-dominated military dictatorship in Rwanda was among the first to be so pressured. While Habyarimana's military dictatorship was unlikely to be sustainable in the long term, a process of democratization carried with it a variety of associated and unintended consequences. External democratization pressure served to weaken the grip of PARMEHUTU, reduce the power base of more moderate Hutu opinion and enable more radical groups to emerge. Furthermore, the evolution of multiparty democracy within Rwanda threatened to marginalize the RPF in its camps on the Uganda–Rwanda border. The 'RPF was an unknown entity inside Rwanda' and it was 'viewed by many as a foreign force'.[10] Nevertheless, its response to this process was swift. On 1 October 1990, three months after the initiation of democratization, the RPF invaded. This invasion caused 800,000 Hutus to flee southwards, further legitimizing and substantiating Hutu fears of Tutsi rule. In effect, democratization delegitimized the Habyarimana regime, dictated the political agenda of the RPF as well as encouraging their invasion.

While the US zeal for spreading democracy effectively eroded the Habyarimana regime, France worked to shore up the budding Rwandan 'democracy'. The RPF's invasion in 1990 was a short-lived affair. By the end of October, Zairian, Belgian and French troops had blocked the RPF's advance and forced a cease-fire agreement. This demonstrated Habyarimana's dependence upon France. Not without some cause, the RPF invasion was portrayed within Rwanda as a Ugandan invasion supported by a fifth column of Rwandans. As such it offered a pretext for the further suppression and exclusion of Rwanda's remaining Tutsi and disloyal (or moderate) southern Hutu.

The failure of the RPF invasion led to a vast increase in essentially bilateral international involvement in the conflict. Habyarimana's army, at the time of the invasion, numbered only 5,200.[11] Regular French troops supervised from October 1999 the massive expansion of the Rwandan Army from 5,200 to over 40,000 a year later.[12] While the French government has not disclosed what armaments were supplied to Habyarimana's regime, Africa Rights has been far more specific claiming that 'at least $6 million worth in 1991–92, including mortars, light artillery, armoured cars and helicopters' had been transferred.[13] The French also played a key role in training the 1,500 strong Presidential Guard, the Reseau Zero (a death squad) and the Interahamwe militia, both of which were complicit in the genocide.[14] However, France did not simply organize, train and equip the militias. It deployed troops in combat and supporting roles in response to both the 1990 and 1993 RPF offensives. In effect the Habyarimana regime was utterly dependent for survival upon French military assistance.[15] This made it unable to resist calls for 'democratization'.

## National liberation exile army: The Rwandan Patriotic Front (RPF)

The RPF began clandestinely in 1979 as the Rwandese Alliance for National Unity. It recruited Tutsi refugees in southern Uganda for service in Yoweri Musevini's Alliance for National Resistance Army (the NRA). The NRA seized power in Uganda in 1986. Tutsis occupied several key command appointments within the NRA. Musevini certainly encouraged Rwandans to join his army. They clearly provided a loyal 'hub' within the organization, helping him to consolidate his grip. However, the Rwandan refugees were willing participants and beneficiaries in this project. Through membership of the NRA they opposed the hostility of the Ugandan State toward its southern peoples. Membership of the guerrilla army also provided the youth with a sense of purpose and individual benefits, vital factors for a displaced and dislocated refugee population. In the resource-starved areas of southern Uganda, membership of a guerrilla army provided a means for social advancement and even survival (for the poorest youths and the orphaned children).[16] Consequently, membership of the NRA, for the Tutsi population, became associated with self-preservation, and a raft of individual social and economic benefits. Most importantly, it promised a return home that would put right the injustices perpetrated against the Tutsi people in the 1960s and destroy a corrupt and unreformable Rwandan government.

By the end of the 1980s many Ugandans resented the presence of a large number of Rwandan Tutsi and their privileged position within the NRA. Musevini found this difficult to sustain politically. Furthermore, Western bilateral and multilateral donors demanded military demobilization as part of 'good governance' conditions attached to aid. This presented opportunities to the RPF who were able to obtain US funding in order to 'demobilise' from the NRA. However, this did not represent genuine demilitarization. Having detached themselves from the NRA, Rwandan Tutsi were able to form homogenous Rwandan units.[17] Furthermore, from December 1987 the movement became increasingly dedicated to the pursuit of the right of return to Rwanda. This obviously implied overthrowing the ethnically particularist Habyarimana regime.

Despite harbouring the aim of returning home, RPF links with the Tutsi population in Rwanda remained very limited; making any return to its Rwandan homeland less of a 'People's War' than a war *for* the people. During the RPF advance into Rwanda in 1990 it failed to develop a wide base of support among the Tutsi population or even attempt to create an effective civilian administration in areas that it had captured. This represented a missed opportunity and, consequently, the majority of Hutu and even Tutsi, fled the liberated areas. Consequently the result of increasing RPF success on the battlefield was only to further polarize Rwandan society.[18] The widespread use of atrocities and terror tactics by RPF and Ugandan troops added to the fear of the Hutu population and stimulated recruitment to the Hutu militias: the Interahamwe (the militia of the revolutionary Movement for Reconciliation and National Development – MRND, the reformed PARMEHUTU party) and the Impuzamugambi ('Those who have the same goal')[19] and the militia of the Coalition for the Defence of the Republic (CDR). RPF troops also destabilized the Rwanda–Zaire and Rwanda–Tanzania borders.

The RPF were as dependent upon external sponsorship as was the Habyarimana regime and, to some extent, this explains the rapid expansion of RPF troop numbers. The RPF was a highly motivated, militarily experienced and well-educated force (allegedly the RPF had the highest percentage of graduates of any guerrilla army in the world).[20]

In October 1990 it numbered only 2,500; however, by April 1994 it numbered well over 25,000.[21] The UK and the US provided training to the RPF through the NRA while Uganda provided training directly. The Americans also provided Paul Kagame, the RPF chief of staff, with staff training at Fort Leavenworth. From 1990 Kagame restructured the RPF and using Western military supplies provided through Kampala, began to wage guerrilla war against the Habyarimana regime.

The process of undermining the Habyarimana regime's power base was accelerated by attempts at conflict resolution brokered by the US and France. After the failure of regional efforts, France and the US hosted a series of negotiations in Arusha, Tanzania, from July 1992.[22] The Arusha Accords, signed in August 1993, represented at best enormous constitutional change, at worst, surrender for the Habyarimana regime. The Habyarimana regime acceded to the settlement from a position of profound weakness. France had withdrawn the last of its troops in December 1993, leaving the regime without external support. Even Western aid donors increasingly channelled aid through the RPF, ultimately cutting even International Monetary Fund and World Bank credits to Habyarimana's regime in early 1994.[23] The creation of a multiparty democracy called for in the Arusha Accord undermined the power base of Habyarimana's regime. The President's role was relegated to an essentially ceremonial position, while reducing ministerial representation to only five out of the 21 Cabinet posts. Arusha also saw a reduction of Habyarimana's control of the judiciary, local government and the army. In contrast, the RPF saw its importance, in terms of control of the structures of government, increased enormously. It was allocated five ministerial positions as well as half of the senior commands within the new Rwandan army. Its troops would also make up some 40 per cent of the lower ranks of the army and a battalion of them would be stationed in Kigali in order to protect Tutsi politicians. For an organization that had little real legitimacy within Rwanda, the Arusha Accords elevated it to a status far beyond what it could conceivably have achieved through the ballot box.

The effect of the Arusha Accords was to further polarize Rwandan society. For Habyarimana's MRND party Arusha was little more than a capitulation to the RPF. The political instability unleashed by democratization and the Arusha process was translated into genocide through the endeavours of hard-line Hutu politicians, including Habyarimana's wife, to prevent the implementation of Arusha. As such, Rwanda's genocide was a means of maintaining political power in a state where the ruling party had been forced to relinquish its grip.[24] The catalyst for this violence occurred on 6 April 1994. Habyarimana's aircraft was shot down over Kigali as he returned from Arusha. Over the ensuing six months 800,000 people died. The violence was aimed at exterminating any that supported the RPF or the process of democratization; in effect anything and anyone who undermined Hutu supremacy. The genocide was brought to an end through the agency of a successful invasion of Rwanda by the RPF. As they advanced, nearly two million Hutus (those responsible for the genocide as well as the 'civilian' population), fearful of revenge attacks, fled Rwanda into neighbouring Zaire and Tanzania. The exiled RPF returned home.

## Widening instability: Eastern Zaire

The flight of the Hutus from Rwanda triggered general instability in the region. The arrival in Eastern Zaire of large numbers of Hutus upset the delicate balance between the Zairian Tutsi and Hutu populations; causing widespread violence in North Kivu province. The events particularly impacted a small group of ethnic Tutsi called the 'Banyamulenge' who resided in and around Mulenge in both South and North Kivu provinces in eastern Zaire. The sense of political identity held by the Banyamulenge had emerged as a response to the Zairian leader's (Mobutu Sese Seko) attempts to deny them Zairian citizenship and property rights from 1981. As a consequence of Mobutu's persecution, the Banyamulenge had increasingly described themselves as 'Banyamulenge' rather than 'Tutsi'; thereby stressing their Congolese rather than Rwandan associations. However, to most Congolese the Banyamulenge could never be anything more than Rwandan Tutsi. In the aftermath of the Rwandan genocide the Banyamulenge became strategically vital to the RPF and to the Zairian rebellion. To the RPF they became a vital component in their security strategy; they could provide a stable western border and hold the vengeful Hutu militias in check.[25] The Banyamulenge, however, were motivated more by an instinct for self-preservation than anything else.

The 1994 influx of between one and two million Hutus strengthened the Zairian Hutu presence in the region and destroyed the delicate relationship between the two communities of exiled Rwandese. The Hutu refugee population settled in enormous numbers around the Zairian towns of Bukavu and Goma and reinforced the Burundian Hutu refugee population that had fled their homeland during the violence that followed the assassination of President Melchior Ndadye in October 1993. This new population, however, did not simply comprise refugees. The camps contained large numbers, perhaps as many as the 50,000, former Forces Armées Rwandaises (FAR) and Interahamwe militia. These militia were armed and immediately began preparations for a re-invasion of Rwanda. They also attacked the local Banyamulenge. Tensions within the region were further exacerbated by the economic burden on the local population caused by the arrival of such a large population. This contributed to conflict between the ethnic groups over basic economic resources: food and land. Consequently, Hutu FAR and Interahamwe militias joined the local Hutu and used the opportunity to attack and ethnically cleanse Banyarwanda Tutsi, particularly in the Massisi hills in North Kivu province. Local Kivu politicians and Zairian troops and police encouraged the expulsion of the Tutsi from Zaire and the latter supported Hutu extremists logistically and militarily. Thus the Banyamulenge faced both marginalization by Mobutu's state and physical threats from the vast and growing Hutu refugee population. The impact upon the Banyamulenge of both Zairian persecution and the threat from the Hutu FAR, the Interahamwe militias and the local Banyarwanda Hutu served to alter their sense of political identity. Instead of being Congolese Tutsi, they became far more associated with Rwandan Tutsi. A similar process worked with the Hutu blurring distinctions between Congolese Hutu and those expelled from Rwanda and Burundi.

In August 1996, Ugandan, Rwandan and Burundian government troops covertly crossed the border in support of the Banyamulenge and concentrated their attacks against the Hutu refugee camps. They drove the incumbents into Rwanda or killed them in what appeared to be a reciprocal act of genocide. The threat posed to Rwanda by the remnants of Habyarimana's army and the genocidal militias led first to Rwandan, and then Ugandan involvement. Rwanda's motives, at this stage, were twofold: helping the Tutsi Banyamulenge to defend themselves while also creating a security zone on the Rwanda-Zaire border. There was also some evidence to suggest that Zaire's Mobutu was actively supporting the remnants of the Habyarimana regime through the shipment of arms to the refugee camps. This represented a profound threat to both the Rwandan and Burundian governments. Simon Massey quotes from an unnamed senior UN official who stated that 'Rwanda is defending its own vital interests, but the military initiative that has recently taken amounts to playing with matches near explosives.'[26]

Yoweri Musevini explained that Uganda's involvement was precipitated by the threat of another genocide: 'There was a genocide pending in eastern Congo. The Hutu was about to move against the Banyamulenge. This provoked the conflict between Rwanda and Zaire and we supported Rwanda materially to defend itself against these barbaric forces.'[27] While this may explain the timing of Uganda's support it is quite likely strategic considerations also drove its involvement. Zaire had been used as a base area by Uganda's own subversive exiled armies, the Lord's Resistance Army, the smaller West Nile Bank Front and the rather mysterious Allied Democratic Forces (located in the Ruwenzori mountains or 'Mountains of the Moon' on the Congo–Uganda border). Ugandan intervention in the unstable Kivu area would therefore help in stabilizing southern Uganda. Kagame and Musevini, however, faced widespread accusations that they were intent on creating the precolonial Tutsi-BaHima Empire, spanning from Uganda to Burundi and from Kivu to Rwanda.[28] Musevini himself did not help this when he rather mischievously asked 'what's wrong with having empires? For me, I am interested in this empire building. In the past empires were built by conquest. Now we should unite people by discussion not conflict.'[29]

## Intrastate exiles: The rise of the AFDL in Zaire

The Rwandan (and Ugandan) strategy for dealing with instability on its western border crystallized in the shape of support for a loose coalition of Zairian rebel forces known as the Alliance of Democratic Forces for the Liberation of Congo (AFDL). The AFDL was in fact an amalgam of four parties: *Parti de la Revolution Populaire* (the PRP and Kabila's own party); the *Conseil National de Resistance pour la Democratie* (CNRD); the *Mouvement Revolutionnaire Pour la Liberation du Zaire* and the *Alliance Democratie des Peuples* (ADP).

Laurent Kabila, a shadowy figure in Zairian politics, led the AFDL. He held this position for a number of reasons. Allegedly he had strong links with Uganda's Yoweri Musevini and Tanzania's Julius Nyere having fought alongside the Tanzanian troops that overthrew Uganda's Idi Amin Dada in 1979. He also fought alongside Musevini's NRA during the 1980s, conceivably also coming into contact with the Rwandan Tutsi exiles who constituted a major part of that Army. Furthermore, Kabila possessed some revolutionary credentials; having the distinction of serving alongside the Cuban revolutionary Che Guevara in the mid 1960s.[30] Whilst Kabila was the titular head of the AFDL, he was not the principal architect nor did he provide the majority of men and material. It is clear that the AFDL was dominated by the Rwandan and Ugandan governments. In such a context, Kabila provided a means for legitimizing the Zairian rebellion and remodelling it from what would otherwise appeared to have been a foreign invasion by the Tutsi peoples. His links with Zaire's domestic political opposition, in particular Etienne Tshisekedi were the key to this. Tshisekedi, as leader of the Union for Democracy and Social Progress had been something of a standard bearer for democratic reform in Zaire. Hence there was a necessity to provide the rebellion with a Congolese character.

The AFDL was also supported by another regional power, Angola, in revenge for Mobutu's long-standing support for UNITA (Uniao Nacional para a Independencia Total de Angola). Angola provided both logistical and direct military support through what was, in effect, another exiled army: the Katangan Gendarmes. Angola had long been the home of Congolese who had fled the bouts of violence during the 1960s. The first wave comprised the Lunda from south Katanga and the Katanganese gendarmes who had originally been mobilized by Moise Tshombe, a leader seeking autonomy for Katanga after Congo's independence in 1960. The second wave of exiled soldiers was from Bandudu province and arrived in the mid 1960s. By 1996 few of these original exiles remained militarily active, but the second generation saw Kabila's rebellion as an opportunity for return. Angola supported the return of the Congolese exiles but, it was 'unclear what the mix of gendarmes and "real" Angolan forces was'.[31]

The AFDL seized Kinshasa, the capital of Zaire, on 17 May 1997 forcing the regime of Mobutu Sese Seko to collapse and consigning the name 'Zaire' to history. The speed with which Kabila's AFDL swept through the forests of eastern Zaire was an enormous surprise. It covered over 1,000 miles in little more than seven months. The success of the AFDL in defeating Mobutu's regime was a product of a number of factors. However, it was clear that it was not simply the strength of the organization but also the weakness of Zaire's institutions that were critical in this. It is difficult to assess the balance between the failure of Mobutu's army and the success of the AFDL. Mobutu's army failed to stand and fight, was undisciplined (manifest in the numerous cases of pillage and rape perpetrated by the retreating army) and badly led.

The AFDL's military 'victory', however, could not be translated into a political one. Rosenblum has argued that 'for some years the people of Zaire had been struggling to liberate themselves without the use of violence'. In effect there was a 'culture of resistance that had undermined the authority of the Mobutuist state'.[32] It also undermined the legitimacy of Kabila's new regime. Kabila's legitimacy was further undermined by his own style of leadership, a style that echoed that of Mobutu. This led to the breakdown of the Alliance, which brought him to power and ultimately to conflict between the various parties that supported him. Kabila's link with Tshisekedi failed almost as soon as Mobutu was swept out of power. Tshisekedi had been elected in 1992 to lead a transitional government drawn from the National Conference.[33] Mobutu's refusal to accept this electoral mandate led Tshisekedi to 'cling to the legal fiction that he remained Prime Minister by virtue of the National Conference'.[34] The National Conference was viewed by the majority of Zairians as 'an indispensable mechanism for setting in motion the democratic transition'.[35] Soon after capturing Kinshasa, Kabila sought to dismiss the National Conference in an obvious attempt to consolidate his own grip on power. However, Kabila's failure to gain legitimacy derives from additional sources. In essence, his politics, steeped in ideological views with its Pan African, pseudo Marxist orthodoxy from the 1960s was no longer fashionable in Zairian civil society.

Furthermore, Kabila's failure to engage effectively with Zaire's civil society ensured that the AFDL could not regenerate the legitimacy lost through the breakdown of Kabila's relationship with Tshisekedi. Under Mobutu, organized elements drawn from civil society, the non-governmental organizations and Church-based groups (particularly the Catholic Church), had assumed responsibility for many functions traditionally performed by the civil services in more functional states. Mobutu controlled state spending directly diverting much of Zaire's revenue into his personal accounts.[36] In effect Mobutu's corruption led to the almost total neglect of public services. Non-governmental organizations also had strong links with donor governments and organizations in the north. Consequently, they could mobilize support domestically and internationally; they also represented a means for scrutinizing the AFDL, the Zairian army and Kabila's new administration.[37] While some authors suggest that Zaire was virtually ungovernable as a result of Mobutu's rule, it was equally ungovernable without the support of Zairian civil society.[38] Thus the failure of the AFDL to effectively win support in Zairian civil society is perhaps its most fundamental error.

Kabila's armed forces also became increasingly divided following their 'victory'. Once Mobutu had been ousted, Kabila and his Rwandan allies turned the attention to restructuring of their disparate and incompatible military forces. Kabila's new army comprised some 4,000 Banyamulenge; 20,000 new recruits or Kadogas (recruited in the Westward march against Mobutu); and 8,000 Katanganese Gendarmes and as many as 70,000 ex Mobutu FAZ (Forces of Zaire). The Banyamulenge proved to be less concerned with Congolese politics than security in Kivu. The former FAZ were the reverse, demonstrating little concern for Tutsi and Rwandan security and resenting the heavy Rwandan presence and role in the Congolese forces. Furthermore, the Kadogas resented

Kabila's favouritism towards his Katanganese allies whom he placed in command appointments and within the presidential guard.[39] An increasingly widespread Congolese resentment of Kabila's linkage with both Rwanda and the Banyamulenge ultimately caused him to shed these allies. In mid-1998 Kabila yielded to anti-Tutsi sentiment. First he sacked his Tutsi Chief of Staff; then he expelled all Rwandan and Banyamulenge troops and 'cleansed' the government of Banyamulenge politicians.

The consequences of this action were, arguably, predictable. Uganda, Rwanda and the Banyamulenge reacted violently; supporting another loose coalition of rebels designed to oust Kabila. In many ways Kabila could, and should, have predicted that Uganda and Rwanda would react so robustly to his attempt to end his relationship with them. It was apparent to many outside observers that Kabila and his external sponsors were bound not in a relationship of love but of convenience and, from Rwanda's point of view, of necessity. Kabila offered Rwanda a means of providing for security on her western border. His refusal to deliver the security zone that had led them to support him in the first place led to both Uganda and Rwanda ending their support for Kabila in order to seek other proxies. One exile army in Zaire was in effect to be replaced by others.

## Conclusion

The RPF's return to Rwanda from its base in Uganda gives it all the hallmarks of the classic national liberation exile army. Traditionally, the concept of an exile army assumes that borders delimit a government's authority and that 'exile' begins once a state's physical and legal borders have been crossed. In the context of the Great Lakes, and perhaps any failing state, such distinctions are far less vital. The lack of consistency between ethnic distribution and legal, international boundaries between different states makes such a distinction lack utility. 'Exile' becomes more one of a question of armies existing beyond the control of a declining central state authority. Thus, it is fair to say that the concept of 'state failure' confuses the idea of 'exile'. Consequently, an army, which exists in an overt form beyond the effective reach of the state, regardless of whether it exists beyond the borders, may be described as existing in a condition of exile. Such was the case of Kabila's AFDL coalition of intrastate exiles.

Many reasons lay behind the Great Lakes region spawning so many exile armies. The formation of 'exiled' armies has been a product of the struggle for political participation and power within a multiethnic state, tensions over the control of basic resources (particularly land) and the increasing availability of conventional weapons, enabling challenges to the state's monopoly of violence. It is also clear that involvement by external actors has a dramatic impact on the fortunes of several of these exiled Armies. Ugandan, American and British support for the RPF; Angolan, Ugandan and Rwandan support for the AFDL and the Banyamulenge; and even French support for the Habyarimana regime (ultimately spawning the exiled Hutu militia armies in Eastern Zaire) were clearly critical in their survival and their differing successes. However, in the case of AFDL the linkage with external patrons was also an element in its demise after the fall of Mobutu. The failure to deal effectively with the issue of external, principally Rwandan, patronage was a failure on Kabila's part.

It is also clear that an exiled army must develop effective links with the population it hopes to rule or suffer potentially devastating political consequences. The failure of the RPF in Rwanda to develop links with both the Tutsi population and, perhaps even more importantly, the Hutu population within Rwanda, led to a further polarization of Rwandan society. In Zaire, Kabila's general unpopularity resulted initially from his unwillingness to introduce democratic reform or to engage effectively with Zairian civil society. His obvious dependence upon the Rwandan Government and the Banyamulenge served to erode what was left of his popularity. In these conditions Kabila, opportunistically, ended his relationship with both external sponsors and the Banyamulenge, an act that spawned yet more rebellion and, arguably, confirming the Great Lakes as the breeding ground for exiled armies.

## Notes

1. The views expressed here are personal and should not be taken as representing the policy or views of the British Government, Ministry of Defence or RMAS.
2. G. Prunier, *The Rwanda Crisis: History of a Genocide* (New York: Columbia University Press, 1995), p. 367.
3. R. Howard, 'Civil Conflict in Sub Saharan Africa: Internally Generated Causes', *International Journal*, 11(4) (Winter 1995–96), 27–53.
4. *Africa Research Bulletin*, 33(10) (October 1996), p. 12421.
5. J. Fenton, 'A Short History of Hutu Authoritarianism', *New York Review of Books*, 15 February 1996, 7.
6. C. Williams, *Aux Sources de l'hecatombe Rwandaise* (Brussels-Paris: L'Harmattan, 1995), p. 46.
7. P. Uvin, Development Aid and Conflict: Reflections from the case of Rwanda (UNU/WIDER/RFA 24: Helsinki, 1996), p. 7, website: http://www.unu.edu/hq

8. Between 1987 and 1992 it fell 17 per cent and in 1993 it fell by 8 per cent alone. *Rwanda Country Report* (London: The Economist, 1994), pp. 1–3.

9. John Pender, 'Understanding Central Africa's Crisis', 9 September 1999, Africa Direct London, website: http://www.africadirect.net

10. *Rwanda Country Report* (London: The Economist, 1994), pp. 1–3.

11. On French military support to the Habyarimana regime see: 'Arming Rwanda', *Human Rights Watch*, London, 1994, website: http://africapolicy.org

12. Pender, p. 6.

13. African Rights, *Rwanda: Death, Despair and Defiance*, 2nd edn (London: Africa Rights, 1995), p. 62.

14. G. Prunier, *1959–1994 History of Genocide* (London: Hurst, 1995), p. 64.

15. See also: K. Rupesinghe (ed), *Conflict Resolution in Uganda* (London: James Currey, 1989).

16. For brief coverage of the problems of demobilizing RPF child soldiers see: 'Operational Focus: Child Soldier Demobilisation', in *The Conflict, Security and Development Group Bulletin* (London: Centre for Defence Studies, October 1999), p. 5.

17. 'RPF is the Ugandan Army Says Expert', *Economist Intelligence Review Briefing Note*, 19 August 1994, p. 1.

18. Federation Internationale des Droits de l'Homme: Commission Internationale d'Enquette sur les Violations des Droits de l'Homme Commises au Rwanda depuis le 1er Octobre 1990, found at website http://www.fidh.imaginet.fr

19. *Occasional paper: Project on Environment, Population and Security* (Washington DC American Association for the Advancement of Science at the University of Tauton), June 1995.

20. K. Marten, 'Eyewitness to Genocide: The United Nations and Rwanda' *Political Science Quarterly* Vol. 117, no. 3 Fall 2002.

21. Pender, p. 6.

22. For an excellent account of the failings of the Arusha process see: A. J. Kuperman, 'The Other Lessons of Rwanda: Mediators Sometimes do More Harm than Good', *SAIS Review* (Winter–Spring, 1996), 221–240.

23. Africa Direct, *From Arusha to Goma: How the West Started the War in Rwanda* (Africa Direct: London, 1995), p. 1.

24. See T. B. Seybolt, 'Co-ordination in Rwanda: The Humanitarian Response to Genocide and Civil War', *Journal of Humanitarian Assistance* – electronic journal, website: http://www.jha.sps, p. 5.

25. D. Shearer, 'Africa's Great War', *Survival*, 41(25) (Summer, 1999), 89–106.

26. S. Massey, 'Operation Assurance: The Greatest Intervention That Never Happened, Posted', *Journal of Humanitarian Assistance* – electronic journal, website: http:www.jha-sps.cam.ac.uk/a/9533.htm

27. Musevini quoted in Reuter's press release dated 16 September 1998, website: http://www.reuters.com

28. Even the Zimbabwean Foreign Minister, Stan Mudenge, added to this. See Reuters Press Release 30 August 1998, website: http://www.reuters.com

29. Reuters Press Release, 16 September 1999, website: http://www.reuters.com

30. R. Lemarchand, 'The Fire in the Great Lakes', *Current History*, 98(628) (May 1999), p. 199 quotes Che Guevara's diary, 'I always thought that he did not have enough military experience; he was an agitator who had the stuff of a

leader, yet lacked seriousness, aplomb, knowledge, in short the innate talent that one senses in Fidel the minute you meet him.'

31. Democratic Republic of Congo Report, No 3, International Crisis Group, 21 May 1999.
32. J. F. Clark, 'Democracy Dismantled in the Congo Republic', *Current History*, 97(619) (May 1998), 193.
33. For an excellent account of Tshisekedi's struggle against Mobutu through the 1990s see S. McCormick, 'Zaire under Mobutu: Master of the Game?', *Current History*, 93(583) (May 1994), 223–7. See also George Nzangola-Ntalaga, 'Beyond Mobutu', *Ibid.*, 219–22.
34. P. Rosenblum, 'Kabila's Congo', *Current History*, 97(619) (May 1998), 195.
35. See George Nzangola-Ntalaga, 'Beyond Mobutu', p. 220.
36. See W. Reno, 'Sovereignty and Personal Rule in Zaire', *African Studies Quarterly*, 1(3) (1998).
37. This was threatening to the Kabila regime given its involvement in, or at the very least acceptance of, human rights abuses within Congo. For a survey of these abuses see 'Hidden from Scrutiny: Human Rights Abuses in Eastern Zaire', *Amnesty International Report AI Index*, AFR 62/29/96, December 1996, p. 6.
38. J. Ayoade, 'States without Citizens', in D. Rothchild and N. Chazon (eds), *The Precarious Balance: State and Society in Africa* (Boulder, CO: Westview Press, 1988), p. 196.
39. Lynne Duke, 'Revolt in Congo Had Multiethnic Genesis', *Washington Post*, 27 October 1998, p. 20.

# 12
# The Kosovo Liberation Army

*Matthew Bennett*[1]

The Kosovo Liberation Army (KLA) more properly the UCK (*Ushtria Çlirimitare e Kosovës*) came to international prominence in the late 1990s, as a product of the crisis in the province of Kosovo-Metohija in Serbia. (For its Albanian population the land is known as Kosova; for cartographers; simply Kosovo.) Although some claim a history for the organization stretching back over two decades, it does not seem to have existed as a functioning institution until 1996 or 1997.[2] There was no coincidence in the sudden rise of an active, military response to Slobodan Milosevic's Serbian government's repressive policies in the region, at that time. The attempted resolution of the Balkan wars that were a result of the break-up of Yugoslavia had been reached via the Dayton Accords of November 1995. While this agreement went a long way to resolving the conflict between the major successor states of the Yugoslav federation established as result of the Second World War, it actually left the ethnically Albanian majority population of Kosovo in a worse position than ever before.[3]

## Background to the conflict

The province of Kosovo has always held a vital place in the Serbs' understanding of their history. This is a result of ancient political structures, religious institutions and military events dating back over hundreds of years into the thirteenth and fourteenth centuries. The medieval period saw the establishment of a Serbian kingdom in the Balkans and northern Greece, rising to greatest prominence under Stephen Dusan (d. 1355). This state, practising its own Orthodox Christian rite, was the victim of Ottoman expansion resulting, in part, from a famous encounter at Kosovo Polje in 1389. Although the outcome of the battle was a strategic draw, the fighting resulted in the death of both the

Ottoman Sultan Murad I and Prince Lazar (Hrebeneljanovic) a prominent Serbian commander. The battle was remembered by the Serbs in their epic poetry and the song of the 'The Field of the Blackbirds' became a crucial part of their sense of national identity during the ensuing centuries of Turkish rule. As the power of the Ottoman Empire waned in the early 1800s, the Serbs were one the first subject nations to strive for independence through their rebellion of 1804. During the course of the nineteenth century Serbian historians and literary scholars created an image of Serbian nationhood to help consolidate the new state. This national myth had at its heart the province of Kosovo with all the resonance of sacrifice and religious inspiration provided by the 'holy geography' of the region. It represents to Serbian nationalists 'the cradle of the nation' with its many monasteries, in one of which prince Lazar is buried. In 1912, as result of a round of Balkan wars, Serbia gained Kosovo. In the words of a soldier who found himself on Kosovo Field: 'Each of us created for himself a picture of Kosovo while we were still in the cradle. Our mothers lulled us to sleep with songs of Kosovo, and in our schools our teachers never ceased in their stories of Lazar'.[4]

This resonance led Slobodan Milosevic to deliver a speech on the 600th anniversary of the battle in 1989, asserting Serbian rights to the province. Indeed, it was as a result of his visit to Kosovo in 1986 that he was able to gain a sufficient political profile to challenge and replace the then President Ivan Stambolic. The fact that Milosevic's political fortunes were entirely bound up with his promotion of the Serbian minority in Kosovo was crucial in exacerbating the dispute with the Albanian majority. For the Albanians have a history as well. Their great medieval hero was George Kastrioti, known as Skanderbeg (a name which calls upon the image of Alexander the Great's military achievements), who defied the Ottomans in the fifteenth century. They formed a majority in Kosovo from at least the end of the seventeenth century when there was a Serbian exodus.[5] Kosovo is also central to Albanian nationalism because it was in Prizren in 1878 that they first tried to create a sense of self-identity (although still within the Ottoman empire).[6] The Serbian victory of 1912, while it expelled the Turks, left the Albanians subject to brutal repression, so much so that they conducted a guerrilla war in the 1920s against the royal government. The only time they held the upper hand was between 1941–45 when the Axis powers controlled the region, and when the Germans took military command in 1943 they formed the SS-Division Skanderbeg, which inflicted many atrocities on the Serbian population.[7]

When the Communist leader Josip Broz Tito and his partisans emerged triumphant at the end of the Second World War, Kosovar resistance continued for six months.[8] Tito's regime owed nothing to the Albanians and was capable of oppressive actions, as became clear upon the dismissal of his Chief of the Secret Police in 1966.[9] Yet at the same time, Kosovo did benefit from federal funding, receiving almost 50 per cent of grants to Yugoslav deprived areas.[10] In addition, although Kosovo is rich in minerals, the province saw little benefit from their extraction as they were almost entirely manufactured outside in other parts of Yugoslavia. In the field of education and culture, demonstrations in 'the year of freedom', 1968, did prompt Tito to allow closer contacts with Albania which were to prove crucial after his death. In 1974, Kosovo was granted the status of 'Socialist Autonomous Province'. This permitted flying the Albanian flag and equalized the use of the Albanian language, including its own university. Ethnic Albanians also now had access to posts in the police and administration. Yet the economic inequalities continued to rankle.[11] In the year following Tito's death (May 1980) mass student demonstrations, later allied with workers' movements, provoked a severe crackdown from Belgrade. This resulted in widespread arrests, a purge of the Party, government, academic institutions and the media, all wrapped up in show trials. Although the boot was clearly on the Serbian foot, that was not how it seemed to the Serbs. Their feeling of victimization was articulated by a group of scholars at the Serbian Academy of Sciences and Arts (in 1985), and was publicized at the Tenth Congress of the Communist Party of Serbia in 1986. They complained of a 'physical, political, legal and cultural genocide against the Serb population of Kosovo' and urged that the province be more closely bound with Serbia.[12] Milosevic took his lead from this approach and so built his popular appeal. In October 1987, this became reality as the provincial police were replaced by federal police and Serbian intervention increased. At the same time, an exodus of ethnic Serbs, and a great increase in the Albanian population meant that the balance in the populations which had been about 60:40 in favour of the Albanians a generation earlier had become 90:10.[13]

## The birth of a parallel Albanian society

So what was the Albanian response to this new oppression? With their elected parliament now declared illegal, they held a referendum in September 1991. In this poll, 87 per cent of the electorate voted, 99.8 per cent in favour of independence; but they had no means of achieving independence.[14] Under its Stalinist leader Envher Hoja, the neighbouring country of Albania had never been on good terms with

Yugoslavia, but even after his death in 1985, did not feel strong enough to challenge the might of the Yugoslav Army (VJ). So what the Kosovars did was to create a shadow state or parallel society within their province. This provided welfare, education and ran a system of taxation, with ministries of finance, justice and information.[15] Money came from abroad with 3 per cent levied on expatriate income, the funds being handled by Bujar Bukoshi who headed a government in exile.[16] The Kosovar president was Ibrahim Rugova, a French-educated intellectual, elected in May 1992, and whose moderate party the Democratic League of Kosovo (LDK) won over 60 per cent of the parliamentary seats.[17] His policy was, from the first, a pacifist one of non-engagement with the Serbian authorities. Instead he preferred to appeal to the international community on the grounds that the Kosovars were non-aggressive victims of state repression. On 16 February 1993, he presented a ten-point action plan for how the Kosovo situation might be resolved.[18] Of course, by this time the plight of the Albanian population must have seemed a side issue in the context of the greater Bosnian crisis. Although the General Assembly of the United Nations did pass a resolution on human rights in Kosovo in late 1994, it was not until the Dayton Peace Accord, of November 1995, that the writing on the wall became clear to the Kosovars.[19] And its message was grim.

## KLA: Opposition and armed resistance

After a decade of non-violent protest and appeals to the international community it was now apparent to the Kosovars that they had been abandoned to the devices of Milosevic's government in Belgrade in order that peace could be brokered in the rest of Yugoslavia and its successor states. Although there had been a couple of attacks on Serbian police in autumn 1995, it may be significant that the first declared action of the Kosovo Liberation Army, the terrorist bombing of Serbian refugee camps in the Krajina, took place on 11 February 1996, representing disillusion with Dayton.[20] It looked as if Rugova's idea of 'internal liberation' was no longer going to satisfy the aspirations of Kosovars. At the same time the money that was coming in from abroad, from the *Gastarbeiter* population in Germany or from the Albanian community world-wide, but especially in America, began to be drawn into more direct action funds such as 'Homeland Calling' rather than going to Bukoshi.[21] All this might still have come to nothing had it not been for the sudden collapse of the Albanian economy (Albania's population had got caught up in a Capitalist pyramid-banking scheme.) The army and police abandoned their posts and the armouries were thrown open. Suddenly large numbers of weapons became available for arming the KLA. Not that this meant that the KLA went onto the offensive, it mostly just occupied Albanian areas. Faced with the Serbian offensive of July 1998, the guerrillas preferred to withdraw into the hills rather than fight.[22] But the Serbs' scorched earth policy against the civilian population produced a potential humanitarian disaster.

The justification for direct action against Milosevic's regime was the increasingly violent behaviour of the Serbian police and paramilitary forces in overwhelming force. It is difficult to be sure how large the KLA was initially.[23] Potentially, the forces could have been very large indeed. Both over the border in Albania, and further afield in western Europe, there were many recruitable young men ready to come to the aid of their perceived fellow-countrymen in Kosovo. Eventually this is what led to the establishment of training camps within Albania to feed men into the conflict in the province. But this all happened on a very short time-scale, from the initial guerrilla attacks of early 1996 to the withdrawal of Serbian forces in June 1999. The actual crisis which led to the KLA's victory was of even shorter duration than that. The key event was the massacre at Prekaz in early March 1998. A man known as Adem Jashari, with a reputation as a local brigand, had been linked to the KLA which encouraged the Serbian authorities to arrest him. In the blood bath that followed, he and some 80 members of his extended family died.[24] In response there was a widespread armed uprising of a very traditional type, not really a guerrilla war. At first the KLA had the Serbs on the back foot, but a counter-offensive in July drove its soldiers back up into the mountains. The episode also provided the impetus for the first widespread ethnic cleansing that led to 250,000 people becoming refugees in the autumn of 1998. This was followed by international intervention, the arrival of the monitors from the Organization for Security and Cooperation in Europe (OSCE) and a period of uneasy peace in the province.[25]

## KLA: Structure and effectiveness

As regards organization, the KLA has been credited with 17 brigades and seven operational areas.[26] In mid-1998 western analysts were suggesting that it controlled about one-third of Kosovo's territory and possessed the capability to deny access to several major supply routes to the Serbs.[27] Yet, despite an open border policy pursued by Albania's President Sali Berisa since 1992, the KLA could not guarantee its own supply lines back into Albania. Also, while its official spokesmen Jakup Krasniqi claimed there were 30,000 men under arms, other sources suggested even higher numbers.[28] Such estimates were important for their propaganda value but probably had little meaning in reality. Interestingly, in late May 1999, towards the end of the conflict, a Pentagon briefing indicated that in March, before the bombing began, there were some 5,000 effectives in Kosovo, backed-up by 1,000 or 2,000 in Albania; and that this had grown to over 15,000 and 5,000 respectively.[29] It is pointless to wrangle over such ill-defined data, though, perhaps the more important point being how much the KLA was able to achieve in its war of liberation.

There can be little doubt that in purely military terms its contribution was extremely limited. This was not for want of determination by its members but due its lack of equipment with which to fight an enemy well-provided with armoured vehicles and heavy weapons of all kinds. KLA equipment handed in under the agreement with KFOR numbered some 10,000 Kalashnikovs and machine guns, with only a few hundred mortars and anti-tank weapons.[30] While this may not represent the totality of the weapons available, there is no evidence that the KLA ever possessed the necessary punch to contest a modern battlefield. This not what it came into being to do, of course, as originally its activities were guerrilla in nature; but the transformation from the war of the flea to a force able to contest ground against the opposition is something that liberation armies generally aspire too. The immediate result of the commencement of bombing by the North Atlantic Treaty Organization (NATO) on 24 March 1999, was the effective expulsion of the KLA by Serbian forces.[31] Its forces were able to regroup under cover of the air assault and begin to make ground against the enemy, but to what extent is uncertain.[32] Despite protestations by Western observers as early as 1996 (repeated during the conflict) that NATO should not become the KLA's air-force, this is effectively how it appeared.[33] Milosevic's submission was more likely the product of the destruction of his nation's infrastructure rather than defeat on the ground inflicted by the KLA. Doubtless he was considering his own political future as much as the convenience his fellow-countrymen; but the result was the creation of a satisfactory environment for the insertion of KFOR – without a ground war. It might be asked why, and as the KLA representatives constantly demanded, NATO did not provide the KLA with the heavy weapons it so palpably needed?[34] NATO's Supreme Commander Gen. Wesley K. Clark consistently refused such requests on the grounds that such supplies would transgress the arms embargo laid up upon Yugoslavia as a whole. This may represent Western fears that such a move might encourage

Russia to arm Serbia in a similar manner so escalating the conflict; and, to their credit, this constraint was recognized by KLA spokesmen.[35]

Indeed, perhaps the most impressive and successful operations fought by the KLA were not on the battlefield but in the media war. The Serbs did not help themselves by physically threatening and then expelling foreign journalists. Also, much of the material put out by the Serb media was clumsy in the extreme, resorting to the crudest 'black propaganda'. While this may have served to convince its home audience, the international reception of its claims was little more than derisive. NATO did direct a bombing attack on the Serbian TV station in Belgrade as this was assessed to be a legitimate target in respect of both Serbian leadership and communications. On the whole though, the Kosovar line was much better received. The KLA set up a website in Albanian and English, while the Kosovo Information Centre (a LDK venture) added German text as well, in seeking to gain international sympathy. The newspaper *Koha Ditore* also maintained a website supported by extensive pictures to convey the message of Serbian oppression.[36] In a sense, there can be no doubt that Kosovar claims of brutality and murder by the MUP were justified, although this does not mean that there were no atrocities committed by the KLA itself. In international terms, certainly, except perhaps in Russia and a few other parts of the former Soviet Union, there can be no doubt that the Serbs lost the media war.

## KLA: Legitimacy and international support

The issue of the legitimacy of the KLA was debated throughout its existence. As late as March 1998, Robert Gelbard, a senior American diplomat referred to it as a 'terrorist organisation'.[37] After all, it was engaged in attacks on the police stations and other representatives of a state whose recognition had been part of the successful negotiation of the Dayton Accords. Only when the severity of the Serbian persecution of the Kosovar Albanians became apparent did the international community begin to admit the acceptability of the violent struggle. There was still the issue, though, of who exactly the KLA represented. Ibrahim Rugova's pacifist regime, although criticized for complacency, still retained a great deal of support within Kosovo. His preparedness to be seen with Milosevic during the Spring of 1999, both before and after the war began, did undermine his reputation; although this may have been more in the eyes of the western media who had already identified the Serbs as the enemy, than in his own constituency. The die had already been cast by then, owing to the failure of the Rambouillet talks in February. That these had been effectively dominated by Hashim Thaji and the KLA voice, is clear, and provides a substantial reason for their breakdown.[38] While the Serbs may have just been biding their time waiting for the Spring weather before renewing their 'ethnic cleansing' offensive, there may have been a mutual desire for outright war. It is possible to argue that, having pressed so far down the road of military insurgency, it was in the KLA's interests to bring the situation in Kosovo to a final decision. This position is little more than a more aggressive interpretation of Rugova's 'Ten Point Plan' of early 1993, which requested United Nations (UN) peacekeeping troops and UN protectorate state as a way forward. The uncompromising line of the KLA pushed western powers into the interventionism which they had sought to avoid in the wake of the Bosnian conflicts.[39] During the fighting there can be no doubt that Hasim Thaji came to prominence as the leading representative of the liberation struggle, and Rugova seemed to have lost his moral authority. Additionally, many of the recruits into the KLA came not from the province itself, but from the economic exiles from the Albanian community, migrant workers in western Europe and the US. Their roots in Kosovo were accordingly more attenuated and their attitude to the Serbs far more confrontational than those of the community which had co-existed (admittedly grudgingly) during the decade of the 'shadow state'.[40] Interestingly, though, following the Undertaking of Demilitarization and Transformation, agreed by the KLA to take place on 20 September 1999, Rugova's party seemed to have regained its popularity. Apparently, polls conducted by Western organizations indicated that Thaji did not seem to have been accorded the gratitude of the liberated to conquering hero that he seems to have expected. The statistics indicated that the LDK still held 80–90 per cent support.[41] Seen in this light the legitimacy accorded to the KLA can be seen as at the best expedient. Yet, how frequent an occurrence in history is it that an exile army, which successfully recovers its homeland, then find itself dissolved on the orders of an international body which is capable of enforcing its instructions? At the dawn of the new millennium it is hard to be sure that the attempted disarming will work, however. Conclusions arrived at in the first year after the insertion of the NATO led Kosovo Force (KFOR) may not accurately predict the direction that will be taken by the main parties involved over a longer time-scale.

## Conclusion

As an example of an exile army the KLA has several distinct characteristics. Its emergence related to a particular political event: the Dayton Accords of November 1995. Prior to their negotiation the pacifist approach had dominated the Kosovars' response to the Serbian domination. Also, although the army was supported by a neighbouring, legitimate government, the relative weakness of the Albanian regime in the face of Serbian power meant that while the country provided a refuge for the rebels it could not get involved in more active military support. It was not until the international community became involved through the actions of NATO that the KLA was able to make any gains in its claimed territory; although the NATO air campaign was intended to coerce the Serbian government, rather to provide close air support to KLA ground forces. Even then, it took time over the ten weeks of the bombing campaign before its commanders were able to put many men into the field. Lacking heavy weapons, its impact was more symbolic than practical. Its ideology was essentially nationalistic, although there were international implications stemming from the largely Muslim beliefs of the Kosovar population. This led to support coming both from legitimate Islamic governments and some of the more radical Islamist and mujahadeen groups.[42] Certainly the former provided humanitarian support out of country; just how much the military experience of the latter contributed to KLA training is uncertain. Clearly, the Western powers who liberated Kosovo, through an overwhelming demonstration of air-power, were uncomfortable with any links to Islamic 'fundamentalist' or 'terrorist' groups. The NATO forces did not want an exile army fuelled by an ideology which they distrusted, to claim too much of a share in running the recovered territories. In this sense, the KLA did not fulfil the normal objective of an exile army of either assuming power or supporting its own civilian government. The enforced dissolution of the KLA , even allowing for its conversion into a 'defence force', meant that a crucial role of such an organization was subsumed into that of an international rescue force. The continuing uncertainty of the actual status of Kosovo – autonomous and independent (as the Kosovars would wish) – or still legally part of the Serbian Federation, might suggest that that KLA still had a role to play were it not for outside interference. However beneficent the intention of the NATO allies, they had deprived the KLA of its main intended function. Perhaps this was for the best. After all, by late 1999 it seemed that Rugova's pacifist regime had regained the political credibility and popular support, which it had ceded to the military wing of the independence movement in the lead up to the conflict and its duration. Maybe the best kind of national liberation exile army is one that can be allowed to wither away once the liberation has been achieved? The leaders of too powerful and successful a force can always be tempted to start throwing their weight around in a region which they seek to dominate through growing ambitions. Under such circumstances an exile army becomes the cause of instability and an instrument for the oppression of others, rather than a force designed to achieve political independence for its own people.

## Notes

1. The views expressed here are personal and should not be taken as representing the policy or views of the British Government, Ministry of Defence or RMAS.
2. The origins of the KLA are much disputed and subject to propagandist variation. See C. Hewitt and T. Cheetham (eds), *Encyclopedia of Modern Separatist Movements* (Oxford: ABC Clio, 2000), p. 160 gives a useful summary of its history up to June 1999. Of particular interest for this subject are: T. Judah, 'The Growing Pains of the Kosovo Liberation Army', and J. Pettifer, 'The Kosovo Liberation Army: The Myth of Origin', in M. Waller, K. Drezov and B. Gökay (eds), *Kosovo: The Politics of Delusion* (London: Cass, 2001), pp. 20–9. See also: A. Heinemann-Grüder and W. C. Paes, 'Wag the Dog: The Mobilization and Demobilization of the Kosovo Liberation Army', Brief 20, Friedrich Naumann Stiftung, Bonn International Centre for Conversion (Bonn: BICC, 2001), pp. 10–14.
3. Noel Malcolm, *Kosovo: A Short History* (Basingstoke: Macmillan – new Palgrave Macmillan, 1998) and Ben Lombardi, 'Kosovo – Introduction to Yet Another Balkan Problem', *European Security*, 5(2) (Summer, 1996), 256–78 makes the point about Dayton on p. 268.
4. Tim Judah, 'Kosovo's Road to War', *Survival*, 41(2) (Summer, 1999), 7.
5. Between 1693–97, '30,000' Serbian families [approximately 150,000 people?] fled from the Krajina into Austrian Habsburg territory following failed rebellions. See: Lombardi, 'Kosovo – Introduction to Yet Another Balkan Problem', pp. 257–8.
6. *Ibid.*, p. 258.
7. Judah, 'Kosovo's Road to War', p. 8. This persecution continued up to 1951 under the direction of a pro-Nazi group, Saban Poluzo. See also: Stephen R. Bowers and Marion T. Doss Jnr., 'Low Intensity Conflict in the Balkans', *Armed Forces Journal* (May 1999), p. 28. There also Serbian counter-atrocities during the war.
8. Tito hit those Serbs who were royalist and Mihailovic supporters equally hard.
9. Lombardi, 'Kosovo – Introduction to Yet Another Balkan Problem', p. 259.
10. Although even this did not prevent the average income being only 40 per cent of the richer regions, sliding to 30 per cent in the 1970s. Dimitrios Triantaphyllou, 'Kosovo Today', *European Security*, 5(2) (Summer, 1996), 285.
11. Lombardi, 'Kosovo – Introduction to Yet Another Balkan Problem', p. 260.
12. *Ibid.*, p. 261.
13. Triantaphyllou, 'Kosovo Today', p. 284 and his Table 1.
14. Lombardi, 'Kosovo – Introduction to Yet Another Balkan Problem', p. 263.
15. *Ibid.*
16. Judah, 'Kosovo's Road to War', pp. 11–12.
17. The Democratic League of Kosovo won 96 of 143 seats. These statistics are somewhat devalued by the fact that the Serbs did not vote and so were unable to take up any of the 14 seats allocated to them under proportional representation. Triantaphyllou, 'Kosovo Today', p. 283 and n. 19.

18. Ten Point Plan: 1. Deploy a significant number of UN or NATO peacekeeping troops to Kosova immediately. 2. Establish Kosova as a UN protectorate. 3. Put in place many more CSCE [now OCSE] monitors. 4. Extend the no-fly zone over Kosova. 5. Stop quiet 'ethnic-cleansing' of Kosova through Serb intimidation. 6. Disarm and disband Serbian paramilitary units; place all Serbian artillery under international control. 7. Re-open Prishtina Airport for humanitarian relief flights. 8. Cease colonization of Kosova by Serbia. 9. Permit the freely elected Assembly to meet. 10. Exempt Kosova from international sanctions imposed on Serbia and Montenegro. Tryantaphyllou, 'Kosovo Today', p. 282 and n. 18.
19. *Ibid.*, p. 287.
20. Lombardi, 'Kosovo – Introduction to Yet Another Balkan Problem', p. 264.
21. Judah, 'Kosovo's Road to War', p. 13.
22. In this respect the rebellion looks more like conventional armed peasant resistance to oppression, rather than a guerrilla campaign designed to over overthrow a hated regime. See for example: *Ibid.*
23. See below for a range of 'estimates' produced by KLA sympathizers and more objective outsiders.
24. Judah, 'Kosovo's Road to War', p. 13 and Chris Hedges, 'Kosovo's Next Masters?', *Foreign Affairs*, 78(3) (1999), 24–42. Hedges had actually met the Jashiris three weeks earlier and he gives graphic details of the Serbian massacre which created martyrs for the KLA's cause see pp. 35–6.
25. Mladen Klemencic, 'Kosovo: 'What Solutions for the Albanians in the "Cradle of the Serbian People"?', *Boundary and Security Bulletin*, 6(4) (Winter, 1998) 57 and Judah, 'Kosovo's Road to War,' p. 13.
26. Zoran Kusovac, 'Croat general to Lead KLA as Part of Reorganisation', *Jane's Defence Weekly*, 12 May 1999, 4.
27. Zoran Kusovac, 'KLA Power Rising', *Jane's Defence Weekly*, 8 July 1999, 21.
28. *Ibid.*, p. 21 refers to Western estimates of 40–50,000 fighting men and Albanian ones of 80,000 with over 50,000 Kalashnikovs available in the province.
29. Transcript of Rear Admiral Thomas Wilson's Pentagon briefing on 'Operation Allied Force', 27 May 27 1999, p. 1 (of 29). USIA Website.
30. Zoran Kusovac, 'Disbanded KLA to Transform in 60 Days', *Jane's Defence Weekly*, 29 September 1999, 5. Heinemann-Grüder and Paes, 'Wag the Dog: The Mobilization and Demobilization of the Kosovo Liberation Army', p. 14 cite KLA commander Agim Ceku's estimate of 20,000 although preferring the lower total of 12,000 under arms and likely fewer effectives.
31. Peter Finn, 'Kosovo Guerrilla Force Near Collapse', *Washington Post*, 1 April 1999, p. A1, URL: http://www.washingtonpost.com/wp-srv/inatl/longterm/balkans/stories/kla040199.htm.
32. Initial reports such as B. Bender, 'KLA Action Fuelled NATO Victory', *Jane's Defence Weekly*, 16 June 1999, 5 were rather over-optimistic in this respect. Gen. Wesley K. Clark, *Waging Modern War: Bosnia, Kosovo and the Future of Combat* (Oxford: Public Affairs, 2001), pp. 330–9 describes 'four or five battalions, perhaps 1,800 to 2,000 men' fighting over Mount Pastrik from 26 May to 6 June. See also Clark pp. 150, 277, 341, 344 and 351 for his cautious assessment of the KLA's military usefulness.

33. Klemencic, 'Kosovo: 'What Solutions for the Albanians in the "Cradle of the Serbian People"?', p. 58.
34. Finn, 'Kosovo Guerrilla Force Near Collapse', pp. A1–A4.
35. Peter Finn, 'Albania Asks West to Arm Rebels', 20 April 1999, p. A20, URL: http://www.washingtonpost.com. and Bender, 'KLA Action Fuelled NATO Victory', p. 5 is much more upbeat claiming that two weeks from the end of the bombing campaign the KLA 'began flushing out' Yugoslav forces to provide concentrated targets for air-attack.
36. Bowers and Doss, 'Low Intensity Conflict in the Balkans', p. 32. The authors are critical of the KLA for stage-managing a battle in Rasak to make it appear a one-sided massacre by the Serbs, p. 34.
37. Howard Clark, *Civil Resistance in Kosovo* (London: Pluto Press, 2000), p. 173 and n. 30 for changing the term to 'terrorist activities'. For the full quote, see Heinemann-Grüder and Paes, 'Wag the Dog: The Mobilization and Demobilization of the Kosovo Liberation Army', p. 15.
38. Clark, *Civil Resistance in Kosovo*, p. 181. According to Heinemann-Grüder and Paes, 'Wag the Dog: The Mobilization and Demobilization of the Kosovo Liberation Army', p. 11 'The KLA never accepted the legitimacy of the elected Rugova government'.
39. Clark, *Civil Resistance in Kosovo*, p. 188 argues forcefully that the interests of the wider Kosovar population would have been better served by 'an alternative international strategy'.
40. Bowers and Doss, 'Low Intensity Conflict in the Balkans' p. 30 and Hedges, 'Kosovo's Next Masters?', p. 31.
41. Peter Finn, 'Support Dwindles for Kosovo Rebels', *Washington Post*, 17 October 1999, pp. 1–5, URL: http://www.washingtonpost.com/wp-srv/Plate/1999-10/17/1931-101799-idx.html. pp. 1–5.
42. These have proved difficult to quantify, and no authority seems able to provide real evidence of their possible role. See for example: Heinemann-Grüder and Paes, 'Wag the Dog: The Mobilization and Demobilization of the Kosovo Liberation Army', p. 14.

# Conclusion

*Matthew Bennett and Paul Latawski*

The military and political challenges faced by exile armies are unique to the circumstances they find themselves in. Most exile armies, however, by dint of these circumstances face a common set of issues that impact on the political and military context shaping their role and their operational effectiveness. These issues include legitimacy, factionalism, ideology, relations with the host or sponsoring country, manpower problems and operational effectiveness.

Legitimacy is fundamental to the political context in which an exile army operates. Given the fact that exile armies are operating outside the territorial base of their homeland, legitimation in the international environment becomes a necessary hurdle to overcome. Most exile armies derive their legitimacy from moral, political and institutional succession from a homeland or through the self-legitimating ideological features of a national liberation movement. Among the case studies in this book, some of the armies associated with exile governments resident in London during the Second World War reflect the idea of institutional succession from governments ousted from occupied homelands. Of the examples examined in this book, Polish and Norwegian exile enjoyed this kind of legitimacy while the Czech and French examples had only a tenuous claim to such legitimacy. In the Polish and Norwegian cases the fact that they were unwilling to capitulate even after the most catastrophic of defeats added to their political and moral legitimacy. The legitimacy of the national liberation exile armies is the most fragile. The perceived justice of the cause (internationally) and the attainment of victory can create a strong base of legitimacy as the cases of South Africa and Zimbabwe illustrate in this book.

Legitimacy may even reside in an individual leader. The stubborn and forceful personality of Charles de Gaulle did much to confer legitimacy on the Free French Forces despite the reality of the re-entry into the war of sizeable forces associated with the Vichy regime. Whether or not the leader is strictly from a military background does not matter as can be seen in the role of Chandra Bose. Legitimacy can also derive almost entirely from the support of a patron power. Stalin's communist Polish army from 1943 onwards and the Cuban exile army of the early 1960s illustrate this point. It is the weakest type of legitimacy as it is derived from an external power rather than the support of the people in the homeland.

The legitimacy of an exile army, however, is a fragile thing. An exile army's legitimacy can be undermined or called into question by a number of factors. The most important of these is the fact that they are isolated from their homeland and thus are unable to consult their domestic political constituency. Re-entry to the homeland as quickly as possible is therefore a vital objective from the point of view of legitimacy. Rival exile armies or armed movements that emerged within the homeland can contest the mantle of legitimacy of any exile movement during the struggle to return and after its return.

The issue of legitimacy is rarely clear and may be disputed by rival claimants. At one extreme, in the Great Lakes example, the doubtful legitimacy of any of the players fuelled continued conflict. Obviously, the behaviour of exiled armies played a part in how they were viewed by their supporters in country. Even failure can confer legitimacy. The activities of the Indian National Army helped to set the scene for post-war independence activities. Rapine and pillage, or terrorist activities can undermine legitimacy in the eyes of that population, although they need not, and could be seen as the natural concomitant of guerrilla warfare if that that was the tool for achieving the political goal. Legitimacy can even be passed from one player to another. In Kosovo, Rugova's legitimacy was bolstered by a mandate from his people, yet he lost it to Thaci during the military phase of the independence struggle, which turned out to be brief, so he recovered his authority soon afterwards. The Norwegians were united behind their monarch who played an important role in the country's recovery. Yet the factionalized Cuban exiles proved unable to command respect from their main supporter, the American government. No matter what the status of the government an exile army seeks to topple (e.g., South Africa and Iraq), a dislocated opposition is unlikely to make inroads.

This last point highlights a very common factor shaping exile armies – factionalism. Most of the case studies indicate to some degree either overarching political division among the exile movement or rival or loosely allied exile armies. The cases of Iraqi exile forces and the multiple insurgent forces of Zimbabwe are extreme examples of this phenomenon. The multiple strands making up the French exile army and the rival Polish exile armies on the eastern and western fronts seem to illustrate how prone exile armies can be to divisions and factionalism.

Ideology provides an essential raison d'être for an exile army. By employing a wide definition for ideology it can include: theism (e.g. Catholicism and Islam), monarchism, republicanism, nationalism and Marxism. The return to the homeland, however, must not be narrowly conceived as a kind of restoration to the *status quo ante bellum* but a modern version of *reconquista*. Return often entails not only the replacement of the political order currently dominating the homeland but a more fundamental displacement that introduces revolutionary economic and social change. During the Second World War, Stalin's Polish army was a means to the end of introducing a new communist regime in Poland and all that entailed politically, economically and socially. Its creators saw the Indian National Army as an anti-colonial tool for ending British rule on the subcontinent. In more contemporary examples, the exile forces of South Africa and Zimbabwe were instruments to hasten the end of white rule in those African states. The real or perceived ideology of an exile army can also be a significant limitation on its efforts. The Kosovo Liberation Army suffered from negative perceptions in the international community of murky links to Islamic fundamentalist groups.

Ideologies are not always clearly defined. For the Czechs it was democracy (to be disappointed) for the Norwegians the restoration of the monarchy. The French desired in their return to the 'metropole', a different kind of restoration although still rooted in the French democratic tradition. It is also natural that the many opposition movements of the 1960s onwards saw Marxism as their defining ideology, especially in central and southern Africa, although the successful regimes that resulted may show little sign of this original impetus.

Ideology serves also to magnify the importance and effort of an exile army well beyond its actual military achievements. The exile army becomes a major symbol of the ideological underpinnings of the effort to regain the homeland and it perpetuates the established ideological symbols of that homeland and sometimes devises new ones to symbolize the advent of a new order. The symbolic role of ideology is most evident in terms of ceremony, badges, uniforms and flags. The adoption of the cross of Lorraine by de Gaulle's Free French forces or the modification by the Polish communist army's of the national symbol (removing the crown from the eagle) both made old symbols into something new to serve a new ideological agenda.

An exile army is inevitably dependent politically and militarily on a host nation or sponsor. A distinction may be made between a geographical host of an exile army and a more distant sponsor that supplies essential ideological and material support. The Soviet Union's role is supporting national liberation exile armies in Africa during the Cold War highlights this distinction. In most cases the roles of host and sponsors are combined as in Britain's example during the Second World War. From a practical point of view, this dependency on a host and sponsor is one of the most necessary yet most frustrating realities faced by an exile army. The scope for autonomous action by exile armies is limited by dependency for finance, training and equipment and the attending operational subordination to host-nation forces. The Norwegian case in terms of the financial independence conferred by the revenues from Norway's large merchant fleet represented an exceptional aspect of autonomy not enjoyed by other exile forces in Britain during the Second World War. In the political and military realm, the most significant risk for an exile army is its total subordination to the political and strategic aims of the host nation and sponsor. It can make the exile force a mere appendage of a foreign power. The damage can be best measured in the lack of legitimacy of the exile force among the homeland population. The ill-fated invasion attempt by the Cuban exiles in the early 1960s is a striking example of the cost of being too associated with the aims of a sponsoring power. Significant tensions can also arise regarding the operational employment of exile forces. By their very nature, most exile armies cannot mount sustained military operations and combat losses without putting in peril their very existence. Therefore questions of operational employment are very sensitive ones between exile forces and their host nations. This is a common point of friction between exile armies and their patrons particularly for larger exile armies that have considerable operational utility as in the case of the Poles in the Second World War. Relations between the exile army and host nation can in some cases be very good especially in cases were there are strong common interests or ideological bonds. At the very least each side benefits from solidarity in a common struggle. Not all of the limitations in the relationship between host nations and exile armies are borne by the latter. The cost to a host state can be great in military and economic terms by providing an operating base for a national liberation army. The case of the Rhodesian war is instructive in this regard as the front line states paid a significant price due to military operations directed against the exile forces they hosted.

Much also depended upon the wider context of the conflict in the relationship between host state and exile army. The allied victory in the Second World War, certainly secured the recovery of their states for the French and Norwegians, with a re-establishment of the status quo. The Czechs and Poles, however, drew the short straw of Soviet domination that was to render their attempts at self-rule helpless for over 40 years. In the India, there was the apparent paradox of an independence movement in arms thoroughly defeated along with its Japanese sponsor, yet the impetus for opposing the colonizing power – Britain – actually gained force and credence. This enabled a negotiated independence, initially at least, peacefully achieved. The ensuing partition was tragically violent, and proof that issues of self-realization had not been fully addressed was the Bangladeshi war of independence a generation later. Here, it was quite apparent, however sterling the efforts of internal resistance that India's role in ensuring the defeat of Pakistani forces was vital. The liberation movements in southern Africa rather found themselves at the receiving end of modern, well-equipped forces. Although the Soviet Union provided some training and weaponry, the eventual success of majority regimes was due to long, attritional conflicts which owed as much to the political arena as to the military. The USA's role in supporting 'freedom fighters' spreads the gamut from incompetence to decisive success across the decades that saw interventions in Cuba, Iraq and Kosovo (although admittedly both the scale and nature of these involvements was different in each case).

One of the central military problems faced by exile armies is the difficulty in acquiring adequate manpower for mounting and sustaining military effort. Indeed, the availability of manpower can determine the degree to which an exile army is a real fighting force. Limited manpower can reduce it to the scale of a symbolic force, one that has little military utility but serves a wider political purpose for an exile government or national liberation movement. From a practical viewpoint, exile armies generally possess an uncertain recruitment base. The core personnel that make up an exile army form part of an exodus – a geographical, political and military transfer of activity away from the homeland. Although recruitment from the homeland represents the most important source of manpower, it is also invariably the most unreliable. Matters are made more complex when the recruits from the homeland come predominantly from one ethnic or tribal group or overwhelmingly from one political movement. Because access to the homeland is curtailed or denied, other sources of recruits become extremely important. Émigré communities and enemy prisoners of war can become indispensable external sources of recruits. The consequences of this uncertain recruitment base are distinct limits on the numbers of soldiers likely to be available. Under such circumstances, commitment to operations can result in a rapid decline of effectiveness due to attrition or battlefield losses. The risk of being 'bled white' is a serious one and could lead to the collapse of any military effort from abroad and indeed to the collapse of the political movement or its exile government. Nevertheless, unwillingness to commit troops to action for fear of losses can risk a heavy political price from another direction if the host country withdraws support for perceived lack of solidarity.

Similarly, the actual size and effectiveness of exile armies varies hugely in the case studies continued in this volume. It was the crucial factor in determining military scale of effort. The Czech forces had to be protected against loss, and Norwegians were capable of producing a bare thousand (although they provided 30,000 sailors to the Allied war effort). The Poles and the French were able to recruit and field much larger numbers, and, in the latter case, actually deploy the Vichy forces in being once that regime had fallen. In the Indian sub-continent, the INA was apparently able to call upon hundreds of thousands of potential volunteers, but barely managed to recruit 40,000 and only fielded some 9,000 (a weak division), too small a force to have a military impact. In contrast, Bangladesh raised an estimated 80,000 militia, turning out 2,000 'trained' men every two weeks. South Africa saw a very slow increase from some 500 in arms in the 1960s, through to the 25,000 who joined the South African National Defence Force (SANDF) in 1993. The Zimbabwe operations were on a similar scale although much more actual fighting went on, and the aftermath of the conflict was more marked. The Iraqi opposition to Saddam Hussein, following the 1991, Gulf War was fractured and largely ineffectual. The KLA, in contrast, was credited with some 30,000 effectives, although they proved very difficult to identify on the ground. About 5,000 is a more likely top limit to KLA numbers.

The effectiveness of an exile army can vary enormously. It can make a genuine military contribution to the outcome of a conflict and realizing the political aims of an exile government or national liberation movement. Sometimes it can have only a symbolic military and political role. Indeed, the military effectiveness of an exile army may only be measured after regaining the homeland. By acting as a 'force in being' during an armed conflict, an exile army provides military seed corn for the new post-war regime. In the cases considered in this book, the exile military forces represent a spectrum of military and political value. Clearly the Polish exile armies made a genuinely significant contribution to allied operations on many fronts during the Second World War while other forces, such as those of Czechoslovakia and Norway played a more symbolic role overall despite the heroism shown on limited operations. Yet when measured in terms of realizing their underlying political aims, the Polish forces in the West failed to regain their homeland while Norwegian efforts were crowned with political success. On some occasions, catastrophic military failure can eliminate an exile army as a fighting force as the Cuban example demonstrates. Often, it came down to an issue of trust between host nations and their sponsored exiles. Because this was entirely lacking in the Cuban context, any operational efficiency the exiles might have had was entirely undermined. The Japanese were not prepared to allow the INA the kind of resources needed to become effective, and its troops suffered from very poor logistics as a result.

In the case of national liberation armies fighting insurgencies, the political and military effort are intimately linked. Given the difficulties in defeating insurgencies, military success is more easily registered even if opponents may possess greater military proficiency and sophisticated weaponry. Its members often possess high morale or greater combat motivation which is a product of their ideological context. In a confused situation such as in southern Africa, guerrilla forces could be a positive danger to their 'Front Line' state supporters. Terrorism can rebound seriously upon hosts in cases like these. Border raids lead to reprisals that can inflict damage on the wider society sheltering the exiles and not just the troops. Of course, guerrilla activity may be just what is required by the exiles – it may their only true way of being militarily effective. So, the Bangladeshi Mukti Bahini lived up to Dr Kissinger's axiom that: 'The guerrilla wins if he does not lose; the conventional army loses if it does not win.' Clearly this was something to which the unsupported and disorganized Iraqi opposition could not even aspire. The KLA's role may have been more symbolical than practical, as well. But is precisely because exile armies are conceived by their creators to embody the spirit of the nation that a representational presence may be enough to achieve the political objective of homecoming. That is what they are for.

The idea of exile armies of whatever kind remains bound up with the idea of seeking a defined piece of territory. In terms of the placement of exile armies in armed conflicts in the international system, the phenomenon of exile armies is bound up with the traditional centrality of the state and sovereignty. Exile armies throughout the twentieth century and earlier have based their struggles in a state or group of states external to the one they struggled to return to or to create. In the post-Cold War international environment, the combined effect of globalization and state failure may point to a very different reality for exile armies. The cases of Iraq and in the Great Lakes region of Africa demonstrate that notions of statehood and sovereignty may not be such important factors in the future for exiled armies.

# Index